To Karen,
    May you enjoy the adventurous Westerners
you'll meet in these pages.
                            Michael Thoele

FIRE LINE

∎ ∎ ∎

FIRE LINE

The Summer Battles of the West

MICHAEL THOELE

FULCRUM PUBLISHING
Golden, Colorado

To Tiffan and Caleb,
my babies who grew up to be firefighters

and

to the twenty-seven who went to battle in the western fire season of 1994 and did not return:
In California, Robert Buc, David Castro, Joe Johnson, and Shawn Zaremba.
In Colorado, Kathi Beck, Tami Bickett, Scott Blecha, Levi Brinkley, Robert Browning, Doug Dunbar,
Terri Hagen, Bonnie Holtby, Jon Kelso, Rob Johnson, Don Mackey, Roger Roth, James Thrash, and Richard Tyler.
In Idaho, Robert Johnson and John C. King.
In Montana, Bob Kelly and Randy Lynn.
In New Mexico, Robert Boomer, Sean Gutierrez, and Samuel Smith.
In Oregon, Sydney Maplesden Jr.
In Washington, Paul Hodges.

Library of Congress Cataloging-in-Publication Data

Thoele, Michael.
    Fire line : the summer battles of the West /
by Michael Thoele.
        p.   cm.
    Includes index.
    ISBN 1-55591-217-8 :
    1. Forest fires—West (U.S.)—Prevention and control—
History. 2. Wildfires—West (U.S.)—Prevention and
control—History. 3. Forest fire fighters—West (U.S.)—
History. 4. Wildfire fighters—West (U.S.)—History. I. Title.
SD421.32.W47T48   1995
634.9'618'0978—dc20   94-40585
                               CIP

Printed in Korea

0 9 8 7 6 5 4 3 2 1

Fulcrum Publishing
350 Indiana Street, Suite 350
Golden, Colorado 80401 USA
(800) 992-2908

Cover photo: Glittering like a fireworks display as it climbs from the ground to the treetops, a California forest fire devours all in its path.

Title page photo: High on a steep slope above the Boise River, a lone firefighter confronts a wall of flame sweeping through brush.

Table of contents photo: Fighting fire with fire in southern Oregon, a sprinting firefighter splashes a volatile mix of flaming diesel oil and gasoline into brush at the edge of the forest.

Contents

Preface

I N THE MYTHOLOGY OF THE GREEKS, Prometheus gave fire to man and was forever punished for his transgression. Fire, the treasure that the gods had wanted to reserve to themselves, changed humankind. The gift of Prometheus became an implement of hunting and of war. With fire, man was able to make weapons and tools, to warm himself against winter's cold, to fertilize his fields with ash, to cook his food and brew his beer, to boil potions, kiln cement, bake bricks, glaze pottery, shoe horses, cast statues, and mint coins.

But fire was not always beneficent. It could burn the hand, the hut, or the house. It could rage through the fields, destroying a summer's work and a winter's sustenance. More distant, it swept through forested valleys and up mountain slopes. It was of less concern there. Humanity's numbers were small, and the earth was large. For millennia, fire romped unchallenged in the wilderness, often aided and abetted by hunters and farmers who valued the way it cleared the land.

But just as civilization sets limits on man's excesses, so it found the need to limit fire. Where humanity flourished, fire in the wild inevitably was recast with the cloak of enemy. The more cities that spread and homes that rose, the more unacceptable wildland fire became. The new reaction was partly visceral; the fire that raged across a plain or up a valley to threaten a settlement or a homestead was a clear and present danger. And it was partly economic and esthetic and cultural; as those settlements and homesteads grew, the forests around them acquired new values.

In the main, civilization had its way. With its numbers and its technology, it tamed the forests, veined them with roads, and created systems that overpowered wildland fire. A few well-settled regions—Spain, southern France, the southeastern United States—still have their share of wildfire. But they have mostly small fires in large number, not landscape conflagrations. Wildfire in the galloping, threatening, primeval sense haunts humanity mostly on its frontiers in the earth's temperate zones. It is still a threat in vast, unroaded sections of Russia and northern China. But nowhere is the battle joined more earnestly than in the outback sections of three still-frontierish nations: Canada, Australia, and the United States. More than any other places, southeastern Australia and the western reaches of Canada and the United States are the venues where man and fire are still coming to terms.

My introduction to wildfire in the American West came in 1987. Somehow, though I had spent nearly twenty years as a Western journalist, forest fire had missed me. I had seen one or two small ones. I had heard of big fire from afar, read some accounts of the great historic fires, and listened to a few old-timers

■ ■ ■

Left: Pounding in hand-dug fire line in the dark at Cameron Lake on Washington's Colville Indian Reservation, an Idaho firefighter gains ground with nighttime humidity and moderating fire behavior as allies.

who had been to battle. But until 1987, I had never been there. That season, bad as it was, will be remembered as the warmup. The forest fire season to end all fire seasons was still a year away. Yellowstone National Park would burn in 1988, commanding the attention of the nation and the world.

But 1987 was a holocaust by any measure. Northern California and Southern Oregon were burning that fall, some six hundred thousand acres torching off in a series of fires that stretched nearly three hundred miles. The fires gobbled forests and homes, and forced the evacuation of communities. For long weeks, they rebuffed the best efforts of tens of thousands of firefighters, the U.S. Army and Air Force, and dozens of National Guard units. Whatever part of my reporter's soul that may have yearned to be a combat correspondent came away from that experience fulfilled. I went to war with the troops. I slept in their camps. I sat in strategy sessions with their generals. And I emerged with the burden of a new curiosity.

Roles of life and work in the West fascinate. In America, with our congenital westering, pioneering, frontiering ethic, we have always found allure in the adventures of those who deal with the challenges of untamed land. Our books and films and plays have limned the triumphs and tragedies of explorers, trappers, homesteaders, loggers, miners, cowboys, railroad builders, bush pilots. But civilization has had its way with them, too. Most of those American icons are seen now only through history's eye. The few that remain are vestigial shadows of their colorful ancestors, dimmed by technology, fettered by regulation, and demythologized by a new set of social attitudes toward that quintessential American matter of taming and using the land. However, those who are called to battle when fire marches across the landscape of the West still do largely the same elemental work as they did a century or so ago, when halting fire began to become a priority on the Western frontier.

Alone among all those other Western archetypes, the fighters of forest fire have been largely ignored in the cultural record of the region. Here and there are some mostly episodic local histories of a single fire or a single region. Beyond that, the cultural record on forest fire and those who fight it is thin. It runs to a couple of films and a handful of books—Stewart Holbrook's colorful and historic *Burning an Empire,* Norman MacLean's nonfiction *Young Men and Fire,* George Stewart's novel, *Fire,* and Stephen Pyne's landmark history, *Fire in America.* How odd. Because far more Westerners have fought fire than ever punched cows, laid rails, or mined gold. Down the decades, forest fire has been a rite of passage for tens of thousands of them, from pickup saloon crews at the turn of the century to footloose young men in the Civilian Conservation Corps to college students in the post–World War II era.

Westerners often refer to the fighting of forest fire as a white-hat job, an image that recalls frontier heroes of another century. In the 1990s it is a pursuit that envelops a subculture of fifty thousand Westerners, most of them seasonal workers, most of them relatively young. It is a world that does not lack for drama. Nor, as it showed us in the horrific, life-claiming fire year of 1994, does it lack for tragedy. This book, then, is an attempt to define that world, the arena in which those who take on fire in the forest live, work, and sometimes die.

Michael Thoele
Cheshire, Oregon

Acknowledgments

A YEAR OF WORK ON THIS PROJECT, including thirty-five thousand miles of travel and research in the Western United States, was funded by a grant from the World Forestry Center, an international educational foundation based in Portland, Oregon. The center's grant, in turn, was made possible through the support of various Western individuals, foundations, and corporations, some with strong ties to the forests, others with valued memories of personal or family involvement in wildland fire.

They include: in California, Fibreboard World Products Company, Michigan-California Lumber Company, Potlatch Corporation, and Sierra Forest Products; in Idaho, Shearer Lumber Products; in Oregon, John and Willa Alvord, Edwin and Marie Baker, Molly Bartlett, John and Ruth Bascom, Cavenham Forest Industries, the Clark Foundation, Collins Pine Company, Columbia Helicopters, Ed and June Cone, David Cox, Crown Pacific, Forest City Trading Group, Ehrman Giustina, Nat Giustina, John Hampton, Ralph Hull, Leonard and Alice Jacobson, the Jeld-Wen Foundation, D.R. Johnson Lumber Company, Richard and Ruth Miller, Ostrander Resources, Evert and Joyce Slijper, Starker Forests, L.L. Stewart, Faye Stewart, Stimson Lumber Company, and the Woodard Family Foundation; in Washington, Murray Pacific Corporation, Port Blakely Tree Farms, Simpson Timber Company, and the Weyerhaeuser Company Foundation. Additional support came from Davidson Industries, an Oregon company.

John Blackwell, president of the World Forestry Center, and L.L. Stewart, an Oregon civic leader, besides being early believers when the project was only a vision, went on to serve as the oversight committee for the grant. Their advice and counsel were invaluable. Allan West, Edwin Baker, Dale Gardener, Nat Giustina, John Manz, Craig Nesbitt, and Richard Stauber likewise played important early roles in moving the project from concept to reality.

Around the West and in Washington, D.C., a platoon of information and photographic specialists from public agencies provided crucial assistance. They include Joan Anzelmo, Scott Anderson, Brian Ballou, Bob Bannon, Bob Beckley, Tim Birr, Lynette Berriochoa, Frank Carroll, Doug Decker, Dale Dufour, Cynthia Forrest-Elkins, Ken Franz, Janelle Hill, Doug Huntington, Tiana Glenn, Randi Jorgenson, Hank Lasala, Matt Mathes, Karen Michaud, Don Parker, Howard Parman, Joe Pasinato, James Peaco, Carolyn Richards, Bill Robertson, Mallory Smith, Ray Steiger, David Steinke, Karen Terrill, Leslie Tucker, Bruce Turbeville, Andrew Urban, Steve Valenzuela, Hans Wilbrecht, Andy Williams, Bernie Yee, Ron Young, Wayne Williams, and Mary Zabinski.

The seed that became this book would never have germinated without years of willingness on the part of The Register-Guard of Eugene, Oregon, and its editors to throw choice forest fire assignments my way each summer when smoke rose in the mountains. I could ask for no better preparation. Professional colleagues and academic friends who provided advice and special assistance were Bill Bishop, Tom Detzel, Arnold Ismach, Barrie and Mary Hartman, Bill Kaufman, Lance Robertson, and Dan Root.

Through twelve Western states and in the nation's capital, I was the beneficiary of time, information, and advice graciously extended by archivists, journalists, public officials, corporate executives, retirees, and, most of all, by legions of firefighters. Those who

helped include: in Alaska, Sandy Ahlstrom, Floyd Alexander, Andy Alexandrou, Dale Anderegg, Kathy Barker, Gary Baumgartner, Jeff Browne, Mike Butteri, Hanna Carter, Clifford Charlie, Roy Charlie, Rob Collins, Greg Coon, Julie Crichton, Dave Dash, Rudy Davis, Rod Dow, Gary Dunning, Jack Dyer, Darrell Frank, Richard Frank, Jeannie Herbert, Dave Jandt, Aaron Jokisch, Sharon Kilbourn-Roesch, Fred Kutzgar, Dave Liebersbach, Frenchie Malotte, Dave Matier, April May, Bert Mitman, John Newman, Judy Reese, Tyler Robinson, Gene Schloemer, Greg Scully, John See, Berkman Silas, Peter Solomon, Joe Stam, Ed Strong, Murray Taylor, Mike Theisen, Charlie Titus Jr., Philip Titus, Jim Tucker, Jim Vanderpool, Paul Van Hees, Cheryl Wilcock, Lynn Wilcock, and Matt Ziomek.

In Arizona, Ed Bautista, Rob Berney, Sarah Cassadore, Jesse Duhnkrack, Gary Garrett, Lou Jekel, Jennie Joe, Tanya Kenton, Gary Kniffin, Bill Krushak, Loren Macktima, Dorothy Lonewolf Miller, Phil Parks, Rose Phillips, Sherry Reid, Evans Rope, Jr., Jim Schroeder, Tony Sciacca, Pat Velasco, Heidi Wilhelm, Hunter Wistrand, and K.C. Yowell.

In California, Hashim Abdullah, Keith Alvord, Chris Amestoy, Dale Anderson, Doug Anderson, Barry Aubrey, Dennis Baker, Steve Barme, Carl Bianco, George Biddle, Bill Bielitzer, Dave Boucher, Jim Boukidis, Phil Brown, John Bryant, Fritz Cahill, Chris Cameron, Howard Carr, Dick Carron, Dick Chase, Joe Clark, Gary Cockrell, Constance Collier, Sue Conard, Jim Cook, Pete Coy, Anna Dinkel, David Drum, Jim Dunn, Herb Edmonds, Freddie Espinoza, Terry Golightly, Greg Greenhoe, Harley Greiman, Tom Harbour, Angela Harris, Pete Himmel, Jack Hinshaw, Joe Hiss, Jeff Holland, Jenny Houchin, Dallas Howard, Ron Hunter, Sue Husari, Ed Isch, Charles Isele, Eric Jack, Ben Jacobs, Wendy Jankel, Felipe Jimenez, James Johnson, Antoine Jordan, Mike Klinger, Andi Koonce, Jerry Koschnick, Ron Lamount, Wayne Leitner, David LeMay, Mark Linane, Mike Linn, Juan Lopez, Erik Makhanian, Richard Martinez, Randy Masters, Casey Maxwell, Arch McKinlay, Dave McMaster, Pat Michael, Blaine Moore, Kirby More, Gary and Wanda Nagel, Pat Nelson, Dale Newton, Tom Nichols, Dave Noble, Deen Oehl, Bob Perez, Ira Peshkin, Milo Petzer, David Phillips, Nick Prodan, Jerry Quigley, Tim Quigley, Ray Quintanar, Tom Reavis, Jan Reifenberg, Paul Rippens, Brit Rosso, Paul Salgado, Don Sand, Frieder Schurr, Robert Serrato, Kumiko Shibata, Wes Shook, Deanne Shulman, Jim Simmons, Miriam Sluis, Derek Smith, Karen Steiner, Stan Stewart, Gary Sudduth, Bob Sutton, William Teie, Art Torrez, Christina Uribes, Adam Vancini, Ted Van Devort, Curtis Vincent, Eric Walker, Mike Warren, Walter Williams, Larry Wright, Keith Zachary, and John Zeigler.

In Colorado, Kim Bang, Todd Bates, Fred Bird, Gary Connelly, Drew Cushing, Bruce Dissel, Terese Florin, Dee Fogelquist, Paul and Eileen Gleason, Lael Gorman, Bill Graepler, Major General Todd Graham, Dennis Haddow, Paul Hefner, Kevin Klein, Dawn Kummli, Ernst Little, J. P. Mattingly, Katy Nesbitt, Dave Niemi, Phil Omi, Larry Roe, Bill Rogers, Darrell Smith, Shelly Strong, Rich Tyler, and Brad Washa.

In Washington, D.C., and several Eastern states, David Aldrich, Mick Amicarella, Roger Archibald, Wallace Behnke, Kathy Burger, Elsie Cunningham, Hank DeBruin, Terese Floren, Fred Fuchs, Elmer Hurd, Bob Joens, Lieutenant Colonel Tom Knapp, Mary Jo Lavin, William Leary, Jerilyn Levi, Bob Martin, Kim Maynard, Steve Pedigo, Bill Sommers, and Dennis Truesdale.

In Idaho, Lanny Allmaras, Jeff Bass, Dick Bovey, Lonnie Brown, Ed Case, Bill Casey, Bill Clark, Jon Curd, John Ferguson, Neal Davis, Lynn Flock, Rick Gale, Craig Irvine, Steve Jenkins, Glenn Johnston, Charlotte Larson, Kelly Martin, Ted Mason, Dave McCoy, Steve Nemore, Elmer Neufeld, Duke Norfleet, Rick Ochoa, Steve Raddatz, Jim Schneider, Skip Scott, Jack Seagraves, Ed Seffel, Mary Sprague, John Scott, Stan Tate, Bill Williams, Woody Williams, Jack Wilson, Mike Wolcott, and Bill Yensen.

In Montana, Leslie Anderson, James Brown, Marshall Brown, Boyd Burtch, Tom Carlsen, Tom Cook, Russ Davis, John Fisher, Charles George, Joan Humiston, George Jackson, Steve Karkanen, Bernard Kiley, Don Mackey, Holly Maloney, Bob Mutch, Robert Old Horn, Fred Oyebi, Julia Page, David Pierce, Randy Pretty-On-Top, Jerry Pretty Weasel, Twilla Pretty Weasel, Ted Putnam, Dick Rothermel, Mike Savka, Brian Sharkey, Bill Summers, Charles Sundstrom, and Philip Whiteclay.

In Nevada, Frank Antos, Mike Dondero, Steve Cassady, Lee Griswold, Alan Kightlinger, Bob Knutson, Will Lotspeich, Mike McCarty, Jody Mothershead, Joe Payne, Tina Pusley, and Dale Warmuth.

In New Mexico, Pete Alcorta, Bill and Kathy Allred, Brett Bower, Ron Dunton, Tom Gregor, Dorothy Guck, Brian Infield, Raymond Kirgan, Leo LaPaz, Bob Lee, Jerome Macdonald, Bill Riggles, Steve Servis, Daniel Sifuentes, Walt Sixkiller, Jerry Soard, Robert Stucke, Neto Villegas, Dusty Voss, and Alan Wyngart.

In Oregon, Ron Barrett, Scott Blecha, R. D. Buell, Cal Butler, Dale Carlson, Mike Carlson, Lon Casebeer, Joe Cray, Sue Clay, Doug Coyle, Dolly Davis, Bob Del Monte, Tom Detzel, Don Ferguson, Lynn Findley, Mike Fitzpatrick, Jon Franklin, Everett Hall, Trish Hogervorst-Rukke, Randy Hyde, Dick Grace, Arnold Ismach, Jim Keefer, Pat Kelly, Wes Lematta, Joel Lira, Willie Lowden, Mike Lowry, John Marker, John Mingus, Laurie Perrett, Tom Quigley, John Roberts, John Robison, Paul Rose, Craig Rothenberger, Jim Russell, Gordon Schmidt, Bryan Scholz, Tom Shepard, Ambrosio Vasquez, Pete Vasquez, Mike Wheelock, Boyd Wickman, and Bob Zybach.

In Utah, Brooke Bambrough, Brian Barber, Glenn Beagle, Lloyd Duncan, Bill Hayes, Floyd Lacy, Colt Mortenson, Jeremy Wilson, and Stephen Youhouse.

In Washington, James Agee, Otis Allen, Lynn Andrews, Tim Brown, Erik Christiansen, Major General Thomas Cole, Max Corpuz, Ashley Court, Dale Dempsey, Chris Di Rienz, Garrett Eddy, Michelle Ellis, Tony Engel, Kyle Engstrom, Bob Gustafson, David Glose, Terry Grogan, John Helm, Ken Hoover, Eric Johnson, Les Kanzler, John Keener, Holly Koon, Louise Kutz, George Marcott, Kathy Marshall, Delcie McDonald, Tom Miller, Bill Moody, Linda Ott, Monnie Overson, Dave Peterson, Les Shank, Len Rodriquez, Max Schmidt, Roger Wallace, Rick West, and Bill Wilburn.

In Wyoming, Dick Bahr, Neil Beisler, Mona Divine, Rick Graham, Caryl Hamilton, Robert Jacob, Kevin Kulow, John Litherland, Terry McEneaney, Gordon McWilliams, Don Mitchell, Phil Perkins, Duane Powers, Gene Powers, Mark Rogers, Dan Sholly, Dave Underwood, and Eleanor Williams.

FIRE LINE

■ ■ ■

CHAPTER 1

The Armies of Summer

BEISLER FELT IT FIRST. Something still, heavy, ominous. Something speaking to him from that place where experience lives, distilled to intuition. Something filtering to him through a dozen years of chasing big fire across the West. Something left with him from the chaparral of California and the big timber of Oregon and the piney slopes of the Rockies. But something that the diggers and the sawyers, sweating, panting, pushing, yellow shirts sticking to their backs, still didn't feel in the waning hours of this 104-degree day.

They were the Wyoming Hotshots, best damn fire crew in the Forest Service if you cared to ask them, and they'd been at it for days, pounding in line and touching off roaring burnouts on first one Eastern Montana fire and then another. It was Thursday now, and they'd stolen maybe twelve hours sleep since Monday. With fire on their flank, they were at it again, shovels and pulaski tools clinking, chainsaws screaming, heads down, elbows pumping.

The dragon seemed complacent today. He crept downhill on their right, close enough that his glow beat back the twilight and his breath cooked the sweat from their faces as they worked the toe of the slope. But his march was slow and his teeth were short, no more than two feet tall as they gnawed through dry grass and the duff blanket of needles beneath the towering ponderosas. Still, it was odd, aggressive behavior for a fire this late in the day.

Bad stuff, maybe, for a rookie crew shanghaied away from painting picnic benches in some national forest. But they were hotshots, this Wyoming bunch—wildfire professionals who ranked up there with the smokejumpers and the best of the West's helicopter rappel crews. They had seen the dragon in worse moods. What was a ground crawler with two-foot flames easing downhill against the wind to them? They were drawing their line in the dirt, stealing the grass and needles and trees that the dragon needed to live, fighting fire with fire by touching off the duff with their long, red fuses, and burning out any sustenance that he might find as he stalked toward their thin trail of bare soil. And behind them were two crack crews of Cheyenne Indians, the seasoned firefighters of Western legend, reinforcing the line, chasing down hot spots.

But in that moment, Beisler's foreboding grew.

Forest fires, like new ships and new babies, are christened. If a fire survives its first day, it gets a name, drawn usually from a geographic feature but occasionally tugged from a creative vein hidden in the psyche of some fire bureaucrat. The great campaign fires of the West have had names as poetic as Sleeping Child and as rude as Hog. The Wyoming Hotshots had drawn the fire named Brewer, after a spring that burbled a few miles away.

Above: Spurred by fierce summer winds, a forest fire in Colorado's Rocky Mountains stretches toward the treetops.

■ ■ ■

Left: Deliberately ignited as a weapon in the battle against a larger fire, a burnout engineered by two hotshot crews rages in the night in Montana's Lolo National Forest.

They were a good crew on that June day in 1988, twenty strong and fresh from spring training. In a season that was off to an eerily early start, they could already claim three fires. Rogers, the ramrod of the Wyoming Hotshots, thought of his crews the way high school coaches talk of their teams. This one was younger and a bit less experienced than some he'd had, but strong and smart, and jelling in a way that pleased him. Officially, in the fashion that hotshot seasonal crews are organized in the nation's wildfire agencies, he was the unit's superintendent. Figuratively, he was captain of an elite little infantry platoon, one of the sixty-six outfits that fire bosses scream for each summer when the dragon goes thundering through the forests. Beisler, the foreman, the crew's nominal top sergeant, had chased the dragon through every state in the West.

In the paramilitary world of wildland fire, smokejumpers are the Special Forces, dropping deep behind the lines, risking that long step between airplane door and rocky landing to catch the enemy when he is small, insurgent, and least expecting opposition. And hotshots are the Marines, gung-ho groundpounders charging up the beach against stacked odds. Hotshots, who number only 1,360 in all of America, go where the big fires walk.

From their base in the Wyoming town of Greybull, Rogers and Beisler had crafted this crew around a nucleus of veterans, returnees such as the squad bosses, Graham and Meier, and the sawyers, Mader and Halvorsen. They'd stirred in a batch of recruits, all new to the hotshot business, but most of them bumping up from lower echelons of the wild land fire game. They were a diverse bunch, with three Crow Indians, a Chicago black, and two women in their ranks. They were as old as thirty-six, as young as eighteen. Among them marched athletes, ranch kids, college students, ex-oil field workers, world-traveled adventurers, locals from Bighorn County, and Easterners from as far away as New Jersey.

Today, the twenty had become nineteen. The fire bosses, sequestered back at camp with their maps and radios, had pulled Rogers off the crew and made him a division superindentent. He'd turned the crew over to Beisler—they'd done it before—and moved up to oversee a five-mile section of the Brewer fire's north flank, a piece of the battle that included his own crew, the Cheyenne, a pair of off-road pumper engines, and a bulldozer. The 'shots had seen Rogers occasionally that evening as he came through their sector and heard him talking on the radio with Beisler.

The engines had never caught up with them. And they'd lost the bulldozer around eight o'clock. It had been easy going until then. Rogers had relayed a helicopter pilot's message to Beisler. Ahead of the crew lay a meadow, an open island of an acre or so, surrounded by trees. It ran just a bit below the slow-moving line of fire, opposite a small draw at the bottom of the slope they were working. A gift. With a bit of a detour, Beisler could get the crew onto kinder terrain just above the meadow. Beisler had passed the word to Graham, his squad boss at the front of the crew. They'd bent the line and headed north, moving well, with the sawyers sprinting out ahead and knocking down trees, the dozer peeling a ten-foot swath, the diggers cleaning up behind and firing out, creating a blackened line to stop the approaching flames.

But the 'dozer jockey was a flatlander, not like the ones they'd seen on so many other fires, the sure-handed artists who spurred their diesel steeds into action like tank commanders in warfare. This one was a grader of subdivision lots, a new hire seeing action he hadn't contemplated. Craning over his shoulder at the approaching fire, he'd pulled up short at the top of a modest sixty-foot grade. Too steep, he'd said. Graham, decisive and always a bit impatient, had argued. Nothing to it, he'd said, the regular fire dozer guys do it all the time. But, face pale and hands shaking, the flatlander had spun his iron monster in its tracks and gone clanking back the way he'd come.

There was nothing for it after that but to dig. Digging, after all, is the quintessential work of forest fire. Birds sing, fires burn, hotshots dig. So they'd set off, tools swinging hard, taking out trees to break the forest canopy and cutting fire line, gouging their two-foot trail through the dirt beneath the ponderosas as if digging were an Olympic event. They'd expected to don their helmet headlamps after dark and to punch in maybe two or three miles of line before their shift ended at six the next morning. Killer work. The hardest work there was. Their work. Beisler had trotted off to ribbon a stretch of the new course with bits of plastic tape. His path took him down across the small draw, then up again to the edge of the tree-rimmed meadow. In minutes he was back.

It was then he felt the strangeness.

The temperature was climbing paradoxically as twilight deepened. It was up maybe fifteen degrees since he'd hiked down the trail. Odd. The uphill wind was dropping, disappearing. The humidity was skittering downward, the air becoming a desiccant that sucked the moisture off his skin. And there was the stillness, the dead calm, the heaviness. The fire still crept at ground level. But up the line, two or three trees torched off in a momentary seventy-foot tongue of flame, as if the dragon had cleared his throat and spit into the sky.

In war stories told by the old hands of Western forest fire, the spooky calm before the monumental blowup is standard fare. The stuff of rustic mythology, the academics used to say, like the business of moss growing only on the north side of trees. But no more. Now the meteorologists and the fire behaviorists know it's so. They can explain how the dragon holds his breath just before he breathes fire across the land in an explosion that comes faster than the fastest runner. They can chart it and graph it, though they can never predict its precise time or place. And they can detail the incidents, tragedies often, where no one read the signals, no one felt.

But Beisler felt it now. He moved to Graham. They shut down the saws, told the diggers to take a break. They listened. Beisler turned and trotted the two hundred yards ahead to the meadow, wondering if it could be a safety zone if things went sour. By the time he returned, Graham, too, had picked up the drop in the wind, the faintest hint of some new vigor in the fire.

A few airborne embers, now without the uphill wind to hold them off, flitted down across the line, dropped into the parched grass on the crew's left, and blossomed instantly into tulips of fire. Graham set the diggers to chasing them. Farther back along the line, toward the Cheyenne, more embers drifted over, more fires erupted. Another tree torched off, then another, momentary Roman candles rising above the ground fire, their resinous needles sizzling like bacon. Spectacular but hardly urgent. The Wyoming crew plunged to the task at hand willingly, chasing down the spots even as more ignited.

Beisler watched for a minute or two, thinking and feeling. Logic battled instinct. Then he turned to Graham: "Get 'em out. Let's get 'em out now. Up to the meadow." In the years that Graham and Beisler had worked together, they had gone toe to toe with fire vastly more threatening. This was not a fire to make a hotshot crew turn tail. But there was a trust between the two of them. Not questioning, Graham began rounding up his spot chasers. The rookies responded quickly. A couple of the sawyers balked for just a moment, reluctant to leave a fray they were certain could be won. Graham moved them out.

The dragon was stirring now. The wind, no longer neutral, blew lightly downhill. Beisler ran back down the line. Below, spot fires were picking up on his right, and up the hill the main fire began to drive down on his left. Graham was leading the crew out of the trees, counting heads. Beisler turned and trotted after them. Behind him, the embers were falling in earnest, like bits of hot, red snow.

The oral history of every Western hotshot crew has a chapter for tales of being chased out. A crew boss makes a decision and the troops retreat to a burned-out black zone, a rock field, a meadow. Like freight cars on a siding, they sit it out and let the fire go highballing past. It is often searing and uncomfortable, so hot that firefighters hide their faces behind hard hats or backpacks. But it always plays well in the retelling: "Fire all around us, three-hundred sixty degrees, and we had our cameras out and were eating lunch." As Graham pushed them toward the draw that separated them from the meadow, the veterans on the crew saw one of those forced respites coming. The meadow would be safe.

But the dragon was growing. More embers were falling. Farther up the ridge in the trees behind them, an insistent roar was building. Kulow, a rookie less than a month out of Greybull High School, picked up his pace as the crew broke from a walk to a jog. He felt the growing urgency but had no perspective in which to place it. This was why he'd joined. It was exciting. It was great.

They broke out of the trees, rushed to the bottom of the draw and hit the upslope on the opposite side. As they reached the meadow, a stand of trees torched off down the line, between them and the Cheyenne. The fire was working harder, growing faster. It had become a crescent pushing toward them, its tips beginning to hook around the meadow. Beisler caught up with them. He and Graham conferred. Their message rippled through the crew. Start preparing shelter sites. Just a precaution.

Across the West, those who head off to do business with wildfire carry a yellow pouch, not much larger than a box of chocolates. It is worn always at the ready, usually at the waist. It seems almost too small to yield what it contains—a tiny, man-sized, aluminum foil pup tent, a floorless, frameless, poleless, doorless pop-up shelter that a trained firefighter should be able to deploy in twenty seconds. A bonded inner lining of heat resistant glass fiber lends the foil strength, so it will not tear like a chewing gum wrapper. Even so, the aluminum pup tent's walls are thinner than a firefighter's shirt, and the whole improbable structure weighs less than four pounds.

The Wyoming Hotshots had renewed acquaintances with the shelter only three weeks before. In a ritual of spring training that plays out across the West, the thousands of seasonals who hire on for fire duty practice with old shelters, like toddlers climbing under cardboard boxes. They learn about the corner straps for hands and feet, the narrow flaps that tuck under the tent's perimeter to be held down by elbows and knees. They are told that the shelter could save them from flames as hot as a thousand degrees. They are also told that they do not ever want to prove the point. There is no fun in facing the dragon in his foulest mood with only a handful of tinfoil. And across the years very few firefighters have—some minuscule fraction of one percent.

So, even as they began to clear spots in the meadow, few of the hotshots expected to pull their aluminum tents. To the most jaded of the veterans the digging was just another Forest Service safety precaution, part of life in an outfit that could sometimes seem more preoccupied with abating risk than with fighting fire. Beisler started back toward the draw, wanting to make a last check on the line. He raised Meier, his second squad boss,

on the radio. Just before the crew had pulled off the line, Meier had dropped back to touch base with the Cheyenne.

Beisler never made it to the draw. From above it, he could see fire surging over the line where the crew had labored moments earlier. The wind clearly had reversed. It was pushing strongly downhill now. Barely a quarter mile away, up behind the line, a thickening column of black smoke climbed into the sky, and fire romped on the crowns of the trees. The dragon, having spent the afternoon preheating and drying the forest canopy above, was coming after it hungrily. And out just a few hundred yards, the crescent of fire was becoming a horseshoe, its two sides driving down to flank the meadow. Meier could not possibly rejoin them. Beisler radioed him to stay with the reservation crews and to fall back. In the meadow, they would be eighteen.

Even before Beisler turned back to the meadow, the pace there quickened. There was an earnestness now to the digging but little progress. Their haven was no grass savannah. It was covered instead with a thick, knee-high, vinelike brush that resisted their tools. Worse, the six sawyers had no hand tools at all; they could only stand and wait. Hamilton, strong and capable from years of work in the oil fields, had cleared only a one-foot square. She found the going almost impossible. She handed off her pulaski to McWilliams, the geology major from Michigan. Kulow stood, watching fire build on the ridge and hearing a new sound, a huffing like a locomotive building speed. Sembach, one of the veterans, heard it too. He shouted at Kulow, "C'mon Kevin, you gotta dig, you gotta dig!" Somewhere in those moments, Graham told them they would deploy shelters. Not all of them believed. It was a possibility too rare. The digging went on.

But it was hopeless work. The strongest among them had hacked out barely two feet. Embers, larger now, fell in the meadow. Momentarily, Graham was gone. Now he was returning. "Up here, up here!" he yelled. "There's a road. It's more open." Nearer to them now, the fire rose in the trees. It was still beyond the closest trees, the thick wall of pine that ringed the edges of the meadow. But its smoke darkened the twilight sky, and in the near distance flames marched across the roof of the forest.

Some of the veterans shed yellow backpacks. They dug out the metal gasoline and oil bottles they each carried to feed the saws, and the flarelike fusees they used to touch off burn-

■ ■ ■

Left: Oregon's Union Hotshots, a diverse collection of adventurers, athletes, scholars, and blue-collar workers drawn from around the West, are typical of the forest fire world's elite crews.

outs, and they began flinging them away. Others took the time to dig the flammables off the backs of the rookies still carrying packs. Through it all they walked, stumbled, ran toward the road. Beisler, returning to the meadow as they were moving out, trailed them. It was a few minutes before nine o'clock. Daylight was waning. Barely fifteen minutes had passed since they left the fire line.

The meadow was not much of a meadow and the road that ran along its north edge was not much of a road. A two-track, really, a pair of wheel lines pounded into the dirt by hunters' pickup trucks. But it was brush-free, covered at its shoulders and center with dry grass. The crew arrived in a rush. The wind whipped their yellow shirts and tore away their words. In the rising noise, the ember shower became a storm. Bits of branches and fist-sized ponderosa cones, resinous firebrands that had been swept hundreds of feet into the air and ignited by the fire's updraft, tumbled from the sky.

Graham sensed time getting away. In the crew, he saw disbelief. The never-never moment was at hand, but most of them still wore shelters at their belts. He stepped to the head of the line, the approaching fire over his shoulder and the crew before him. He ripped his shelter from his pouch and flipped it open into the wind. He shook out the last folds and hooked his boots into the foot straps. Then he looked down the line and saw with satisfaction that shelters were coming out.

Beisler reached the road as his crew wrestled their foil tents in the wind, like Kansas farm wives trying to clean off the washline before an approaching tornado. Hamilton had her tent unfolded. She looked fearfully at Beisler. "You can handle it," he yelled. "You'll be okay." As he tucked into his shelter, Antos, the recruit from New Jersey, saw spot fires dancing downwind in the meadow and the trees beyond. The horseshoe was closing. They were encircled. The seconds raced. Beisler turned to see Mader, the sawyer, with a shadow of resigned doom on his face. His hand protruded through a huge seam split in his shelter. "No, no, you're okay," Beisler yelled. "Remember the training film. Grab the rip. Tuck it under you."

As he rushed to throw his own shelter down, Beisler stole a glance at the fire. He had watched fire race across grassy hills faster than an antelope could run, and he had seen it thunder up the chaparral canyons of California, eating houses like popcorn. But he was seeing something different now. He looked into a firestorm, a panorama of flame. Down low, sheets of fire danced beyond the trees at the meadow's edge. Farther up the ridge they whipped above the forest and licked at the sky. The smoke column boiled ten thousand feet into the air. The embers and ash blew so fiercely that he lowered his head and squinted his eyes against them. Down the line to the south, a stand of trees was crowned in fire. To the north, like an image in a mirror, a second batch raged. Pillars of fire, to the right and left.

And then, in the second that Beisler watched, the pillars connected and became a wall. As if marinated in gasoline, the trees at meadow's edge, the last barrier between the hotshots and fire, crowned out in an eighth-mile sheet of flame. Like it was driven by a bellows in a forge, the ground fire had simply lifted, vaulting to the canopy above. It matched nothing in Beisler's experience. And it roared and seethed now, a giant red-orange picket fence, with flames spiking 150 feet above the treetops and bending before the wind, stretching toward the meadow. The dragon was at the door.

Beisler was in trouble. Along the line of shelters, elbows and knees poked and bumped behind the foil, hands reached out to pull in flaps and tuck down tight. The fire was close now, and waves

Above: A wildland firefighter in California's Santa Barbara County emerges from a fire shelter in a training exercise. Thin, bordering on flimsy, the lightweight shelters are credited with saving scores of lives since their development in the 1970s.

■ ■ ■

of heat rolled over him. Near the spot Beisler had chosen for himself, Bates, the recruit from Colorado, stood alone, gloved hands fumbling with his still-folded shelter. Beisler ripped it away, shook it out in the rising wind and handed it back. "Get in! Get in!" he yelled.

Out of time now, Beisler spun to his spot, shaking out his shelter, falling to the ground. As he went down, pulling the shelter over his shoulders like a cape, a sheet of flame rolled out of the trees and swept horizontally over the meadow. The grass at his feet ignited. He pulled the shelter in around him, hurrying, hurrying. He stole a final look at the meadow and took into the tent with him a vision of surrealist hell. Before a backdrop of orange flame, giant maroon and purple balls of unburned gases rolled toward them. They coursed two feet above the meadow, like an armada of great, malevolent, sinuous, airborne steamrollers, seeking oxygen so they could explode into flame, while white vapor streamed off their tops like foam off an ocean curler.

And then the fire was on them.

The shelters were arrayed across the road in rows of two and three, packed in so tightly that some of them touched. They were boulders now in a river of flame, and the rapids eddied and curled and broke over each of them differently, with a venomous sort of whimsy. At the head, Graham felt the superheated wind buffet his shelter and push it down against his back. Beneath the edges he saw a thin line of flickering light, like a racing dynamite fuse, as the grass outside his tent erupted and the fire swept over him. On his right, he could hear Beisler struggling, still working to secure the edges of his tent and coping with tiny grass fires inside. Beisler had been caught with gloves off and sleeves rolled up. But he had a plastic water bottle in each hand and, as he secured the edges of his shelter, he used the canteens to beat out fire and to hold down the front corners.

The fire's first wave was the curtain of flame sweeping off the trees, igniting the volatile gases ahead of it. It was a flash flood, a stampede of flame that filled the meadow and swept over the road. It buffeted the tents and lifted their corners. Into most, it drove heavy smoke and into some, fire. Stewart, one of the Crows, was in the tallest grass along the road. He took fire inside the back of his tent and then in the front. He beat the flames out with his legs and hands, taking more searing air beneath the edges of his tent, choking on smoke. He fought the urge to do what he had been taught would be instantly fatal— to stand and run.

McWilliams had fire. Old Horn had fire. Bates had fire. Red Horn had fire, and in his tent he lifted himself to his fingers and toes, and watched little tongues of flame run beneath his body. Kulow saw that the shelter had pinholes, tiny openings that glowed red-orange, just as the training film had promised. The walls of his tent were too hot to touch, and the temperature inside was climbing. But, with an eighteen-year-old's sense of immortality, he was still fascinated and excited. Then the corner of his tent lifted. He took fire and smoke. In the next moments, he thought about dying. And he heard the screaming begin.

It came first from Trummer. The shortest member of the crew, she had struggled with the long stretch between the foot and hand straps of her shelter. Now wind lifted the back of her tent and for the briefest moment a wave of fire washed inside. Even as she screamed she fought the flaps back into place. Beside her, McWilliams cursed in frustration and shouted above the wind, "Don't panic, Lori! Don't run!" She beat flames out with her hands and rolled onto her side to smother a patch that was searing her leg. As Trummer's cries died, they could hear others. Long, tortured, repeated. Sembach. Those closest to the back could hear him screaming, thrashing in his tent, then screaming again.

Among the tents there was talk. Names were called out, and people checked in with each other even as they fought their interior fires and struggled for breath. They could hear McWilliams swearing colorfully at each new scream, voicing for them all the frustration of being able to do nothing for the others. Up front, Beisler and Graham talked over hand-held radios. They had heard the screams, too. They were certain that some had stood and run, entering the race that could not be won. Graham narrated each moment into his radio, not knowing if his transmission was reaching outside the meadow, wondering if his words would be the only record of what happened there. Kulow had heard nothing from the four crew members between his tent and Sembach's, and he counted them for dead.

Some in the crew sensed the briefest of pauses. The flame front from the trees roared past them, into the forest downwind from the meadow. It had been a prelude, an airborne attack that passed so quickly and claimed so much oxygen that it had burned only the lightest fuels around them. Now the dragon would send an army of towering flame marching at ground level through the brush of the meadow. It came with a volcano of sound, as if they were standing in the afterblast of a battalion of jet engines. It was on them with winds that approached sixty miles an hour. The tents filled with smoke, much thicker than before, and new fingers of fire crept under their edges.

They had heard of the noise and the wind that came with big fire. Some had experienced it before, from a distance. But mere humans were not meant to be at its epicenter, with breakers of flame washing over their tinfoil tents. The shelters shook and flattened and flapped and filled with thick smoke. Inside, as the temperatures rose toward two hundred degrees, the hotshots fought fire with water from their canteens and pressed their mouths close to the dirt, cupping their arms around their faces and struggling for breath. In the enveloping noise, each was alone.

In her tent, Hamilton thought over and over, "Some of us are dying." Bates had weathered the first blast of fire, but he was suffocating now, wrestling with the impulse to run. Hearing nothing but the roar, Kulow began to think that he was the only survivor. Alone in his shelter, Antos had a crystalline vision of the faraway New Jersey girl named Donna and wondered if he would make their wedding, just two months off. McWilliams took a shallow, searing breath. He ripped the earth with his fingers, trying to create a hole for his mouth and nose. There was little oxygen in the smoky air he had drawn; he held it perhaps twenty seconds, then let it go and pulled in another breath. Worse, much worse. Now he was frantic, digging the ground with his fingers, and finally with his teeth, as if some reservoir of sweet air could be chewed from the earth beneath him. He could hold the second breath only thirty seconds. Face in the dirt, he let it go and drew a third. He was dizzy now, choking, losing concentration.

And then, in all the tents, the smoke was gone. Some curious passing eddy of the fire drafted it out as quickly as it had come. A few on the crew felt the smallest whiff of cool air as the smoke exited, though the fire still raged around them. At the rear of the formation, Sembach no longer screamed. But they heard his moans, heard him calling out, heard him thrashing in his shelter. Up front, Graham and Beisler still talked. They listened for a while, felt the foil walls cool slightly. Briefly, they raised the edges of their tents and peered out. Still too hot. Beisler waited another minute, then rose to his knees. A fifty-mile-an-hour wind pulled his shelter from his hands and rolled it back. But it was wind without fire, and he called to Graham as he rose to his feet.

Beisler turned, and he was sickened. Twilight had given way to the first edge of night. He noted vaguely that the racing flame front was gone, already out of sight beyond the next ridge. The meadow had become a blackened moonscape, with clouds of ash and smoke whipping across it. On its edges, as far as he could see, the seared skeletons of pines stood, their branches fingering the night without a single needle. Here and there, small fires burned in the gloom, and several of them were very close— burning clumps of yellow. Yellow, the color of fire shirts. For the briefest moment Beisler saw bodies that had fallen where they'd run. The nearest of the fires was on the road and he went to it. It was a backpack, a piece of fire gear discarded in the headlong dash into the shelters. And so, he realized, were the other yellow lumps, because the tents, battered and misshapen, were shining there before him, row on row.

He and Graham went down the line, shaking shelters, softly calling names and hearing answers in smoke-rasped voices, bringing people out into the darkness and the wind. They found Sembach, rolled in his shelter, delirious from pain. He was burned, seriously, and he had inhaled superheated air. He had deployed at the edge of the road. The fire winds had swirled most cruelly around his shelter. The brush and fuel next to it were heavy, and they had burned with extreme heat. For long moments, as he fought his solitary battle, the winds had curled back both ends of the shelter. His legs, arms, and face were burned. But he would live, they would all live.

They would be alone for almost an hour in the dark before help arrived. Beisler and Graham, sensing the shakiness of the moment, spun the crew into action—gathering packs, counting heads, inventorying equipment, digging out first-aid gear and canteens. The medics, Antos and Bates, treated Sembach. They gave him water, swathed his burns in gauze, and talked him through the pain. The first van into the meadow carried him away, starting him toward a Montana hospital two hundred miles distant.

The crew was alone for most of another hour, treating its minor burns, talking, sharing food salvaged from the packs, waiting for transport. They swapped stories. Mader, the sawyer with the huge rip in his shelter, had survived unscathed. McWilliams had risen from the ground to see his silhouette etched in burned grass, like the police outline of a murder victim chalked onto pavement. Their sense of family was heightened. In the spirit of their moment, they posed for a group photograph, facing the retreating fire and mocking it with the universal one-finger salute. The T-shirt committee conducted its first meeting. Though they didn't know it that June night, they had survived the opening round of the fire siege of 1988, the season like no other. The blazes that would burn until November already were up and running in Yellowstone Park. The grapevine would do its work, and in the fire camps that never seemed to close in that endless summer of drought and flame, others would nod knowingly when they saw the shirts that read, "Been to hell and lived to tell. Brewer Fire."

At dawn they walked through medical checkups. Hamilton called her parents in Wyoming. Like so many other young people who wander onto fire crews, she was a second generation firefighter. Decades before, her father had cut line on Western fire. He had supported his daughter's decision to chase the dragon. He listened knowingly to her story. His memories of other fires in other times were keen. So was his fire camp humor. "See," he said, "I told you it wasn't dangerous."

When the doctors and the training counselors were done with them, the Wyoming Hotshots faced a choice. They knew that Sembach would live. And they knew that, most often, crews that have survived an entrapment go home, take a week off,

regroup. The choice was theirs. It was no choice at all. They went back to the Brewer Fire.

■　■　■

They always come back. From Arizona to Alaska, from California to Montana, they come back. By the thousands, by the tens of thousands, they show up every season to re-enlist for the summer battles of the West. They turn out from villages in the Yukon and cities in Los Angeles County. They trickle in from ivied Eastern campuses and dusty Western ranches. They muster from the tarmacs of boondocks airports and from helicopter platforms in the North Sea, from the asphalt of inner cities and the valleys of the Rockies, a budding of spring as predictable as New Mexico cactus flowers or Oregon apple blossoms.

They come to fight a war, some as ground troops, some as paratroopers, some as combat pilots. Their war has its own Pentagon, its own command structure, its own air force. Their war costs as much as 600 million dollars in an average year, 1.2 billion dollars in a big year, and fields a force of nearly fifty thousand full-time and seasonal troops. Their theater of operations covers nearly two million square miles of mountain, valley, desert, tundra, rangeland, and suburbs in a dozen states, from Alaska southward to Arizona and New Mexico, and east through Colorado, Wyoming, Montana, and the fringes of the Dakotas. The enemy in their war is forest fire, or more correctly, the varied species of wildland fire that march annually through Western forests, deserts, and mountain brush fields. In an average year, the troops will battle thirty-five thousand fires across more than a million acres, in a big year, forty-five thousand fires on six million acres. In their war, civilians will lose homes and businesses. But in virtually every year that the war is waged, some of the troops—young men and women who volunteer for the campaign—will lose their lives.

The conflict is covered in the media but only perfunctorily and episodically. The public often is unable to see the war for the battles. The world glimpses only a few of the moments of high drama when fire rages through a national park or gobbles yet another mountain suburb in California. But to most of America, to most of the West, the larger shape of this annual campaign remains obscured. Its sweep, its patterns, its costs, its effects, its internal tactical and philosophical debates are barely understood.

On the ground and parachuting from the sky, the troops in this war serve in a patchwork army so variegated and so ponderous that it should not work at all. Their operational force is an alliance stitched together in improbable ways across the jurisdictional boundaries of a half-dozen federal agencies, the various state forestry departments and some county jurisdictions. Despite that fractionation, it has awed the U.S. military establishment with its blitzkrieg ability to mobilize rapidly, to move fire crews and equipment thousands of miles in scant hours, and to integrate interagency command functions. At its highest echelons the wildfire alliance has forged links with NASA and with the U.S. armed forces. On occasion, in the truly monumental fire years, it pulls in even the military itself, and puts soldiers and Marines on the fire lines of the West.

In the skies the aircraft and pilots of this conflict are often veterans of America's wars. In a corps so small that it is little more than a fraternity of adventurers, they bring the techniques of combat aviation to a peacetime pursuit that is one of the most hazardous occupations in the nation. Regularly they fly into impossible situations, diving deep into forested canyons in horrific weather and smoke conditions. Some of their aircraft date from World War II. Every season, some crews fly out and do not return.

The nominal generals and colonels of this paramilitary army are full-timers, fire hands who have fought the great battles of the West. They fill billets in the federal and state land management agencies, representing operations as large as the U.S. Forest Service and the federal Bureau of Land Management and as small as the Wyoming State Forestry Division. They are the Pattons and Eisenhowers of their world, strategists and tacticians whose tool kit runs to flanking movements and troop deployments and holding actions and frontal attacks and aerial bombing and, on occasion, strategic retreats. A few decades back, they were always called fire bosses. Now the system prefers to bill them as incident commanders. Like generals everywhere, they rely on technology. They make the tough calls with help from fire meteorologists, lightning detection systems, infrared photographers, fire behavior analysts, fuels technicians, operations specialists, and satellite telemetry.

When big blazes, called project fires, are up and running in the West, the generals and their lieutenants and tacticians and technologists—overhead, they are all called in fire parlance—pursue their crafts in instant cities. Created overnight to house and feed up to two thousand seasonal warriors, fire camps bristle with an eclectic sort of energy, like some odd combination of Arab bazaar, D-Day beachhead, and class reunion. Generators chug away, trucks raise billows of dust, crews march off to battle, aromas waft from kitchens, clipboard warriors charge about earnestly, television cameras whir, tents bloom in rainbow colors, communiqués on briefing boards riffle in the wind, Indians and Hispanics converse in native tongues, firefighters who last met two years ago in Nevada renew acquaintances, Frisbees fly in the background, radios babble, exhausted night shift crews chase sleep in the noonday sun.

Despite all the organizational infrastructure and the professionals who guide the campaign, the battle on the fire lines is largely carried by the seasonal combatants, a group so diverse that it could qualify as America's equivalent of the French Foreign Legion. They are rocket scientists and doctors and architects in training, the best and the brightest signing on for the most punishing work they will ever know before the harness of career settles onto their shoulders. They are murderers and petty thieves, working their way out of the prison systems of the West by building up good time on inmate fire crews. They are Apache and Athabascan, Crow and Cheyenne, beating out a new definition for the warrior tradition in their tribes.

They are aging guerrillas, with the surgeon's signature tracked across their grating knees, college degrees tucked away in some forgotten pigeonhole, and the world's expectations on indefinite hold, convincing themselves that their bodies will do this for one more season. They are blue-collar types from a thousand small towns, off for some excitement before accepting the pleasant inevitability of the jobs and lives their fathers knew. They are daughters loving a job their mothers could not have imagined. They are diggers of potatoes and pickers of lemons, speaking with the accents of Sonora and Oaxaca, and forsaking the fields of the West when smoke rises in the mountains. They are lawyers and dentists, improbably abandoning their families and offices each summer to recapture remembered glories.

For many of the seasonals, the annual battle against Western wildfire, with hundred-hour weeks, twenty-one day shifts, and the most grueling sort of dirt-throwing manual labor, becomes a consuming avocation. Bill Moody, a former smokejumper boss and now a consultant on wildland fire, sees what might be the best aspects of the attitudes of the 1960s filtering through the troops of the wildland fire community. "In our society, we see more and more people who aren't locked into economics or status," he said. "They concentrate on the things they enjoy, the things that give them satisfaction in life. People who like the wildfire environment, the physical challenges, the traveling, the excitement, they don't see themselves as limited by economics or marital status or the pressures that people respond to in pursuing other careers. They find that they can do it. With the proper physical conditioning and lifestyle, they perpetuate the exciting part of their life."

Despite the exhausting work and the danger, some keep at it like professional athletes, back for every season until the legs go. For them, the pursuit of forest fire becomes life-altering passion. Some will be fire bums in the summer and ski bums in the winter, one penchant for excitement supporting the other.

Many extend educations, delay careers, postpone marriages, all to continue battling fire. Since the 1960s, the average age of seasonal forest firefighters has climbed steadily. Some have abandoned college educations. Many have completed them but refuse to leave the fire game— PhDs throw dirt on the fire lines of the West every summer.

In Washington state, David Glose goes after forest fire by rappelling down 250-foot ropes from helicopters. He took a white-collar job after college but gave it up to come back to fire and helitack crews. In his late twenties, he cannot foresee an end to it. "I know there are people who think that with two college degrees, I should be getting on with my life. My father, for one," he said. "He never says it outright but he always asks if I'm going to be doing this again next year. He always talks about long-term plans. When I was in college he thought this was a great summer job. Now that school is over, he expects me to move on. But not yet. Not just yet."

In the West, every stratum of society has adults who have shared this experience; most rank it as a formative influence in their lives. Few expect others to understand. "This type of experience, and it really *is* a rite of passage, is becoming increasingly rare in our society," said Bob Lee. He pursued fire for eighteen years, with the state of California, with the Forest Service, with the Bureau of Land Management. Despite a college degree, despite the tug of conventional responsibility, he kept at it until age forty, then endured a year of acute withdrawal pangs when he stepped into a fire desk job with the BLM in Albuquerque. "You do something that's a tough job," he said. "You become part of this subculture. You go out and face occasionally insurmountable odds in very uncomfortable situations. It has all the challenges of war but none of the drawbacks. You fight a war but you don't kill people. It's about risk. A life needs risk to be truly alive. And so many lives have no risk."

For those who catch the disease, who become passionate about the seasonal pursuit of fire, it is an open secret that the game is not kind to romantic relationships. "There was a smokejumper who got married a few years ago in Alaska," said Jon Curd, who jumps for the BLM out of Boise, Idaho. "Before the wedding, the guys did a bunch of research and put together this little program for him. Flip charts on the lawn. Ninety percent of the jumpers

Above: Oregon smokejumper Margo Freeman, a former college athlete and an off-season coach at the University of Washington, is one of fewer than fifty U.S. women to qualify for jumping since 1981.

■ ■ ■

had been married at one time or another, and of that bunch, ninety-five percent had gotten divorced. And then a bunch of those guys got married again, and eighty percent of them were divorced a second time. The guys who got married a third time were able to get the rate down to seventy percent."

Two or three decades ago, twenty-five was old for a seasonal firefighter, and thirty was ancient. Now there are hundreds of hotshots who will never see thirty-five again, and a few smokejumpers still stepping out the airplane door after age fifty. In the slow times, the perennial seasonals talk wistfully of the firefighter's Holy Grail, a full-time job in fire, even as they admit of its improbability. Regardless, most of them will be back next spring, and next, and next.

"I was a student in New York. I thought I'd go West and fight fire for a summer and then head back East for more school. But it's never happened," said Dave Niemi, a firefighter on a crack National Park Service hotshot crew in Colorado, and a veteran of fire crews in three states and two government agencies. "Fire and the West have just captured my life. It was a chance to see places that normal people don't see, in ways they don't see it. I liked the excitement. I liked the rush of being up against a running crown fire. I liked working six months, making a lot of money, then skiing for the winter. I got into the lifestyle. I became a fire mercenary."

■ ■ ■

Military towns, places such as Jacksonville, North Carolina, and San Antonio, Texas, dot America. So, too, fire towns punctuate the West. Missoula and Boise and Fairbanks, by common consent, are in the first tier. But there are others. Redmond, Oregon, and Carson City, Nevada. McCall, Idaho, and Redding, California. Grand Junction, Colorado, and Wenatchee, Washington. They are places where tanker planes and helicopters have taken to the skies for ages, where smokejumpers

■ ■ ■

Right: In the Southern California wildfires of 1993 a helicopter battles fire sweeping through an Altadena neighborhood. The hazards created when residential developments shoulder their way into stands of wildland vegetation regularly deliver fire to the doorsteps of thousands of Westerners, with catastrophic results.

or fire crews have trained and gone off to battle, where fire is woven into the fabric of local history. In those towns, the ripple effect of big fire anywhere in the West will always be palpable.

In the fire towns, the traditions of the summer battles of the West sometimes are preserved with monuments and small museums. School teachers haul in busloads of pupils for base tours. In the populace, a certain savvy about the wildland fire game is common, and a bit of boosterish local pride is often obvious. The tales of the tanker pilots who anchor at the community airport will be the stuff of legend, the epic bar brawls waged by the local smokejumpers a decade ago will grow even more epic with each retelling by citizens who weren't there, and everyone will remember the year the fire crew stormed out of its barracks to stop the blaze on the hill just above town.

But outside those places, the fire warriors of the West mostly work with the anonymity of infantrymen, though their battles command increasing public attention. That attention is new. Through much of the history of the modern West, the war against forest fire was a closet war, fought largely in isolated forests and mountain ranges. For the most part, the historic "fire busts" of the West—Idaho's 1910 conflagration, Oregon's Tillamook Burn in the 1930s, or any one of a hundred blazes in Southern California before World War II—burned far from the public doorstep. But from mid-century on, wildland fire has come knocking on the door ever more often. It's not that the dragon has marched to town, but that town has marched to him. As cities and subdivisions and hobby farms and ranchettes and housing developments and country clubs and resorts and summer cabins have sprawled into the foothills and mountain canyons of the West, their occupants have set themselves in harm's way.

It is, in a sense, a habitat issue. Now that they no longer talk of the total eradication of fire like epidemiologists chasing some rogue virus, the foresters say that the timber stands and the brushy mountain slopes and the sagebrush desert are fire's natural home. The ecologists speak of the intriguing symbiosis of fire and forest, of the ways that flame is as vital to forest health as rain and sunshine. When humanity claims forest and canyon and range for its own habitat, the deer and the antelope may cede the territory and go quietly. But not fire. In the West, from elegant Southern California suburbs to picturesque subdivisions in Colorado mountains, fire is the evicted occupant who does not go graciously, who returns periodically to haunt his old homestead.

As a consequence of it all, the business of fighting wildland fire in what is now called the interface zone—the margin where homes and forest meet—grows ever more hazardous. "You look up into the mountains at night and you see lights, lights, lights, and then a line of blackness," said Tom Harbour, a California fire boss. "The line is the edge of the national forest. The homes are just built up solid right to the edge of it, in all the canyons and on all the ridges. We had a fire where two Los Angeles County firefighters were killed—wildland firefighters off a helicopter crew. They were trying to keep fire away from houses. It was a neighborhood, a narrow street, a ten-foot strip of land, and then the national forest. They didn't have any room to work."

When Harbour speaks, he could be a fire manager anywhere in the West. His description fits the eastern slope of the Rockies, from Fort Collins to Colorado Springs. It covers the hills around Spokane, Washington, and the pine forests of the eastern Cascade slope in Oregon. It is all too accurate for a thousand canyons in the Southwest, for the Sierra Front in Nevada, and the Boise Front in Idaho. Firefighters once could choose where to make their stand. Like generals in military battles, they chose advantages that the land offered—rivers, roads, rocky ridges—so that terrain became an ally. But now the presence of homes and lives to be protected has robbed them of choice. Too often now they must draw their line on inopportune ground and make their stand in dangerous places. Sometimes the price is high, as in 1990, when six Arizona firefighters died, backs to the wall, trapped on the line they defended in a canyon below a forest subdivision. Or in 1994, when fourteen firefighters died at the South Canyon Fire on the flanks of Colorado's Storm King Mountain, battling an upslope blaze within sight of a rural subdivision.

"The amount of housing in the in the wildland environment is just exploding," said Elmer Hurd, who heads fire operations for the National Park Service. "We're fighting fires to save buildings in places where we used to have the luxury of backing up a mile and waiting to take it on at a natural barrier. We have lost the options."

As a result, wildland fire and those who fight it have vaulted out of the subtext of Western life and into the headlines. Forest fire and the citizenry began intersecting more regularly after 1960, as the postwar construction boom put more and more homes in fire's habitat. The 1970s brought a series of disastrous Western forest fires, some that raged through remote forests and others that claimed homes and lives. In response, government pumped money, personnel and equipment into the wildland fire army. Then a seven-year drought that began in the mid-1980s crinkled the West to parchment and delivered a horrific series of fires—Northern California and Southern Oregon

• • •

Right: Tanker planes, such as this DC-6 swooping low to drop chemical retardant on an Arizona's Harquahala Fire in 1993, are flagships in a dangerous air war. Fifty of the ships fly in the West; almost every season one is lost, without survivors.

in 1987; Yellowstone National Park in 1988; Colorado's Black Tiger Canyon in 1989; Arizona's Mogollon Rim and Alaska's Tok River in 1990; Oakland, California, and Spokane, Washington, in the same week in 1991; big chunks of Idaho in 1992; and, with the drought ostensibly in remission, the horror of Southern California in the fall of 1993.

For the wildland fire community, all of it was prelude for the summer of 1994. In that season, tens of thousands of fires visited the West and exacted the ultimate price from firefighters in seven states. Fourteen hotshots, smokejumpers, and helitack firefighters died on the slopes of Colorado's Storm King Mountain in July, the worst forest fire catastrophe since 1953. Nine of those who fell were from Oregon's Prineville Hotshots, and the attention of the nation was riveted on that quintessential little Western town as it dealt with its grief and paid tribute to its heroes. There was little respite, from fire or from tragedy. Within days, three firefighters died when a helicopter went down in New Mexico. Then, with the wildfire system stretched so thin that the U.S. military was called to action, came the death of a contract fire worker in Washington state and an engine crewman in California. Within weeks a pair of fire-retardant bomber crashes killed two fliers in Montana and three in California. In late summer, a heavy equipment operator was overrun by flames in Southern Oregon. As the fire season ebbed off into fall rains and snows, the firefighter death toll stood at twenty-seven, the worst in sixty years.

Across those same drought-plagued, fire-seared seasons, Western wildfire found its way into popular culture, with artists as diverse as the filmmaker, Steven Spielberg, and the best-selling author, Norman MacLean, weighing in with works built on Western fire and the subculture of people who battle it. Newspapers, even Eastern newspapers, devoted entire pages to the summer battles of the West. The Yellowstone Fire of 1988 produced a spate of books. The ABC television network singled out the anonymous yellow-shirted groundpounders of forest fire for its "Person of the Week" feature. The Storm King fire spawned a run of television specials, magazine articles, and analytical newspaper pieces. Magazines with audiences as diverse as the home-and-garden set, the aviation community, and the outdoor adventuring bunch found their readers fascinated with forest fire.

In a reversal of physics, fire begets friction. As flames come out of the trees and into the public consciousness, forest fire becomes political. It is no longer a remote and vaguely romantic cataclysm, like a volcano on some Indian Ocean island. The mythic image of man versus fire in epic struggle now fits not so handily. More immediate realities intrude. The state and federal agencies and the timber and land companies that manage vast expanses of the West now face a public and a press corps that no longer sees forest fire in simple terms.

Americans are proprietary about resources, so proprietary that public furor over the Yellowstone Fire reverberated through the halls of Congress long after green grass and tourists had come back to the charred meadows. And politicians of all stripes have learned that forest fire at the backyard gate produces an even stronger public reaction than fire in some remote wilderness or national park. Before the 1980s journalists who might have covered one big forest fire a decade could buy into the man-versus-fire script easily enough. Raging flames and heroic firefighters were an easy story. But Western journalists who had seen five fires, or a dozen, inevitably noticed that some were fought better than others. So have their readers. And hard questions sometimes follow.

Other questions are launched from inside the forest community, where debate circles the question of whether decades of aggressive fire suppression have harmed the forest. Increasingly, the conclusion emerges that fire suppression might be the cause both of catastrophic forest die-offs and of some of the monumental blazes of the 1980s and 1990s. In Southern California, the battle is joined over a corollary question, the continuing hazard posed by the fire-based ecosystem of chaparral brush fields that cloak the region's mountains. In the San Gabriels and the Santa Monicas, fingers of urbanization poke into every valley and onto every ridge line.

In the natural order of things, the brush fields—the indigenous amalgam of chamise, manzanita, California lilac, oak brush, buckthorn, and mountain mahogany—would burn off every decade or so. But the natural order has been supplanted with an environmental high-wire act from which there is no retreat. With aggressive, constant fire suppression made an unrelenting necessity by the invasion of homes, the chaparral grows and grows. It stands so thick that its lower limbs die, shielded by the canopy of leaves. Characteristically it is a thin icing of greenery over a thick cake of kindling, tons of it per mountainside acre. Too late comes the realization that blocking holocausts in the brush fields only ensures larger holocausts, that in lower California fire is as inevitable as earthquake, that he who rides the tiger can never dismount.

In the environmentally conscious America of the late twentieth century, the bodies of government assigned to stewardship of the public lands take their licks. They face accusations of cutting too much, grazing too much, mining too much. Environmental lawsuits, stiff media coverage, industry demands, legislative pressure, and protest demonstrations have descended upon the governmental land managers. More than a few timber sale administrators and grazing lease program managers have looked with envy at the fire shops, the fire fighting arms of their agencies. With some of them, it's become an axiom that fighting fire seems to be the only white hat job left in public lands. But lately the fire shop has begun to feel the heat—from those who charge it has allowed too much of the West to burn, or paradoxically from those who argue that it has been too successful in stopping fire, and perhaps spent too much in the process. The fire shop's grant of political immunity may be waning.

Still, in the dominant Western view, the fighting of forest fire, especially the down and dirty fighting of it at ground level, remains a white-hat job. To this day, there is no small town or large city so jaded that it does not heap gratitude and reader board plaudits and commendatory editorials on the itinerant warriors who come, often from thousands of miles away, to fight fire in the surrounding hills. In Thousand Oaks, California, hardly a rural western town, the community buried a fire camp in home-baked treats during the catastrophic fires of 1993. Thousand Oaks proved itself not so different from tiny McCall, Idaho, a quintessential blue-collar timber and recreation community where a crew of Forest Service hotshots, in town for a Saturday night after a tough stint on a nearby fire, enjoyed their beer but had their money refused.

For generations, Westerners have known the battling of forest fire as a rite of passage, whether the job is an introspective summer on some lonely lookout tower, or a test of stamina and will on the fire lines. Tens of thousands of college educations have been financed by paychecks from seasonal fire. Among Westerners, most can count an uncle or a cousin, a college roommate or a coworker, a daughter or a son, who once spent summers fighting fire in the forests.

The East has forest fires, too, after a fashion, just as it has mountains. But Westerners prefer to see the fighting of forest fire, especially big forest fire, as a Western institution, like cattle ranching or rodeo or serious whitewater rafting. "The West has the bigger fires, the conflagrations," said Steve Pedigo, a Forest Service fire planner who grew up fighting fires in the East. "The East has thousands of fires, but just little ones. When you were on an Eastern fire crew, what always made your season was getting hauled out West for one of the really big fires. In the West, you have all the elements. You have the remoteness that brings in the smokejumpers and the hotshot crews that can take off and live in the wilderness and fight fire. In the West, you have the helitack operations and all the air tankers. It's all bigger on Western fires."

A sense of adventure, a love of risk, and a veneer of the unconventional have been the perennial common denominators of the West's forest fire troops. But beyond those traits, fire always has been a pursuit that spanned every subset of the Western experience. Jack Kerouac, the hip chronicler of the beat generation, held a place in the armies of summer; so did Louis L'Amour, the novelist of the traditional Old West. And always it has been difficult for those who have done it to make those who have not understand the punishing physical demands of their work. L'Amour once summed it up for the adventurers and the risk takers who take on big fire with a shovel and will power. "Fire fighting is desperate work," he said. "There is no work so demanding as fire fighting. There is a desperation in fire fighting that is born of man's ancient fear and his present realization of the danger."

Risk comes with varied faces. One of them is the opportunity to risk being wrong. To an extent almost unfathomable to those outside its culture, the forest fire community confers extraordinary decision-making responsibility on very young people. No decision timetable impedes, no written proposals change hands, no board of directors meets. Battlefield urgency prevails. Get on with it. On an Idaho blaze in the early 1990s, a campaign fire of monumental proportions, a young hotshot crew member was handed a radio and posted on a ridge to monitor a roaring canyon fire. Like some combat forward observer, her job was to call in strikes by four-engine retardant bombers. She was a student, only twenty-three, not even a squad leader. But her superiors respected her experience, trusted her judgment. Through the afternoon, each time she sent a pair of pilots and their million-dollar ship winging into the canyon, she spent four thousand dollars.

"It's scary how much money and expense I'm responsible for" said Kim Bang, a former firefighter who has been a BLM fire dispatcher in Grand Junction, Colorado, since her mid-twenties. "If I send in a light helicopter, it's nine hundred to fourteen hundred dollars an hour. If I have just an average fire where I send some smokejumpers, some retardant planes and helicopters, it could be seventy-five thousand dollars just in an afternoon. We think about catching things when they're small. If you go too easy and it becomes a big fire, that's what's truly expensive. But you can't do this without being conscious of what you're spending every time you make a decision."

For every groundpounder who waxes philosophic and poetic about fire in the forest, there are hundreds more from whom the equation is more elemental, more visceral. They yield to no one in their honesty, and when they talk, even the philosophers on their crews nod in agreement. "What it's really about is adrenaline," said Drew Cushing, a second-generation Western firefighter who spends his summers with the Forest Service at Fort Collins, Colorado. "You go along for weeks or months with little fires that don't amount to anything. And then you hit the good one that makes it all worthwhile. More than anything, that's why I do it. I just hang on for the ones that give you a good rush."

CHAPTER 2

The Moral Equivalent of War

I T IS 1944. September. Like a sparrow swooping over the battlements of a castle, a single-engine Fairchild bounces in the updrafts above the Coast Range Mountains in Northern California. Below, the Six Rivers National Forest is a green cape draped over steep slopes and chiseled finger valleys. Streams, thin now in late summer, glint silvery in the sun, like strands of tinsel woven through the trees. Flying south from an airstrip at the Oregon hamlet of Cave Junction, the pilot can count off the six watersheds—Smith, Trinity, Klamath, Van Duzen, Mad, Eel. As the plane swoops lower, the pilot focuses on the column of smoke that rises from the timbered flank of a steep ridge. Lightning has done its incendiary work.

In the rear, in the plane's cramped cabin, three men rise, clip their parachute static lines to an overhead cable, then do a last check of their gear. They stoop-walk to the open door. In this, the era of the great war in Europe, Africa, and the Pacific, they are clad much like soldiers. In their packs and boots, helmets and harness, they look not so different from the men who took democracy's battle past the beaches of Normandy and parachuted into St. Mère Eglise only a few short weeks before.

With World War II on, there are few men available to fight fire in the West, fewer still young enough, strong enough, and, yes, foolhardy enough to do it by jumping from airplanes. But these men, tumbling from the Fairchild's door and rocketing toward the twenty acres of flames they can see below, are veterans of fire now. The trio swinging beneath the chutes and steering hard for the only patch of clear ground the valley offers are conscientious objectors. Members of traditional peace churches, they know their unwavering principles are questioned and resented by many in wartime America. But their bravery is not wanting. This is the war they have chosen.

"We had something to prove," said Elmer Neufeld. And when he had proved it, he elected to stay with his chosen war. He jumped the fires of the West for twenty-five more years after that other war against Japan and Germany was won. He trained generations of new smokejumpers. It is no accident that in retirement Neufeld lives close to the fire game in Boise, Idaho, a command post city in the summer battles of the West. "When you signed up for jumping as a CO, part of it was to show that you weren't short on courage—you just didn't believe in shooting people," he said. "And the other thing for a lot of the guys was that it was a chance to do something important. We had this service we were required to do, and too many of us had been put on make-work projects. I signed up for jumping because it was something that could make a difference."

Above: U.S. Army pilots gather before taking off on fire patrol over the forests of Washington state in 1920. Army fire reconnaissance was the earliest application of aviation to Western fires.

■ ■ ■

Left: Recruited for fire and forestry work during the Great Depression, a truckload of Civilian Conservation Corps volunteers heads off for a blaze in Idaho's Kaniksu National Forest in 1934.

The history of wildland fire fighting in the West is a history of groups being called to battle. The conscientious objectors, who quite literally saved the fledgling smokejumper program during World War II, is but one of the groups. At various places in various eras, fighting forest fire has been the province of soldiers and settlers, of loggers and railroaders, of barflies and hobos, of Indians and students, of unwilling conscripts and enthusiastic seasonals.

The early history of wildland fire in the West revolved not so much around the question of how to fight it but whether to fight it. Much of what modern Americans regard as the "natural" forest, the forest primeval, did not exist when Columbus landed. Historically, across most of the North American continent, Indians fired the woods and the prairies. They did it to clear underbrush, to create grazing areas that would attract game, to make their camps more defensible, to threaten the camps of their enemies, and, on occasion, for pure amusement.

The forest the Native Americans created and maintained was far different from the forest that evolved after settlement. From sea to shining sea, explorers and the earliest settlers noted in their journals the prevalence of Indian fire. Repeatedly, as they took over the land, the newcomers mentioned open, treeless valleys and forests free of underbrush. But as new settlers aged to become old settlers, they noted that after four or five decades the forests had filled in, and that foothills that had been bare when they arrived had reverted to stands of young timber or thickening blankets of brush.

In a pattern that began in the East but was carried west, frontier factions endlessly debated the problem of fire. Typically, in the first cycle of settlement, fire raged unchecked in the

Hired for fire fighting in Washington state in 1918, a squadron of volunteers lines up with the Army officer who commanded them. Military involvement in fire fighting was common in the early part of the century.

▪ ▪ ▪

mountain forests and desert grasslands. Often, the pioneers imitated the Indians they had displaced. Fires begun to clear homestead land would jump the traces and run for months and miles with no effort made to slow them. Lightning fires likewise were ignored. One pioneer-era fire in Oregon rampaged for eight hundred thousand acres, an area larger than Rhode Island, with essentially no suppression effort. In a time when trees were seen as weeds, when the forests of the West were sometimes known as "the green desert," when the doctrine of Manifest Destiny called for shouldering back the wilderness, few saw wildland fire as cause for concern. Near settlements, the hills were fired each fall by grazers, to stimulate pasturage the following spring. From San Diego to Seattle, from Portland to Denver, frontier newspapers spoke of smoke that hung in the air through much of the year.

For many, smoke symbolized progress. But inevitably civilization had its orderly way. The controversy over "light burning" dragged on in California and Oregon until the 1920s, with timber owners contending that small, seasonal clearing fires prevented catastrophic blazes and herders arguing that smoke was the price to pay for a growing livestock industry. But long before that, the forces of business, government, society, and the new field of professional forestry were marshaling to promote forest fire suppression as a public good. For civic boosters of the late nineteenth and early twentieth centuries, ridding the air of its perpetual pall was a cause on par with paving mud streets, closing bawdy houses, and building libraries. And a few visionaries were beginning to talk of the esthetic value of the forest, or of the possibility of a timber famine if the wildland fires of the West were allowed to burn unchecked.

In the frontier West, forest fires were fought in much the same fashion that stagecoach robbers were chased, with the equivalent of an impromptu sheriff's posse. No state or federal force stood ready to deal with them. If wildland fire threatened a community or a farmstead, townspeople and neighbors would turn out en masse to give battle. Such horse-drawn fire equipment as a prosperous town might have for house fires was useless against fire raging in timber stands or galloping up canyons choked with brush. For that sort of fire, the most experienced firefighters, those who understood such ideas as digging fire breaks and setting counter-fires, often were the homesteaders, grazers and timber owners whose deliberate fires drew so much criticism.

The first vestige of organized protection of forest and rangeland in the West came with the creation of Yellowstone National Park. The U.S. Army was assigned to fire patrols there in 1886. The soldiers were successful in curbing fire starts in Yellowstone, even though they were so meagerly equipped they sometimes had to rely on public donations for buckets and axes. As a system of federal forest reserves evolved outside the parks, fire suppression responsibility for the forests, such as it was, passed in 1897 to the General Land Office, a branch of the federal Department of the Interior.

Woefully underbudgeted for its task and never seeing fire as a high priority, the General Land Office established a system of fire rangers. The rangers patrolled the back country of the West, subdued small fires, and marshaled local forces for fighting large ones. Meanwhile, railroads, which stood at risk of losing wooden ties and timber trestles in conflagrations started by their own fire-belching steam engines, formed fire patrols that sometimes used handcars to patrol sections of mountain rail. When big fire hit along the main line, railroad section gangs would be thrown onto work trains and sent off to battle. More than one small Western town threatened by an engulfing blaze was saved by the timely arrival of the trains and their fire crews. Occasionally, tiny communities were abandoned to fire, their residents evacuated in wooden-sided train coaches that sometimes caught fire themselves as they crossed blazing timber trestles.

With creation of the Clearwater Timber Protection Association in Idaho in 1906, the concept of organized fire fighting among the owners of private timberlands began spreading in the logging regions of the West. In later years, the timber protection associations would have their own standing fire crews. But first, they established a system of patrolling fire wardens. The associations also brought some regimentation to the established informal practice of dispatching logging crews and sawmill gangs to fight forest fire. In all the timber regions, the millhands and loggers became a formidable part of the armies of summer.

However, the modern era of wildland fire fighting truly began in 1905, with the transfer of federal forest reserves from the General Land Office to the newborn U.S. Forest Service, a branch of the Department of Agriculture. For the agency, home to America's fledgling corps of professional foresters, the possibility of letting forest fires have their head was never a consideration. "The necessity of preventing losses from forest fires requires no discussion," declared Henry Graves, one of the early chief foresters of the new agency. "It is the fundamental obligation of the Forest Service and takes precedence over all other duties and activities."

In the decades that followed, the Forest Service defined the wildland fire game and defined itself through the fighting of fire. The service became the model, the adviser, the researcher, the godfather, the ally, and, to a significant degree, the financier of emerging state forestry and fire operations. With the leverage provided by federal money that it could distribute to the states, the Forest Service managed to stitch together cooperative agreements that provided, in a rudimentary way, for pooling of manpower and equipment in big fires. The Department of the Interior, meanwhile, became a minor presence on the wildland fire stage. It would be little more than a bit player for half a century, but then, through the BLM and the vastness of its responsibility in Alaska, it would carve out an ascendant role for itself.

Looking back to the Army's successes in Yellowstone, the Forest Service quickly evolved a paramilitary approach to wildland fire. Though its leaders never sported collar bars or shoulder stripes, and its troops were never required to salute, it found much to imitate in the military model; bivouacking in remote camps, studying maps and reviewing intelligence from the field, planning flanking attacks, taking and holding ground, puzzling out logistical problems, lacing together field communications systems. The parallels were abundant, and, since the beginning, they have dominated the conversation of the wildfire community.

In 1910, an essay by the American philosopher and pacifist William James attracted wide attention. Titled "On the Moral Equivalent of War," it was published during a period of extreme forest fires in the American West. Despite his pacifist ideals, James saw much to respect in the values fostered in the crucible of military combat. He not only conceded that the warmaking urge seemed an irreducible component of the human condition, but he suggested that men were ennobled by the experience. Though James did not mention forest fire specifically, he spoke of the value of battling the forces of nature, of securing the character-building benefits of war without the killing. He proposed formation of a corps of young men who could garner the best of the military experience by being sent off to test themselves and serve their country in the wilderness. Ever since, no thoughtful discussion of the world of wildland fire in the West is complete without an observation about "the moral equivalent of war."

■ ■ ■

Caught in the epicenter of an Idaho firestorm, forty-five men ran for life itself. Wind-lashed flames roared louder than an armada of locomotives, towering trees fell like wheat before a scythe, the afternoon sky turned black, and air as hot as the breath of an ironworks forge swept over them. Their leader, Edward Pulaski, a Forest Service ranger, found their path to safety blocked by fire. In a mounting holocaust that raged like a volcano, they were surrounded. But Pulaski, like so many of the early rangers and fire wardens, had been recruited from the land he worked. Now, in the historic fires of 1910, he would prove the wisdom of that policy.

He had been at times a prospector and a miner, and in the conflagration that now encircled the men he led, he had not lost his bearings. He left his troops momentarily, threw a wet gunnysack over his head, and sprinted into the blazing forest. Moments later, he returned to lead the men to the abandoned War Eagle Mine. A man who lagged too far behind, or perhaps sought his own route to safety, was killed by a falling tree. Pulaski got the rest to the mine. At the back of the tunnel, they found a seep of water, enough to wet their clothing and dampen cloths to place over their mouths. As the flames bore down on them, Pulaski hung wet horse blankets across the tunnel opening.

Like a great, red avalanche running uphill, the fire roared across the mouth of the mine. It generated its own winds, probably well over a hundred miles an hour, and they filled the tunnel with thick, choking smoke. Outside, 150-foot trees snapped like jackstraws and crashed across the mine entrance. Inside, men wept. As the air in the mine grew fouler and fouler, some rose in panic. A stampede to certain death seemed at hand. Pulaski drew a pistol and promised a bullet to the first man who bolted. Some accounts say he actually fired between the legs of one man. The men retreated to the back of the tunnel while their ranger stood his ground at the entrance. One by one, the firefighters fell unconscious, and, finally, so did their leader.

In the rear of the tunnel, some of the men revived in the early morning. They found all but five of their group still alive. Helping each other, the survivors crawled and stumbled toward the entrance, making their way toward a black, ashen world where the trunks of fallen trees still burned. Pulaski's body lay by the entrance, and the firefighter who spotted it first turned to report that the ranger was dead. But the body spoke, and it said, "Like hell he is."

A hero of early Western forest fire fighting, Edward Pulaski distinguished himself in the Northern Rockies fires of 1910 and invented the fire-fighting tool still used around the west.

On that day in 1910, Edward Pulaski established himself as one of the legends of Western fire. He would cement his niche a few years later by devising the combination ax-hoe that bears his name and is still the most common fire line weapon in the summer battles of the West. But the siege he survived did more than merely deliver a colorful hero. In the American West of the twentieth century, a handful of forest fires became pivotal events, like Gettysburgs and Pearl Harbors. Changes flowed from them. Because they happened, the world of wildland fire would never be the same again. The Northern Rockies fires of 1910 were such an event.

Arizona burned in that long, dry summer. California burned. And so did Oregon and Washington. Five million acres burned in all, but Idaho and Montana took the worst of it, more than three million acres consumed in 1,736 fires that began in midsummer and raged into fall. Sometimes hundreds of them burned at once, each large enough to stoke a winter's storytelling in a normal year. Officialdom mobilized militias and the U.S. Army. The railroads moved in every available train and man. Thousands of firefighters and immense resources were thrown at the blazes. Here and there, a heroic stand made a difference; at Wallace, Idaho firefighters halted a juggernaut of a fire after it had consumed a hundred homes and business buildings. But mostly the Northern Rockies fires burned at will. And when the first winter snows finally shut them off, seventy-eight firefighters were dead. No Western fire, before or since, ever exacted such a toll from those who fought it.

Still, the disaster was a boon of sorts for the fledgling Forest Service, then just five years old. Underfunded and underequipped, it had patrolled its vast Western holdings with a thin line of horseback rangers. The Northern Rockies fires brought the agency new attention, and new funding. Its network of ranger stations, fire lookouts, and working foresters increased. Over the ensuing decades, it steadily promoted the creation of state forestry departments for fire suppression on non-federal land, and timber protection associations for commercial forest land. The subculture of Western forest fire was born.

The Forest Service regulars and their counterparts in the other organizations became recognized as the first line of defense for routine fires. The rangers, fire wardens, and other employees of the public and private forest agencies choked off thousands of small fires and prevented them from becoming large ones. Epic stories from that era tell of rangers spending days fording whitewater streams and traversing steep cliffs to reach distant fires. But the big fires still came regularly in every sector of the West, chewing up ten thousand, twenty thousand, a hundred thousand acres. For those conflagrations, the rangers and fire wardens still had to pull in farmers, loggers, and laborers, and make firefighters of them. As the society around the forests became more settled and less frontierish, the pool of available volunteers shrunk.

The mission, after all, had evolved toward fighting fires in the backcountry, not just fires that were bearing down on towns to threaten hearth and home. No ranger could realistically expect to find willing, unpaid firefighters to battle remote blazes. The days when fire fighting was a community event, like a barn-raising, were passing. With organization and with expansion of the mission came fire fighting paychecks,

Through the first half of the twentieth century, fire detection outposts such as Washington state's Sleeping Beauty Lookout, sprouted on mountaintops around the West.

■ ■ ■

buttressed by laws that gave rangers and fire wardens conscription rights, like sheriffs seeking deputies for a posse.

Even with money to spend and the law behind them, fire bosses often found themselves cruising the saloons and skid rows of Western towns, sobering up the dregs of local humanity to go chase smoke in the hills. With the new way of business came the problem of "job-hunting fires" deliberately set by those who coveted the earnings of a few days on the fire line. On big Western fires, the pattern of a few agency regulars leading a hastily assembled army of mostly untrained, often unwilling, spur-of-the-moment firefighters would prevail—with one major interruption—until well after World War II.

In the two decades after the fires of 1910, the technology of fire fighting spread its wings. By 1920 fire-spotter airplanes were patrolling Western forests. Experiments in dropping water and chemicals to extinguish fires began a few years later. Radio communications became part of the game. The first brush engines, fire trucks designed for back country work, began showing up on forest roads. Thousands of miles of telephone line were strung on trees to connect remote ranger stations to the world, and to permit the swift dispatch of fire crews. The first generation of the hand-operated backpack water pump, a five-gallon load to be hated by entire generations of forest firefighters, made its appearance. Other rangers joined Pulaski in designing hand tools for the fire line. Some bear their inventor's names, like the McLeod, a combination rake-hoe. Most, including a brush hook styled after a hay-cutting tool, and a combination shovel-hoe, are still in use on the fire lines of the 1990s.

On the mountaintops and ridges of the West, lookout cabins and towers sprouted like daffodils in spring. The most visible symbol of the expanding campaign against wildland fire, they ultimately would number nearly four thousand, with 966 in Idaho alone. Every outfit that had an interest in fire—the Forest Service, railroads, timber companies, the state forestry departments—built the lonely, rustic skyscrapers. The first lookouts were little more than crude platforms anchored to rocky peaks or spiked to the tops of trees. But they evolved to a distinctive form of Western vernacular architecture, eventually to become the subject of books and preservation efforts.

Most were constructed at great pain, with every board, nail, and window hauled on mule back into the wilderness. Some, like the lookouts built atop Oregon's Mount Hood and Washington's Three Fingers Rock, were feats of both engineering and mountaineering. Usually twelve to fourteen feet square, the one-room aeries were ringed with windows and provided the most spartan of accommodations—stove, bunk, table. At the center of each stood a pedestal, bearing like an icon the Osborne Firefinder, a sighting instrument that could produce a precise direction heading on a distant smoke.

The lofty observation posts provided the first significant jobs for women in fire fighting. The West's very first lookout, a perch in a pine tree in Idaho's Clearwater Forest, operated with the eyes of Mable Gray, a logging camp cook who climbed to her station each day after the breakfast dishes were done. Lookouts also became the job of preference for firefighters a bit past their prime. The lonely outposts attracted college students, more often poets, writers, and musicians than football players. Although occasionally a couple took over a tower, lookouts usually worked solo.

Some lookouts had to hike an hour or more for fresh water. Some lived in such splendid isolation that they went weeks or months without seeing other humans. But they could look out across the roof of the forest and see the towers of their neighbors twenty to a hundred miles away, and at night they could all yammer away on the radio. The early lookout workers, especially those without radios, had a broad job description. Sometimes they would spot a distant smoke, then load up a backpack and head off to extinguish it.

Each lookout station had a stool with glass-ball feet that could isolate its user from electrical currents. The stool was the perch of choice, and of survival, when "lightning busts" rocked the mountains, testing the lookout buildings' lightning rods and grounding wires. The units regularly took direct hits, and the tales their occupants told of those experiences were spectacular. Inside the lookouts, fixtures often glowed with eerie St. Elmo's Fire, the phenomenon commonly seen in ships' rigging when electrical currents charge the air. Over the years, a few lookouts died in lightning strikes.

One of the West's most colorful lookouts was Helen Dow, a stylish young woman of the 1920s. Through much of that decade she was the keeper of the Devil's Head Lookout in Colorado's Pike National Forest. She lived in a small bunkhouse at the foot of the tower and climbed a series of thirty-foot poles to reach her glass-windowed observatory. Clad in jodphurs and riding boots, she entertained hikers and wilderness visitors who stopped by at her retreat. Partly because of her colorful history, Devil's Head remains the only operating lookout in Colorado. Across the years, lookouts became a casualty of aircraft fire spotting programs and forest road networks, which made the towers less important. Even smog took its toll, leading to closures of historic lookouts in Southern California and other regions where urban pollution spilled into mountain airsheds and compromised long-distance visibility. Around the West, barely a thousand lookout structures remain. Only about four hundred are staffed. In many cases, their operation depends upon volunteers.

■ ■ ■

Fire lookouts who surveyed miles of Western vastness from thier lonely aeries have always been colorful figures, but few were more colorful than Helen Dow, who stylishly operated Colorado's Devil's Head Lookout in the 1920s.

Lying between the towering Cascade Range and the Pacific Ocean, the Coast Range Mountains of western Oregon are a soggy place, an American rain forest where temperate, wet winters and rainy springs invite nature to turn rococo. An exuberance of fern and salal and vine maple and blackberry creepers and goatsbeard and skunk cabbage and stinging nettle and exotic mushrooms cloak its damp canyons. In shades of green to put grass to shame, moss feathers the cathedral columns of leviathan firs and carpets the spongy earth in velvet. Brooks chuckle bank-full through lush, deep-shaded valleys where storms off the Pacific can run the rain gauge up to 120 inches a year. Winter fog hangs like cotton candy on the treetops of twisting canyons, roofing them into gray-green rooms where the rain falls and falls. Coaxed by nature's atomizer, the vegetation builds to a thousand tons per acre.

But the myth of the Pacific Northwest is that the rain never stops. It stops in summer. Decidedly. Definitively. Especially along Oregon's western edge. Though thunderstorms and gully washers dampen summers in other regions of the West, the Coast Range can cook from July through October with barely a teacup's worth of rain, and sometimes the temperature can push beyond a hundred degrees Fahrenheit. In those parboiled summers, the fern dries, the moss browns, the brooks dwindle to trickles, the humidity tumbles to perilous lows, and loggers rub their sunburned necks and hope against the arrival of an east wind.

On an August day in 1933, the east wind came. It blew in from the desert 150 miles distant, and its hot breath spurred another of those milestone conflagrations, a blaze remembered as the Great Tillamook Fire. Though history's long view suggests that two fires may have begun in separate locations at almost the same hour on August 14, legend lays the Tillamook at the feet of a private "gyppo" logging crew that worked too long on a day when the humidity skittered too low. A log rubbing against another log, or perhaps a cable running over a stump, was enough to unleash a tiny tongue of fire. With optimal conditions, it exploded to become a wall that went racing up-canyon like a cougar running down a deer.

Though aggressively attacked, the blaze staked a four-hundred-acre perimeter by nightfall. Then it slowed for an evening's rest. As Oregon fires go, it was not much of a fire at that point. But at morning, the mercury began a climb to 104 degrees, and the fire set off on a ten-day romp. In short order, every logging company in northwestern Oregon came on the run. The Army was there, with the National Guard and the Civilian Conservation Corps, and the forces of the timber protection associations. Some days the east wind would drop and the combatants would think they had their adversary corralled, but on the new dawn he would get up and run again. With brands pushed aloft by the fire's up-draft and kited eastward by the wind, the fire sometimes would spot ahead ten miles or more. Worse, some arson fires were touched off in the middle of the battle. Gradually the collection of fires pushed itself out to forty thousand acres. The blowup came on August 25, lashed by another sirocco of east wind.

In less than twenty-four hours, the fire stampeded across 220,000 acres of America's best forest land. Trees that had grown since before the time of Columbus perished that day, as three thousand firefighters fled the forest with flames at their heels. The smoke column from the Tillamook climbed forty thousand feet into the troposphere, and ashes fell on ships five hundred miles at sea. Noon was as dark as midnight. One firefighter died beneath a falling tree. Others escaped the flames by huddling in creeks, shar-ing their pools of refuge with deer. Women and children were evacuated on railroad flatcars from logging camps and small towns. Behind them, wooden trestles burned and collapsed.

By the end of the day, the half-circle fire front stretched almost a hundred miles, from a few miles west of Portland to the doorstep of the coastal town of Tillamook itself. Finally the Coast Range reverted to form; enough rain and fog rolled in to give exhausted fire crews a toehold. When the fire was finally contained, it totaled 311,000 acres. The timber loss ran to more than twelve billion board feet, and the financial toll was calcu-lated at 375 million in depression-era dollars. But the Tillamook was not done. Millions of tons of charred, dead timber remained in the Coast Range and, on an almost predictable six-year cycle, massive reburns swept through portions of the scarred land. The last came in 1951.

Much later, the Tillamook Burn would become an Or-egon success story, a miracle of salvage, reforestation, and rejuvenation. But, in truth, successes and harbingers of suc-cess swirled in the smoke of that first horrendous month. In 1933, much that would define the future of wildland fire fighting in the West was afoot. Around the West, the fledg-ling state forestry departments had been growing in size, capability, and experience. The California Department of Forestry was en route to becoming the giant fire-fighting agency that it is in the late twentieth century. And then came the Tillamook, an epic battle managed and fought from its inception by the twenty-two-year-old Oregon Department of Forestry, with the U.S. Forest Service as a bit player. It was a watershed event for the Oregon department, which had been organized with fire as its prime mission. But it was also a signal that many of the state wildland fire operations in the West had come of age. The cast of characters in West-ern fire had expanded.

But the Tillamook had a federal element, too, a new and huge and historic one. The Civilian Conservation Corps was just five months old when the big fire erupted. Created by Presi-dent Franklin D. Roosevelt as a Depression-era job provider, the CCC would eventually enroll half a million men in conser-vation camps across America. Pre-suppression fire work—build-ing trails, clearing firebreaks, burning dead fuel, constructing lookout towers—had been envisioned from the outset as an element of its mission. But fire fighting was not in the plan. Not until that August day when the corp's national director found that opportunistic Oregon officials had shanghaied two hun-dred of his troops. Before the battle was over, nearly a thousand CCC men would fight fire there, and many would remain for the massive reforestation effort launched in its wake.

For nine years, until World War II broke up the camps in 1942 and hauled the enrollees off to a different sort of combat, the men of the CCC would fight fire. Forty-seven of them would die in the process, fifteen in one fire. But they did their work well. Their accomplishment spelled the beginning of the end for untrained, pickup fire crews composed of tottering barflies, reluctant conscripts, and the flotsam of local labor pools. In every CCC camp in the West, firefighters were organized and trained. They went off to battle as teams, working beside men who were their compatriots and under others who were their year-round leaders. The CCC troops had multiple jobs. But when fire came, they received the call. As a result, the job-hunting fires created by local arsonists all but disappeared.

In the postwar years, the lessons of the CCC would be revived to become the basis for the organized crews which now stand as the backbone of Western wildfire suppression. The standard twenty-person fire line crew, the Indian firefighter pro-gram on Western reservations, and even team techniques of fire-line digging all would be anchored on concepts that flowed from the CCC camps. The conservation corps may have con-tributed as much to esprit as it did to organization. At its peak, it fielded designated special crews of elite, give-no-quarter firefighters—the ancestors of the modern hotshot crews—and it awarded medals for heroism on the fire lines. If the 1910 northern Rockies fires had created the beginnings of a forest fire subculture at the command level, and had fostered the be-lief in wildland fire fighting as the moral equivalent of war, then the Tillamook Fire and the CCC had legitimized the concepts for the rank and file.

Though America limped through the thirties under the weight of the Great Depression, the decade was a paradoxically prosperous time for the Forest Service. The stars sat in perfect alignment. In the CCC, the service had a reliable and steady fire fighting force beyond its wildest dreams. In Roosevelt's conser-

Breakfast over and another grueling day's work waiting, Civilian Conservation Corps firefighters board trucks in Idaho's Kaniksu National Forest.

■　■　■

vation-oriented recovery programs it had money to operate the forests and to protect them from fire. It seized the moment and used it to squelch forever—so it thought—the let-burn and light-burn advocates of the West. In 1935, the service announced the 10 A.M. policy. Any fire anywhere in a federal forest would be attacked with sufficient resources to assure that it was contained by 10 A.M. on the following day. If it were still burning then, the resources would be increased to assure that it was out by 10 A.M. on the following day.

The policy would not be cheap. It would guide federal fire fighting in the West until the late 1970s. Because the Forest Service was a pipeline for money, equipment, and ideas, most of the West's state forestry departments also bought into the aggressive fire fighting dictated by the 10 A.M. policy. And so,

in their fashion, did the timber protection associations, which were strongly motivated to protect lands on which expensive investments in reforestation had been made.

The associations, with their ability to call logging crews and millhands to the battle, were in their heyday from the thirties through the fifties. "If we had a big fire, we could bring people from every mill and woods crew for miles," said Garrett Eddy, chief executive officer of Port Blakely Tree Farms and a former president of the Washington Forest Protection Association. "The trucks would come from everywhere. It was a system that worked." For the Forest Service, the 10 A.M. policy was, of course, useless against "escaped fires," the rambling conflagrations which would always consume a week or more. But it worked on the vast array of lesser fires, where a quick and substantial deployment of firefighters and equipment could prevent small starts from growing large.

Before the lessons learned in the CCC era could be permanently applied, a war had to be waged in Europe and the Pacific. While that went on, five fire seasons, from 1942 through 1946, were fought on the home front with an army that was more diverse and more unlikely than the old pickup crews. Conscientious objectors like Elmer Neufeld, who jumped on that September day over the Six Rivers Forest, were moved into the old CCC camps. In that era, they were mostly from the historic American peace churches—the Church of the Brethren, the Mennonites, and the Friends, or Quakers. Mustered into an operation called the Civilian Public Service program, they were forced to work without pay and picked up fire duties across the West.

The bravest of the CPS firefighters, some two hundred of them, volunteered as smokejumpers. The controversial parachute program, only two years old

While the plane that dropped him circles overhead, a Forest Service smokejumper searches for a landing spot amid the trees of Montana's Lolo National Forest.

■ ■ ■

when the war began, was still not universally accepted within the Forest Service. The conscientious objectors kept it alive until the veterans returned from war. But they were not the only firefighters dropping from the sky in those years. Sabotage in the forests ranked as a huge federal concern. Some balloon-carried Japanese incendiary bombs actually made it across the Pacific, but did little damage. The balloon bombs spurred the War Department to ship to the West the 555th Parachute Regiment. The all-black unit had been denied the opportunity

for overseas combat in the segregationist Army of the day. The "Triple Nickel" stationed its men at Pendleton, Oregon, and Chico, California, and jumped fires for the 1945 season.

The concern over sabotage and damaging loss of wood resources needed for the war effort brought others into the game, too. A forest fire prevention campaign, Keep America Green, spawned state chapters and enrolled legions of school pupils as junior fire wardens for the duration of the war. In the 1990s, chapters remain active in several Western states, pushing a broad fire prevention agenda and even putting some teenagers through basic fire training. A World War II advertising effort to raise public awareness of forest fire danger evolved into the Smokey Bear program. Eventually it would acquire a living symbol in a bear cub rescued from a New Mexico fire.

Federal and state governments reached far during World War II to put crews on the fire lines. Teenage boys were formed into units. Old firefighters who thought they would never chase smoke again found themselves back in action. Prison firefighter programs were launched, many of them to become permanent institutions. And at Soledad, California, the first female fire crews in history rolled into action. Organized in the spirit of the war effort, the women who shouldered pulaskis and shovels were the fire line equivalent of Rosie the Riveter. Like Rosie, they were expected to give up their wartime job when Johnny came marching home. But they were the spiritual ancestors of the women who, thirty years later, would fight a different sort of battle to earn a place on the fire lines of the West.

■　■　■

The series of fires that erupted outside Elko, Nevada, in the summer of 1964 raced to three hundred thousand acres in just two days. The BLM's district office clearly was outstripped, so its fire boss tapped some newly strengthened cooperative agreements with the Forest Service and with Nevada's excellent state forestry fire forces. In short order, the cooperators' network reached across the boundaries of ten states and delivered twenty-eight hundred firefighters, sixty-four aircraft, and nearly three hundred trucks and bulldozers. But Elko was not the only smoke in the sky in that dry, dry summer. Soon, other fires reared around the West. From neighboring Utah, the Forest Service asked for the return of some of its crews, sorely needed to fight battles on the home front. The Nevada BLM director, sitting tight and holding all the cards, flatly refused to release them.

In the checkered history of interagency cooperation for the battling of wildland fire, the Elko incident was a watershed. The story of that fractious standoff has been retold ten thousand times, because it catalyzed a process that produced the intricately dovetailed command and logistics structure that handles wildland fire in the West of the 1990s. That system can still deliver the occasional intemperate turf battle, but mostly it is a marvel to those who work inside it and to those who view it from the sidelines. The U.S. military, which still plays a periodic fire-fighting role, publicly admits that it has drawn lessons in rapid deployment from the West's fire command system. Respect for the interagency fire alliance surfaces in academia, too. "Some of us who watch the various public land agencies think it would be wonderful if they could achieve a level of overall cooperation that would match what the people in their fire operations have done," said James Agee, a professor of forest ecology at the University of Washington.

If 1964 was a pivotal time for the world of wildland fire, it was also a good vantage point for assessing the changes delivered by World War II. By then, the lessons of the CCC had been assimilated. Except in the most extreme emergencies, the system was mostly past the days of using untrained conscripts on the fire line. Trained seasonal crews, most often college students, had picked up much of the load. After experimenting for years with crews that ran as large as fifty members, the federal and state agencies had largely settled on the twenty-person configuration that is the modern standard for the federal agencies and many of the Western state operations. The smokejumper program was thriving. Interagency hotshot crews, Forest Service outfits organized to go wherever big fire erupted, had proved their worth and taken on a commando sort of esprit.

The Indian firefighter program had grown from modest beginnings with the Apache in New Mexico, and was spreading across the West. The helicopter, a gift from the war, seemed made for the reconnaissance, supply, and troop delivery needs of the fire-fighting task. And most spectacular of all, the air tanker—the converted military plane capable of delivering thousands of gallons of chemical retardant in the face of advancing fire—had soared rapidly from experiment to acceptance.

As always, change in the federal wildland fire operation had been mirrored, or refracted with intriguing variations, in the state forestry departments. In the postwar years, the Forest Service was the designated pipeline for surplus military hardware for wildland fire. Along with its usual distribution of federal cash for state fire operations, it had channeled to the states tons of military surplus equipment. Thousands of military trucks in that distribution were ingeniously converted to battalions of brush engines, with water tanks, pumps, and hose.

The California Department of Forestry had grown dramatically in the postwar years, even developing its own fleet of air tankers. In places such as Colorado and Wyoming, which would never have strong state fire operations, energetic county-based systems, heavily reliant on volunteers trained for wildfire work, grew in strength. Such local involvement in wildland fire, particularly in rural areas, would grow steadily over the next three decades. In the lumbering regions of the West, some of the timber protective associations had begun stepping out of the fire game by the sixties, bequeathing an even larger fire role to state forestry departments in Washington, Oregon, and Idaho.

Despite that change, the larger timber companies often remained strong players in the game, involved in intricate preseason planning with state and federal agencies, and prepared to roll equipment, logging crews, and even sawmill hands to fires. "You learned," said Max Schmidt, long-time woods boss for the Simpson Timber Company on Washington's Olympic Peninsula. "You got so you could take that call at three o'clock in the morning from the Forest Service or the state, and have seventy-five loggers on the line in the morning. In a way, some of your reputation depended on how well you could do that."

The most robust new kid on the block in that era was the Department of the Interior's Bureau of Land Management. Except for fire operations of the National Park Service, also an Interior agency, Interior had largely disappeared from the fire game in 1905. The BLM was born in 1946 as a consolidation of several Interior agencies. Its new domain included vast expanses of desert and rangeland, as well as substantial amounts of timber. Historically fire protection for that land had been provided through contractual arrangements with the Forest Service and the state forestry departments. Initially the BLM left that arrangement in place.

But in the territory of Alaska, the BLM had a huge, virginal task. Later, in the 1970s, well after Alaska had gained statehood, the BLM and the state's new Division of Forestry would divide fire-fighting responsibility for most of Alaska. The state, with its command ranks largely recruited from seasoned fire hands in the federal agencies, would take the lower third of Alaska, while the BLM chased fires in the vast outback region to the north. But at the outset the BLM *was* fire protection in Alaska. In fact, with its Alaska territory, the agency administered more than one-eighth of the land mass of the United States, more than the combined acreage of its federal brethren, the Forest Service, the National Park Service, and the Fish and Wildlife Service.

Regularly, Alaska had known tundra-gobbling, million-acre fires. The first organized fire protection, the Alaska Fire Control Service, had been launched by the Interior department only in 1939, but its growth had been truncated by the war. With the Forest Service as only a minor presence, Alaska was a frontier waiting for wildland fire protection. And it was a frontier that could not have been protected without aircraft, which had begun arriving in war surplus quantities in the very year the BLM was born.

In relatively short order, the BLM created a fire system, compressing into a dozen years or so the development process that had spanned half a century in the Lower 48. The BLM launched its own smokejumper program, established a paracargo system to supply firefighters in Alaska's sprawling, roadless backcountry, and built in the native villages a network of fire crews similar to those on the reservations of the Southwest. Then the agency bundled up its newfound expertise, headed south, and began reclaiming fire responsibility on much of the land it had let others protect.

So it was that the BLM came to be running its own Elko fire in 1964 and playing high-stakes logistical poker with its sister agencies. For over half a century, the wildland fire outfits of the West had signed one cooperative agreement after another. Too often they symbolized the good intentions of top bureaucrats, but seemed never to trickle to field level. Fed by natural agency rivalries, a complex mythology evolved, centering on purportedly fearsome liabilities that would certainly come into play for any fire outfit that dared step unbidden or unauthorized onto the territory of another.

At the hangar of Missoula, Montana's Johnson Flying Service, a wilderness flying company that played a pivotal role in the early history of smokejumpers, a contingent of jumpers prepares to head to a fire in the 1950s.

A story, a true story, is heard so often among old fire hands in the West that it could be a script. It played out in perhaps a hundred different places. Only the respective roles of the agencies changed from one incident to the next, but the outcome was almost always the same. In a typical version, the tale goes like this: "I was on a BLM crew and we were right at the edge of our district, busting our tails to stop this fire. Only there weren't enough of us to get a handle on it. We looked up, and there was a Forest Service crew on the other side of the boundary, just waiting for it to cross onto their land, but not doing a thing to help. When the fire got to the line, we stopped and they started. Only there weren't enough of them either, and they chased it over the hill."

But Elko would begin to change that. For the remainder of the 1964 fires, the BLM's national director created a fire coordinating center at Salt Lake City, Utah. He invited other agencies to share the responsibility. That arrangement was succeeded by a Great Basin Fire Center to handle crew, equipment, and supply allocation in the region between the Rocky Mountains on the east and the Sierras and the Cascades on the west. The operation was located in Boise in 1965 and renamed the Boise Interagency Fire Center. It was still regional in scope, and primarily a BLM operation. But in an unlikely half-dozen years, a set of key fire officials in the Forest Service and the BLM carved out a national role for the center. Sometimes, in the process, they were as awkward and uncertain as new in-laws meeting for the first time at a wedding reception. But, in a fashion that few would have predicted, the rivalrous clans of fire fighting were pulled together. It was a remarkable development, because the Forest Service—by far the larger and more senior national fire service—willingly let the newer and smaller BLM fire operation step into a role of vast importance.

The Boise center, renamed in 1993 as the National Interagency Fire Center, evolves constantly. Conceptually it is the logistical Pentagon of wildfire fighting in America, the place that oversees the distribution of fire crews, airplanes, helicopters, radios, and tens of thousands of supply items for the mammoth fires of the West. Its tough decisions are made—always by consensus and never by vote—by a sort of Joint Chiefs of Staff. Its members, the directors of the center, represent all the federal agencies that fight wildland fire, the BLM, the Forest Service, the Bureau of Indian Affairs, the National Park Service, and the Fish and Wildlife Service, with a representative of the U.S. Weather Service in an advisory capacity. In times of multifire emergencies, representatives of the National Association of State Foresters, the federal General Services Administration, and the U.S. Army join the deliberations.

Though officially a BLM facility, NIFC is a sort of inter-agency temple, and the shoulder patches of all of the member agencies work side by side in the offices and warehouses of its seventy-three-acre site at the Boise airport. The center does not dictate strategy or tactics on Western fires, although the hard decisions it must make on the availability of crews or aircraft can have a profound effect on the strategic options available to on-site fire commanders. Instead, the center sits atop a pyramid of state and regional coordination centers. If a fire in a given region grows too large to be met by local resources, NIFC brokers the exchanges between regions, whether the need is more crews or more headlamp batteries. If so many fires are burning in so many places that not all needs can be met, NIFC sets priorities, and makes the inevitable tough choices.

When a planeload of Navajo and Zuni firefighters arrives from Arizona to help on an Oregon project fire, when a federal air tanker stationed in Denver is shifted to a state fire in Southern California, when a Utah prison crew shows up on a Montana fire line, NIFC has done its work. NIFC alone can start the process that will activate the military for fire duty. It can secure the assistance of NASA for special satellite observations on monster fires. Through its close link with the federal General Services Administration, it can even put East Coast factories on double shifts and overtime when long-running campaigns like the 1988 Yellowstone fire threaten to exhaust the supply system.

It is, in short, a far cry from Elko in 1964. "It's a system that happened because some people cared enough about the idea of cooperation to give up some territory, to take some risks for their agencies and even for their careers," said Jack Wilson, the retired BLM director of the center and one of the pioneers who created it. "It's more than just a place. It's a concept. And the concept is that fire is the enemy, and the rest of us should be able to work together."

In its beginnings in the sixties, NIFC offered the first real possibility that the patches of wildland fire protection could be stitched into an operational quilt. The 1970s began with cataclysmic wildfires in Southern California and Central Washington, and touched off an era of technological development and creative administration in which more of the fences between agencies were torn down. The National Wildfire Coordinating Group, a high-echelon blending of the federal and state wildfire agencies, was born to create training standards, procedures and mobilization processes, and a comprehensive firefighter safety program.

The coordinating group's greatest contribution may have been the development of the red card system. The system provides a single coordinated training approach and multiple levels of certification for every wildland firefighter—from the greenest rookie groundpounder to the crustiest and most experienced fire general. It is the core of a mobilization scheme that makes it possible for a crew trained in Georgia to be inserted into a Western organization fighting a fire in California. In addition NWCG launched at Marana, Arizona, a generalship school, a facility that would become the national center for training top wildland fire commanders.

Nomex, the fire resistant fabric that has become the yellow-shirt, green-pants uniform of the armies of summer, emerged in those years from the laboratories of the DuPont corporation. It is not fireproof, but it can sustain temperatures up to a thousand degrees and give a fleeing firefighter the thirty seconds of protection needed to reach safety. Crafted first into military flight suits, it performed well in tests where mannequins were swung above a flaming pit of jet fuel. In the 1990s, most of the wildland fire community cannot imagine going to battle without Nomex, but old DuPont hands remember a tough sell. "We did the tour," said Wallace Behnke, a retired DuPont chemical engineer. "We did the Forest Service in Missoula and the California forestry people. I carried a propane torch. I'd lay a piece of Nomex across my arm and hit it hard with the torch. And those fire bosses would say, 'Wow. Turn the lights off. Let's do that again.' "

The fire shelter was perfected in those years, too, and became standard issue with the larger wildfire agencies by the late seventies. The shepherd of its continual improvement is Ted Putnam, a researcher and equipment specialist with the Forest Service. Putnam has become a recognized national expert on fire fatalities and entrapment situations. He has helped investigate many of them, work that much resembles both forensic pathology and archeology. Trained as a research psychologist, he has developed a set of observations about human performance and behavior in burnover events. He has cultivated a working knowledge of microclimatic effects that surround a shelter in a fire storm. And he regularly analyzes shelter and clothing fragments to establish how much heat entrapped firefighters have sustained.

"Since 1976, there have been roughly six hundred shelter deployments," he said. "In some cases people opened shelters even though they didn't really need them. But what we do know is that, by our analysis, about two hundred forty lives have been saved and one hundred sixty serious injuries prevented because of the shelters. We've seen fatalities where people were under the shelter, but panicked and stood up. What I have never seen is a death in a situation where a person got under the shelter and stayed under it. We've never found a body in a well-deployed shelter. The physical evidence that you find doesn't support the idea that that has ever happened."

The technological explosion of the seventies also handed the fire community a sophisticated lightning detection system for Alaska and for the Western states in the Lower 48. Both systems are run by the BLM, but the data are shared with other wildfire agencies. Remote sensors—thirty-seven in the Lower 48 and nine in Alaska—feed the strike data back to central receiving stations instantaneously. The NIFC at Boise receives the sensor data for the Lower 48, and can tally as many as fifty thousand strikes a day for the eleven states it monitors. It can pinpoint virtually all of the strikes within ten miles and many within a mile. Computers package the strike information and ship it out electronically, so that regional dispatch centers get instantaneous mapping of all strikes in their area. The centers receive their information within sixty seconds of the lightning strike. From there the information is broken down and transmitted to the field, so that aerial observers and fire crews can begin scouting for fire starts.

The 10 A.M. policy died during the sweeping changes of the 1970s, though some of the old fire hands battled to keep it. Its demise came with the realization that technology made it possible to throw ever greater resources at fire, sometimes outstripping any practical cost-benefit consideration. Beyond that, the thinking about fire itself was in flux. Although the wildland fire community thought it had driven a stake into the heart of deliberate wildland fire in the 1930s, controlled burning returned.

Ironically this time deliberate burning was the child of the land agencies themselves, and it had a new name, prescribed fire. As the beginning of official recognition of fire's role in forest ecology, prescribed fire came in two forms. Prescribed natural fire was first espoused by the National Park Service. It is the concept that under a certain set of conditions—a prescription—a naturally caused fire, almost always a lightning strike, will be allowed to burn in a national park or a forest wilderness area. Often the prescription will contain pre-set boundaries or other conditions that call for extinguishing the fire if it grows too large or too threatening.

The second category was prescription fire ignited by man, usually in nonwilderness areas, for specific forestry, vegetation control or hazard reduction objectives. Often, its aim is to mimic natural fire. The 1970s were the heyday of such prescribed burning. As fuels buildups in federal and state forests were attacked by foresters and fire crews, smoke rose in towering columns around the West. Sometimes they used low-intensity fire to remove undesirable undergrowth; sometimes they stoked infernos to obliterate collections of deadwood or logging debris. "It was a great laboratory, something you could do only once," said Hank DeBruin, who later became Forest Service director of fire management. "People had days and days to play with fire. You learned how to backfire, you learned how to hold a fire in place, you learned how to make it do what you wanted

A B-17 bomber, a relic of World War II, drops bor·· ·····Vashington's Wenatchee National Forest in 1970.

■ ■ ■

it to do. We learned such ··
years. It was just bef·
concern about air
do again. Bu·

   Mean·
the Califor
dubbed FIR·
and the think
organizational ar.
mass fire. Out of th·
tem and a network o·
foundation of fire opera·

   Perhaps most importa·
program called the incident
crease in size and complexity
operational scheme used to fight ·
Over two decades, ICS has been r·

gift to the world of emergency services. Across the country, it is
now a universal system adopted by a variety of federal, state,
·d local agencies for dealing with large emergencies. In the
·s, when the World Trade Center was bombed in New York,
·flood waters spilled over the levees of the Mississippi,
·rricanes struck Florida and Hawaii, the incident com-
·m was the framework for emergency response.
·m also has become the management structure of
·diverse problems as environmental spills, ma-
·wilderness search and rescue operations. Be-
·o any one-time situation that creates large-
·ions and logistical demands, it has even
·coordination and staging of such
·nts as the fiftieth anniversary observance of
·r Pearl Harbor in 1991 and President Bill Clinton's
·ummit," the 1993 Northwest Forest Conference in
·and, Oregon

CHAPTER 3

The Two-Faced Enemy

A S PREDICTABLE AS THE POSTMAN, hell arrived every day at noon. In that summer like no other, the fires that rose on every quarter baked and stewed and grumbled and fermented beneath the lid of the morning inversion. In air curdled with smoke, they gathered their strength, bided their time, and toyed with the yellow-shirts who thought they could stop it all. Then, day after wearying day, as the inversion broke, the humidity would drop, the winds would rise, and the smoke would chimney upward, as if the damper had suddenly been opened on the flue of some giant blast furnace. Flexing their muscle, the fires would rise out of the canyons and kick the yellow-shirts back again.

Up and running, the fires leaped precious miles of hand-dug line, the agonizing work that had been pounded in by headlamp on the night shift. Roaring up the ridges, they came on louder than a rocket in a railroad tunnel. Clawing skyward like a cat climbing curtains, they changed the climate, they changed the wind, they created their own weather. In their fury they tossed aside trees like giants marching through cattails, and they jumped rivers as easily as urchins hopping puddles. Their flames licked a thousand feet into the Wyoming sky, and pieces of them floated off to lives of their own—gaseous, pulsating fireballs rolling for long moments above the earth like miniature suns. In the hurricane winds that marched ahead of the fires, forests fell by the mile before the flames ever arrived, like small children dying of fright before an approaching horror. Releasing the energy of a thousand Hiroshimas, the flames sent up smoke plumes so great and so tall that they generated their own hail and lightning, and the bolts arced above Yellowstone National Park.

With thirty-two thousand other firefighters in that summer of 1988, Dick Grace fought the battle of Yellowstone. The fire brought him and his special niche of expertise to the park, like it brought all the others. They came from across the West, from across America. They would be thrown into the fray for three or four weeks of long shifts and sleepless nights. They would give all they had to give, then be shipped out to make way for fresh replacements. The fires that burned on every flank of Yellowstone abused Grace, as they abused the others. As they marched across 1.4 million acres of forest and meadow, they showed him things he had never seen. They taught him lessons he did not want to learn. They rebuked the certainties of his professional life.

Grace was Forest Service, out of Oregon, a mid-career manager who had never forgotten that it had all begun for him on the fire lines. His groundpounding days as a college student in the Olympic National Forest lay years behind him. But, like so many in the state and federal land agencies, he had built a career that

Above: In the dark of a New Mexico night, a ground fire creeps through a pine forest. Often such fires do little more than clear ground, and most of the trees in their path may survive.

■ ■ ■

Left: Pushed by wind and aided by low humidity, a fire in California's Klamath National Forest licks skyward.

never wandered far from fire. No matter what his assignment, he had always led two lives—the routine, official, predictable job of winter, and the infinitely variable job of fire in the summer. He had been an incident commander, a fire boss. He had served on a national fire command team, been at some of the great battles of the West. In Marana, Arizona, where the generals and staff officers of wildland fire learn their craft, he had been a teacher. Now, when big fire called him from his desk at the Willamette National Forest, he served on one of the system's area command teams, an elite group qualified to carry the umbrella of top responsibility when multiple fires barraged a region of the West.

When Grace arrived at Yellowstone, he was only one among the many experts hauled into the greatest battle since the 1910 fires of the northern Rockies. He was a logistics specialist for the very biggest fires. He was known as a worker of miracles in the wilderness, a mover and provider of crews, meals, tools, showers, buses, sleeping bags, paper clips, trucks, fire hose, aspirin, radios, gloves, canteens. Almost overnight he could push the buttons and pull the strings that would outfit several small, functioning cities, each home to fifteen hundred or more firefighters. He was conditioned by training and by his logistician's experience to believe that any fire—any fire—could be corralled in a matter of days. It was, as all the old fire dogs knew, simply a matter of deploying enough resources, and then seizing the moment when the inevitable break in the weather arrived.

For twenty-one days Grace would be the supply master of the Yellowstone battle. The entire might of the U.S. government was galvanized for the multiple fires that ravaged the park that summer. Even Canada was shipping equipment to the battle. And much of it, millions upon millions of dollars worth of it, passed through Grace's hands. A year earlier, Grace had been on a two-month series of southern Oregon fires that commanded the nation's attention. When that siege was over, the Southern Oregon fires had claimed ninety-six thousand acres. On a single day during Grace's stint at Yellowstone, the fires there *grew* by 165,000 acres.

Some days at Yellowstone he would take to the air with a pilot in a twin-engine plane and go slaloming through the 35,000-foot smoke columns that rose in a hundred-mile line from Storm Creek to Jackson Hole. It was, he would say later, like seeing the mushroom of an atom bomb explosion on every horizon. There was, quite literally, no larger war on earth at that moment. Grace was in the ultimate fire, with the resources of his nation at his disposal. And when he left Yellowstone to return home, the fires still raged as if he had not been there. Like so many others that summer, he was left questioning all that he thought he knew.

"I was in Washington the day Mount St. Helen's erupted," he said. "At Yellowstone it was like seeing the eruption again and again. Every afternoon, for days and weeks on end, the inversion would break and these spectacular columns of smoke would go up thirty thousand or forty thousand feet. Then the column would dip a little and start dumping embers out ahead, into the next valley, or across a river. Chunks of trees and rocks and roots were coming out of those updrafts. It was bizarre. I would not have believed it possible to have the amount of resources we had assembled, and not beat that fire. We deployed 'em and we used 'em for weeks. And we didn't make a damn dent."

■ ■ ■

Why does one forest fire creep meekly along the earth, and another explode to run through the treetops? Why does one sweep horizontally through the forest, broadcasting its smoke and flame before it, and another pull flames inward as it climbs straight to the sky like Jack's beanstalk? Why will a hillside of California chaparral burn with flames of four feet on one day and forty on another? Why does fire run faster uphill than down? Why does one tree in the forest erupt into a pillar of flame, while others around it do not ignite at all?

Fire appears as inscrutable as granite. If the land is dry enough, and the match or the lightning bolt or the abandoned campfire is applied, then the forest will burn. Beyond that, fire seems imponderable. So imponderable, in fact, that just three centuries ago, science could explain combustion only by postulating the existence of a wondrous element called phlogiston. From the vantage point of the atomic age, phlogiston seems a scientific version of the ancient fable of the emperor with no clothes. It was never isolated, never seen, and measured only by its purported absence. Phlogiston was, the best minds of the eighteenth century said, the element that made burning possible. Contained in all things, it was consumed in burning. Its weight disappeared when wood or paper or cloth were reduced to ashes. And if certain metals gained weight in burning, then phlogiston was said to have "negative weight," so that—paradox of paradoxes—it added weight by disappearing. Ultimately, after a hundred years of richly undeserved credibility, phlogiston was ushered to the scientific ash heap by the work of the French scientist, Antoine Lavoisier.

In the realm of pure science, laboratory work by Lavoisier's scientific successors has long since demystified the fundamental mechanics of combustion. However, the infinite variation of wildland fire has yielded its secrets more grudgingly. It still defies perfect predictability. But to an amazing degree, it is quantifiable, measurable, knowable. Even the chaotic, defiant, maelstrom sort of fire that swept Yellowstone must follow physical principles and obey a set of rules.

Across the decades of the twentieth century, the few practitioners of the science of wildfire behavior have fathomed ever more of those rules and have rushed each new discovery to those who fight the battle on the fire lines. After Neil Beisler pulled the Wyoming Hotshots off the line on the Brewer Fire and got them to safety with scant seconds to spare, his rookies thought they had been the beneficiary of some sixth sense in their leader. Perhaps. But it was also a case of preparation meeting necessity. Beisler, like so many of the seasoned crew chiefs and foremen of the summer battles of the West, had been to school on fire. His considerable fire line experience was buttressed with the findings and teachings of the fire behaviorists.

As a science, wildfire behavior is nurtured mostly by Americans, Canadians, and Australians. Worldwide, the community of wildland fire behavior researchers and analysts numbers barely five hundred. Most work in the field, called to duty when big fires erupt. The pure laboratory scientists, the ones who experiment with wind tunnels and fuel bed models, are but a small percentage of the group. Bob Mutch, at the Intermountain Fire Sciences Laboratory, a Forest Service facility in Missoula, Montana, is one. An ex-smokejumper who headed into experimental forestry, he did some of the pioneering research in fire behavior. Then he moved to technology transfer—seeing that the discoveries of fire behavior research are delivered quickly to the troops.

"For decades we thought that all a firefighter needed to know was that if it was dry and the wind was blowing, then any fire you had was going to be a problem," he said. "What we've learned since the late sixties is that the vegetation itself affects the flammable properties of any ecosystem. This was a new dimension. It wasn't just how dry it was, or how strong the wind was. It was a matter of the chemical composition and the physical nature of the material, of the waxes and oils and resins."

Every rookie on a wildland fire crew learns first about fuel, weather, and topography. If the rookie grows to be a grizzled firefighter, spends a lifetime in the game, and rises to the job of fire behavior analyst or of fire boss, the triad of fuel, weather, and topography still will be inescapable. Every consideration will swing upon those three hinges. In the West, each wildland firefighter learns the rudiments and comes to some understanding of such factors as fuel moisture content, up-canyon winds, and microclimatic fire effects. They learn, too, about such regional weather phenomena as foehn winds, the blast-furnace breath of the desert that sweeps from the east, vaults over the Cascades or the Sierras and becomes godfather to historic fires.

Many of the seasonal warriors, if they stay in the game, become aficionados of fire science. Around the campfires of grimy smokejumpers and in the smelly crew buses of macho hotshots, a few curbstone meteorologists always stand ready to discuss the intricacies of adiabatic processes, orographic lifting, convection heat ranges, thermal outputs, and the lightning-breeding portents of cumulonimbus clouds.

All of it, arcane though it seems, is rooted in scenarios that, to the layperson, seem random and chaotic, but are in fact measurable and understandable. Now, for example, it is a simple matter of applying known formulas to compute the tons of fuel per acre in a Pacific Northwest forest, on a brushy chaparral hillside in California, or on a rolling desert in New Mexico. Each of those "fuel models" is identified and described in tables that range from Alaska tussock tundra to mature timber. The ways in which fire spread is affected by the steepness of terrain have been demystified, as in the axiom that every twenty percent increase in slope will double the rate of fire spread. The notion that localized wind conditions, some of them induced by fire itself, can produce dangerous whirlwinds, downdrafts, and updrafts is better understood now. And the crucial aspect of humidity in ignition, fire spread, and flame length has been recognized.

Not until the late 1960s did the fire community begin to comprehend the staggering quantities of heat energy released in forest blazes. In that Cold War era, common interests united the fire scientists and the federal civil defense researchers, who feared mass fire as a byproduct of nuclear war. Montana's Sundance Fire in 1967 became a case study and produced stunning figures. In a day it ran sixteen miles in the Pack River Valley and consumed fifty thousand acres. It threw firebrands ten miles in advance of its flame front. It uprooted mature red cedar and white pine, and tossed huge chunks of them skyward.

Such tales the old fire hands had heard before. But the researchers who were turned loose on the fire spawned another set of figures. The self-generated winds of the Sundance topped 120 miles per hour. At the peak of its run it consumed a square mile of prime forest every minute and a half. In its hottest sectors, the fire released the equivalent of a twenty-kiloton Hiroshima atomic bomb every two minutes. And in a run up a mountain called Roman Nose, it released an atom-bomb energy equivalent once every three seconds.

For crew bosses on the line, wildfire behavior is distilled into operating principles they can take into action or teach to their troops. For the professional fire behavior analysts, who play a key role in command-level strategy sessions on the big fires, the principles are woven into complex formulas. The formulas often are programmed into hand-held calculators or graphed out on work sheets called nomograms. On a campaign

Microclimatic fire effects spawned by unpredictable winds and varied topography are the firefighter's nemesis. Above a Southern California home near Ojai, a strong upslope wind in a ravine generates tall, racing flame, while a mild downslope wind in an adjoining ravine nudges modest flame downhill.

fire, the analysts, plugging in data from federal fire weather forecasters, hourly local humidity measurements, and field observations of fire activity, will begin each twelve-hour work shift by projecting how far and how fast the fire might run, what flame lengths can be expected, and what special hazards will be posed. Their batting averages are remarkably high on ground fires. Only since Yellowstone have they come up with an approach to predicting and estimating running crown fires, the blazes that leap from the ground to the tops of trees, then explode into racing hurricanes of flame and wind. Now they are building a new body of knowledge to pass on to the groundpounders.

The principles of fire knowledge are applied in a thousand ways. Fires burn vigorously in the heat of the afternoon, when humidity is lowest, and usually lie down at night, when the humidity rises. Hence, burnout operations and major pushes to establish sections of fire line often are done on the night shift. The combination of falling humidity and rising wind can kick moderate four-foot flames into towering thirty-footers in minutes. For that reason, experienced crew leaders and fire line bosses are constantly attuned to weather; many pack small instrument kits, and take periodic wind, temperature, and humidity readings.

Narrow rock chimneys and low saddles in ridgelines generate venturi effects that quicken wind speed and spawn extreme fire behavior. Because fire preheats fuel on upslopes and can run dramatically faster as terrain steepens, crews are taught never to work with fire below them. A fire that suddenly "hooks under" is an instant danger signal. Certain fuels, such as the oily chaparral of California, are known as high-risk, fast-burning environments. "When the chaparral is dry and ready to burn, it's probably the most volatile natural fuel in the world," said Mark Linane, who goes up against chaparral fire on foot as a hotshot crew boss in the Los Padres National Forest, America's most fire-active piece of public land. "There's nothing like it. It makes the rate of spread on a woods fire look like a piker. It is so incredibly fast and the heat is so intense. You're talking about speeds far faster than a man can run. We've had trucks trying to keep up with the head of wind-driven fires and falling behind at seventy-five miles an hour."

The most common wildfire is, in fact, wind-dominated. It runs before the wind. How it runs, slow or fast, large or small, depends, of course, on the variables of fuel, weather, and topography. Because wind speed is greater above the ground, the fire may accelerate markedly if it finds fuel twenty feet, or a hundred feet, above the surface. If it leaps to the crowns of trees, it may burn in two passes—racing ahead through the treetops and advancing more slowly at ground level. The wind-driven fire is always pushing outward, usually in one direction, with a defined head and flanks.

Its flames and heat roll ahead as it moves. Sometimes, even though a fire runs mostly on the ground, the ladder fuels of tall brush and low branches intersecting at a lone tree will invite fire to climb upward. The flames will mount the ladder, rung by rung, and finally, in the midst of the forest, the tree will stand as a solitary, spectacular 150-foot torch of flame.

As wind-driven fire rolls onward it generates massive amounts of heat. A plume of smoke, or convection column, begins to rise above it. Under the right confluence of conditions, the column rises more and more vertically as the force of rising hot air begins to overpower the driving wind. If the power of the fire becomes greater than the power of the wind, the threshold of fearsome, sometimes fatal, fire is at hand. The plume dominated fire draws wind to itself and begins building a towering, mushroom-shaped thunderhead that can climb forty thousand feet. Its foot may spread a mile or more in diameter. But the fire behavior surrounding it may be modest, with fire being drawn toward the center of the rising smoke column, rather than pushing outward. Firefighters on the outside of the circle may not perceive what is happening, because they are too close to the plume to observe its growth.

Richard Rothermel of the Missoula fire lab has fathered understanding of plume-dominated fire and its hazards. "It is the nastiest one," he said. "You get this big convection column. The fire isn't moving very fast. It's the type of fire you often try to produce when you're doing deliberate prescribed burning. You want to get a large column that will draw the fire in from the sides. That's good. But the truth about the plume-dominated fire is that it's like the forward pass in football. Three things can happen, and two of them are bad."

The good outcome is that the modest, in-drawing fire permits itself to be encircled and contained by fire crews. The second outcome is that the plume may march off across the landscape, usually uphill, seizing fuel and growing in power. And the third, the worst, is the triggering of a horrific series of events. As the column grows and rises thousands of feet, the hot air at its top mushrooms and cools rapidly, so that a mass of heavy, cold air builds above the rising, lighter warm air. A few raindrops, called virga, may even fall, often the only warning of what is impending.

Suddenly, the wind direction reverses. Cold air falls downward outside the rising column, like water tumbling from the peak of a fountain. At ground level, firefighters are confronted by fierce downburst winds that reverse the direction of the fire and drive it outward on every quarter, like confetti blown off the top of a table. The fabled calm before the storm of a fire blowup is real; it is the brief period of dead stillness that marks the wind shifting from inflow to downburst.

At Yellowstone, Rothermel, the fire theoretician, had his first field encounter with the downburst phenomenon. He was away from the fire front, but saw the wind uproot and shatter trees for three and a half miles. "Later I met two fellows who were caught in those downburst winds in helicopters," he said. "They descended very rapidly before they were able to pull out. The fire operations chief was in one of the helicopters. He thought they were going in for a closer look. What he didn't find out until later was that the pilot was giving it full power and they were still going straight down."

■ ■ ■

In the house-to-house combat zone that was Altadena, California, in autumn of 1993, the Arrowhead Hotshots faced a multimillion-dollar decision. The Santa Ana, the devil wind that whips in from the desert in fall, was scouring fire-prone Southern California. Like a panzer division fueled on napalm, it marched westward along the slopes of the San Gabriel

When creeping ground fire finds a "ladder" of brush and low-hanging limbs, it can torch off into pillars of fire that consume one or several trees without harming others nearby.

■ ■ ■

But not many were there to take in the view on this October day. All but a few had gathered what they could, then fled. The fire had mostly had its way as it ran down the San Gabriel front. Sometimes it would lay back on the mountainside, like a bully walking menacingly on the opposite side of the street. Then, pushed by the wind, it would make another sortie off the slopes. Where it chose, it had kicked its way into neighborhoods, leapfrogging from one rooftop to another and leaving a trail of burned-out automobiles and blackened fireplace chimneys to mark where homes once stood. In its wake the startled eyes of bright blue swimming pools stared skyward from the face of a charred wasteland. Now, a half mile out, the fire began another run.

Marshaled from around the West, firefighters were rolling in by the thousands for what would be a two-week siege in Southern California. The Arrowhead Hotshots, a National Park Service crew, were in the first wave of an extended attack force that would eventually total fifteen thousand firefighters. An organizational structure was still being hammered into place when the Arrowhead crew arrived after a two-hundred-mile drive from Sequoia National Park. They had simply been sent into the guerrilla battle in the neighborhoods, with no orders other than to find fire and stop it.

Mountains, raging through thick chaparral, blowing fifty-foot walls of flame before it, and incinerating expensive neighborhoods at will. Along the foot of the San Gabriels, at the north edge of the Los Angeles basin, the comfortable suburbs of Glendora, Azusa, Monrovia, Pasadena, Altadena, and La Crescenta were stacked against the toe of the mountains. The builders had gone as far as they could go. The upscale homes with green, watered lawns and shading trees bumped up against the dry chaparral slopes and canyons. From their decks, which jutted above the sere brush of the lower canyons, the owners of houses that ran to over a million dollars in value could look up toward the Angeles National Forest.

Freelancing and looking for targets of opportunity, the Arrowhead 'Shots chose for their beachhead a neighborhood at the north edge of Altadena. Before them, at the edge of a sea of resinous chaparral, sat a row of sixteen upscale homes, each 300,000 dollars to 1.5 million dollars in value. They were moored like ships at harbor's edge, with a tidal wave approaching and nowhere to go. Across a narrow street, block upon block of similar homes stretched away to the south and west, residential dominoes waiting to be tumbled by fire. Some of the front-row homes were separated from the dry, ten-foot brush by meager strips of lawn. Others were built on the lips of a draw that bisected the neighborhood, and their decks, cantilevered above the chaparral, were an open invitation to fire. The most expensive of the homes, just completed, stood on a peninsula site that jutted into the brush.

A few residents who had not evacuated were gathered on the deck of one of the homes, sticking with their neighborhood until the last possible moment, socializing with forced gaiety in a party that had the feel of an Irish wake. City fire engines were arrayed on the streets in front of the homes, and another crew had cut a small fire line at the edge of the brush. None of that would be enough to stop the fifty-foot flames that were bending horizontally in the wind and marching downhill toward the homes. The structural firefighters were trained to take over when homes ignited. But the world beyond the edge of the green lawns was not their world. They had seen homes torch off all day, and they were openly skeptical that the approaching fire could be stopped. Jim Cook, the Arrowhead crew's superintendent, conferred with two Forest Service wildfire bosses standing behind the homes.

There was a chance to be very, very wrong here. Doing nothing in a patently hopeless situation would ensure that the fire would sweep onto the houses. That would be a blameless calamity, and in the triage mentality of the day the hotshots could have been forgiven for walking away and choosing another battle. But Cook was weighing a slim-chance alternative. Lighting an intercepting burnout in the teeth of the wind that was gusting at twenty-five miles per hour seemed as likely to succeed as rowing up a waterfall. It carried the risk that the deliberate fire itself would touch off the homes, and that those who lit

The drip torch, the ubiquitous weapon of wildland firefighters from Alaska to New Mexico, ignites a mixture of gasoline and diesel oil with the burning wick at the tip of its spout.

■ ■ ■

it could be held to blame. And yet, done perfectly, it might work.

The wildfire bunch made its decision. From their gear, the hotshots broke out the bright metal canisters with the odd, curlicue spouts. They ignited the spouts, so that each burned like a small candle atop the pitcher of gasoline and diesel fuel. Behind them, the city firefighters muttered derisively. One of them shouted, "Never trust a bozo with a drip torch." With hoses, the 'shot crew wet the grass and the brush closest to the houses. Then two firefighters—one from the hotshot crew and one from the Forest Service—moved out. From their hand-carried torches, they began splashing bits of liquid fire into the volatile brush. Cook had watched the rhythm of the gusts. He shouted directions as the crew worked the intervals. The wind never quit, but they played its fluctuations, choosing their moments for touching off spots that roared into flame.

As the main fire advanced nearer and nearer, they worked the line in small sections. Moving fast now, they were incendiary Rembrandts painting a black ribbon onto the earth. In some spots they unleashed momentary leaping flame within twenty feet of houses. Around the mansion on the peninsula lot and down in the draw, beneath the overhanging decks, they turned in their best work. Gradually the black strip grew. The flames from the burnout climbed. They wavered in the wind, leaning hungrily toward the homes, and the smoke blew back on the hotshots who patrolled the burnout's edge. But as the new fire built in intensity, its rising heat overpowered the wind. Its smoke plume swung to vertical and then slowly tipped toward the main fire. It was over in minutes. Uniting in a common updraft, the two fires came together, wrestled, and starved themselves to death a scant two hundred yards from the homes. On the burning mountainside, it was as if someone had suddenly turned out the lights in hell.

While the hotshots checked the perimeter and gathered their gear, a few of the neighbors moved among them, dispensing gratitude. But there was little time to bask. More fire awaited the crew on that day when all of the Los Angeles basin seemed to be erupting in flame. The Arrowhead 'Shots moved on. They would battle fire through the night and far into the next day, forty hours in all, before they would get any real rest. Later, there would be a bit of time to savor the small victory at the edge of Altadena. "Maybe once every couple of years you get a situation where you absolutely know you made a difference," said Brit Rosso, as he savored the riskiest burnout of his career. "It makes all the other days worthwhile."

■ ■ ■

In the war against wildland fire, the foe wears two faces. The enemy becomes ally. So often, the truly big fires are stopped with fire. In many cases, the bulldozer trails, the hand-dug lines, the air-dropped retardant stand as accessories, before or after the fact, to the deliberate burnout or backfire. Fire is the adversary, but fire is also the tool that stops fire. Even in some of its most powerful manifestations, fire can show its other face and be brother-in-arms. Hotshot crews, the aces of big fire, regularly work the edges of plume-dominated conflagrations. Like matadors twirling *veronicas* with capes of smoke, they use the in-drawing wind to propel aggressive burnouts that pull to the center and rob the fire of its fuel and momentum. In so many ways, this counterpoised yin-yang defines the roles of fire and those who fight it.

The strategy and tactics of battling wildland fire lie far from the urban concept of shiny red trucks and limitless amounts of water. At ground level, forest fire often is fought with no liquid at all, with dirt-throwing tools and fire itself as the prime implements. On initial attack of a small fire, one crew or several will work the fire's flanks, digging line to keep it from spreading outward as they race to pinch off its head. The digging chore, different for each type of vegetation, is the sweaty, backbreaking essence of fighting fire. In a forest, it begins with a fifteen-foot chain saw swath through the brush, with trees felled to open a firebreak in the canopy of limbs. Then comes a two-foot-wide gash of clean earth, with every leaf, branch and root removed. A good hotshot firefighter does a chain—a measurement of sixty-six feet—every hour. A crew of twenty hotshot diggers and sawyers equals perhaps fifteen chains an hour, all while packing a forty-pound pack stuffed with drinking water, gear, rations, headlamp, batteries, saw fuel, and tools. Maintaining that output for sixteen hours is the world's worst way to travel three miles.

If the approaching blaze is large, the line-digging is mixed with burnouts. Triggered with drip torches or flarelike fusees,

the deliberate fires are set loose between the hand-dug line and the oncoming flames. By burning out the intervening area and creating a black zone to reinforce the line, the line crews hope to halt the fire in its tracks. Ideally the two fires burn together and die for lack of fuel. The more problematic the wind and terrain conditions, and the taller the approaching flame front, the greater the black zone required to block the fire. Some burnouts become spectacular fires themselves, accelerating as their smoke columns are tugged into the updraft of the main fire.

Though the term "backfire" often is used by outsiders to describe the business of fighting fire with fire, it has specialized meaning for those who do it. The burnout, used often, is a relatively small-scale firing effort, no more than a quarter-mile deep and often only a few feet wide. The backfire, used much more rarely, is a large-scale fire in its own right. Often launched from a geographic barrier such as a river or a rock face, it usually means ignition of hundreds or even thousands of acres. It almost always represents a command decision to surrender a big piece of territory in an attempt to halt a major blaze.

On many fires, bulldozers will clank to action where terrain permits, working tightly against flames, and pushing over trees and brush to create their own wide version of a fire line. It is some of the riskiest work in the business. In fire regimes such as Southern California, bulldozer operators have died in roaring walls of flame. "The fire is always there after you," said Doug Anderson, a full-time fire bulldozer specialist with the California Department of Forestry. "Your job is to be right on the edge of it all the time. We did it for years without closed cabs. It was common to have fire everywhere—over the tracks, over the hood, and once in a while in the cab with you. I had it come in real good once in an open cab. I got singed on the neck, but I made it through. It let me know it was there."

If necessary, hand crews follow the bulldozers, burning out as they go. On flat or well-roaded terrain, brush engines come into play. They pack relatively small amounts of water, often less than a thousand gallons. But by using it wisely and well, they can run the same flank-and-pinch operation as ground crews. Often, they can work closer to tall flame fronts than crews without water. Thousands of Western wildfires are handled every year by engine crews working alone, using their machinery or their shovels, as the situation demands.

Large fires stir in all the possible mixings of manpower and equipment. A fire that is born on flatland and marches into hills may have engines attacking its low flank, and bulldozers and hand crews punching in fire line and burning out on the high side. Water often plays a larger role in mop-up than in initial attack. After the furor of initial attack has passed, long hose lays from engines or from portable pumps set on creek banks can provide water for working stubborn hot spots. Or, last and worst, the firefighters may turn to slogging up and down hills with five-gallon backpack hand pumps. Still, hundreds of fires are fought to the last wisp of smoke with no water at all. Such fires end with firefighters "cold-trailing," constantly turning the ashes until the mix is cool enough to be probed with an ungloved hand.

No matter how wet or dry the tactical approach taken at ground level, the troops usually can count on air support with chemical retardant or water drops by planes and helicopters if a fire proves stubborn. In some locales, particularly in tight interface zones where homes built in wildland trees or brush stand at risk, aircraft may even be part of the initial attack. The retardant tanker's drops can slow a running fire's charge, back up a crucial burnout operation or take the heat off a 'dozer operator or an engine crew. The longer a fire runs, the more helicopters will fill its skies, swooping over ridges to discharge belly tanks or massive buckets on long control lines. As the fire edges into mopup, the tanker planes will retreat to their airstrips and the helicopters will take over the aerial work, making countless sorties to douse hot spots and to cool burning snags before they are felled. In Alaska, helicopters sometimes fill another role. Dangling spectacular torch devices filled with a napalmlike fuel, they take over the task of touching off burnouts and backfires.

Alaska fire fighting, in fact, differs in many ways from the Lower 48 version. Out on the fragile tundra, which covers much of the state and is underlain by permafrost, the basic flank-and-pinch attack strategy still works. But precious little digging goes on because the tundra carries scars for decades. For moderate fires, the weapon of choice is a spruce bough. Wielded like a five-foot fly swatter, it is the perfect tool for beating out low flame in the spongy, mossy ground cover, which can be as thick as two feet. If a true firebreak is needed, firefighters sometimes produce it with chainsaws. After running a pair of parallel saw cuts through the tundra, the ground crews can lift out blocks of it, as if they were thick lawn turf, and set them aside. Later, as part of post-fire rehabilitation, the excised sections are set back into place. With its low resource values and vast spaces, Alaska, more than any other place, is the home of the giant backfire. Sometimes, tactical fires of a hundred thousand acres are set loose on the tundra.

Western wildland fire sears more than a million acres of public and private land in a slow season, and nearly six million in a heavy season. A typical year delivers more than thirty thousand fires. Small fires, quickly contained, are the rule. Every summer the West experiences thousands of fires that never grow beyond ten acres and never make headlines. Even those that race out to a hundred acres or more may require only a day of serious firefighting. Statistically less than three percent of the fires account for more than ninety percent of the burned acreage.

Across the decades, the number of those monumental project fires seems to approach some irreducible minimum and diminish no further. Typically the West each year experiences two hundred to five hundred fires of a thousand acres or greater, and sixty to one hundred seventy-five of five thousand acres or greater. Virtually every season brings a dozen or more mammoth fires of ten thousand to a hundred thousand acres, although the occasional dampish year with no fires that large is possible. In 1988, the record fire year for modern times, the system coped with more than twenty fires that exceeded twenty-five thousand acres, including a half-dozen that went beyond a hundred thousand acres. There is little correlation between fire size and physical danger; the ten-acre fires can deliver death and injury as regularly as the ten-thousand-acre ones.

In some remote areas of the mountain West, almost all wildfires flare from natural causes, specifically lightning. In some areas on the fringe of the urban West, especially Southern California, almost all wildfires are human-caused, very often arson. Year in and year out, about thirty percent of the West's fires are spawned by lightning. The rest are the product of humans. Arson and the escape of fires that were started to clear land or burn debris account for most of the human-caused fires. Smokey Bear has done his work: Escaped campfires and discarded cigarettes account for less than ten percent of the total.

Forest fire can roll up astronomical damages in timberlands, as much as 90,000 dollars per acre in extreme cases. Typically fires with high loss potential are attacked much more aggressively, with heavy commitments of crews and equipment. The financial loss from such blazes can be mitigated with salvage logging, because many low-intensity forest fires kill trees without consuming them. But on public lands salvage logging has become a political and environmental issue, with environmentalists arguing that erosion and other ecological damage is increased by harvesting a burned-over forest. In other Western fuel types, particularly desert brush and the characteristic chaparral of Southern California mountains, the fuel itself has little commercial value, and the direct financial loss to fire on the landscape is often inconsequential. However, in many locales those fires can threaten structures, or introduce the possibility of devastating winter mudslides from denuded slopes.

But no one has ever devised a scale for measuring the total economic and environmental impact of wildland fire. "I have always believed that the measurements we have applied to fire are too heavily weighted toward short-term economic considerations,"

said Jack Wilson, a respected fire general, now retired, who directed the national interagency fire center at Boise for years. "They ignore long-term environmental effects, off-site effects, and long-term economic and social accountability. Take a tree in the Pacific Northwest of thirty-six inches diameter at breast height. It probably took two hundred twenty-five years to reach that size. If a fire kills it, the log can be salvaged. But consider the idea that the land on which it grew for two hundred twenty-five years was not used for anything else. Society invested fire protection costs, perhaps fertilization costs, in-lieu-of-taxes expenses, and revenue losses because the site was idle. With the fire it sustains soil loss, changes in microclimate and habitat for unthought-of birds and animals. Then add another two hundred years to grow a tree the same size. Now the loss takes on a completely different perspective, and it is huge."

Outside the forest, the greatest losses, in human and financial terms, come when wildland fire rages through homes. The Southern California fires of 1993 took two lives, destroyed eleven hundred homes and rolled up damages that totaled a billion dollars. The toll for the Oakland Hills Fire of 1991 was 25 lives, 3,354 houses, and 1.5 billion dollars. For firefighters, interface fires often come with an aspect of the surreal. To stand on a hillside and watch twenty million dollars worth of homes disappear in twenty minutes is an experience almost too large to be assimilated.

"Now eighty-five, that was a good year," said Bill Krushak, a Forest Service fire officer in Arizona and the veteran of six years at the helm of a hotshot crew in the 1980s. "Wheeler Fire,

south zone, California. That was pretty good stuff. Helicopters dipping out of swimming pools. Walking down the sidewalks of Ojai with chainsaws, dropping eucalyptus trees. These big expensive homes going up right and left. It was quite the urban interface. Lost a lot of houses, but we saved a bunch, too. The homeowners were glad to see us. Right in the middle of it all, with fire everywhere, they were hanging over the back fences with lemonade. We fought the fire out of Ojai and chased it off into the wilderness. We were cutting 'dozer lines without 'dozers. Lines that were six 'dozer blades wide and all by hand, because we couldn't get the 'dozers. Great fire behavior, some of the most spectacular fire behavior I've ever seen. When it sucks up gravel and rains it back down on you like hail, that's pretty good stuff."

At the Riverside, California, fire lab, a Forest Service facility similar to the fire laboratory in Missoula, the burgeoning interface fire problem has driven researchers to turn their attention to houses as a fuel, an idea that once would have seemed alien to forest fire research. Richard Chase has been in the forefront of that work. "One thing we've learned, which people don't seem to want to hear, is that, contrary to conventional wisdom, houses don't burst into flame because things near them are hot," he said. "The heat coming from surrounding vegetation has little to do with it. Homes are ignited by contact with burning brands and embers. They burn because they're built on hillsides, in ways that allow fire to get under them. They have a high nook-and cranny-factor, too many spots that are just a catcher's mitt for flying brands. And people don't want to hear that, because

Left: Hitting a fire high and low, a Forest Service helicopter and a California Department of Forestry bulldozer work in tandem on a thousand-acre range near San Diego. California agencies field full-time fire bulldozer specialists who regularly brave rugged terrain and extreme fire behavior.

■ ■ ■

Right: For most of a week in 1991, Oregon's Warner Creek fire lighted the nighttime skies outside the small town of Oakridge.

Shafts of sunlight compete with rising smoke from a fire in Oregon's Wallowa-Whitman National Forest.

■ ■ ■

they want to believe that all they have to do to protect themselves is keep the vegetation cut back. But what's really important is the way they're building their houses."

Fire is popularly seen as the destroyer of the forest, the ravager to be stopped at all costs. But the last third of the twentieth century has renewed the debate of the first third. Now, just as in the let-burn and light-burn debates of the 1920s, fire is championed as the necessary friend of forest health. The debate is all but over. Among the state and federal wildfire agencies, the National Park Service was the first to jump ship from the idea that all fire is evil. Though small, the park service fought forest fire as aggressively as its brethren until the mid-1960s. Then it began to reconsider fire in light of the agency mission to maintain land in its natural state. Fire, after all, had been a part of the forest ecological cycle long before the land was converted to parks. And the results of excluding it were already obvious in fuel buildup patterns and changing vegetation mixes.

Starting in Sequoia-Kings Canyon National Park, the park service began experimenting with the concept of prescribed natural fire—letting certain lightning-caused fires in the parks burn themselves out or allowing them run to predetermined boundaries. "We simply came to feel that fire, like wind and avalanches, is part of the natural scene," said Tom Nichols, a prescribed fire specialist with the park service in California. "If the intent of Congress was for us to protect these areas in their natural setting, then to include fire occasionally on some natural cycle is fundamental to complying with that charge."

In Alaska, the BLM followed the park service lead and embraced a new philosphy of letting some fires run, depending upong the value of the resources threatened. Then in the early

With only a tiny amount of its underlying flames visible, a Colorado fire in the Pike National Forest sends a towering smoke column into the sky.

. . .

When all the prescription conditions were in alignment, the fire would be touched off. Control strategies, usually firefighters using customary fire-line tactics, would be employed to keep the fire within prescribed boundaries. In that era, more than ever before, fire was used outside the wilderness as a tool to return forests to original vegetation patterns, to remove logging debris, to improve wildlife habitat. But, though it was a great learning tool for fire crews and future fire commanders, declining budgets and increasing concerns about air pollution radically scaled back the concept of deliberate manmade fire in the 1980s.

Prescribed fire remains an important implement in the tool kit of foresters. More and more, it is seen as crucial to creating healthier forests, to reducing the hazards of fuel buildup and to correct-

seventies, the Forest Service introduced the same policy to wilderness areas. Beyond that, the Forest Service, the state forestry departments, and private timber owners plunged deeply into use of prescribed nonnatural fire for nonwilderness forests and rangelands during the 1970s. By definition, prescribed fire meant establishing a geographic boundary and a set of fuel and weather conditions—a prescription—for a section of forest or range.

ing ecological imbalances which may have been created by fire suppression itself. But the frontier is long gone, and nearly all of the West's forest land lies within easy burning distance of homes and communities. Even as the need for fire becomes more and more evident, the politics, costs, and risks of deliberately introducing fire to those forests stand as formidable obstacles to putting the ally to work.

CHAPTER 4

The Groundpounders

O N HIS KNEES, ALONE, Paul Gleason wept in the ashes. The blowtorch winds of a hundred-degree Arizona day swept over his shaking shoulders and riffled his blackened shirt. Here and there, small fires still burned on the shoulders of Arizona's Walk Moore Canyon, and as Gleason knelt and sobbed the smoke rose in wisps around him. His last summer in combat, his last tour of duty as a groundpounder on the fire lines of the West, had brought him to this.

At forty-four, though he would not have claimed it for himself, he ranked as one of the lesser fire gods. A Pacific Northwest hotshot crew boss, he was something of a legend in his own time, a tough, aggressive, intellectual firefighter who was the stuff of stories told in fire camps from Alaska to New Mexico. In the world of Western wildfire, only two or three hotshot bosses were seen as his equal.

It had all started so long ago. He had charged out of high school and landed a beginner's spot on a Forest Service engine. But before the season was out he had wangled a transfer to a hotshot crew. And he had never let go of ground-level firefighting. He had squeezed in college, with a degree in mathematics. There were plans for a doctorate and perhaps college teaching. But fire had taken over his life. He had spent time with crews in California, Washington, and Oregon. He had ranged the West. On his ticket were the punches from the big blazes, the infernos that the veterans of Western fire always recall with the sort of reverence that old soldiers reserve for battles such as Belleau Wood and Iwo Jima and Khe Sanh. He had been to more than five hundred of them. He had marched through all the ranks in the infantry of forest fire. He had paid his dues, earned his spurs, and landed the only job he'd ever really wanted—running a 'shot crew and taking on big fire.

Hotshot crews stand as the shock troops of wildland fire. Fielded by four federal agencies, the Forest Service, the Bureau of Land Management, the Bureau of Indian Affairs, and the National Park Service, they go where the action is. In the game, the legendary smokejumpers and the lesser-known helitack crews are initial attack specialists who chase small fires and, when the mix of skill and luck is right, keep them from becoming big ones. But hotshots are the chasers of conflagrations.

When it's down and dirty in the brush, when the mountain's steep and the risk is high, when the fat's in the fire and the fire is everywhere, hotshots get the call. Across America, the system counts only 1,360 of them, on sixty-six crews, and all but one crew in the West. In fire camps, they are easy to spot. Older on the average than rank-and-file groundpounders, they show up in matching T-shirts, hats and attitudes, their gear stacked in a disciplined line, their yellow fire shirts invariably filthy, their aura of camaraderie and family palpable. Cross one and

Above: Chasing fire up a near-vertical ridge, an Idaho crew races to establish a control line in the Boise National Forest.

■ ■ ■

Left: Veiled in flame and clad in fire-resistant clothing, Arizona firefighter Brent Underhill has only dirt and a shovel as his allies in taking on a wind-driven fire at the Fort McDowell Indian Reservation.

you get to fight the whole bunch. In the mountains, they like to steam past other crews on tough uphill slogs, and there is no race quite like the tool-clinking, elbow-pumping, dirt-throwing sprint that comes off if a pair of hotshot crews wind up digging adjacent sections of fire line.

This was Gleason's world. His crew, the Zig Zag Hotshots out of Oregon, knew him as a man who quoted Chinese philosophers, read books on the art of warfare, and, in the off-seasons, was a rock climber who took on big walls all over the West. He was summoned often to teach fire tactics to others. He talked about risk, and he was given to introspection, to saying things such as, "You get these situations where the fire blows up and it's making a big run and it's chewing through the forest and all the regular firefighters have been pulled back. And they're standing alongside the road when we go by. And you hear them say, 'Here come the hotshots. They're gonna take care of it. Throw them in the middle of it. They'll pick it up.' You have to be careful not to let that stuff get into you too much. You've got to work on the edge. But when you get close, you've got to know what close is."

Twenty-four years of the pursuit of fire had led him to his final season as the tool-packing ramrod of a fire crew. For a long time now, the fire world had pushed for him to put his time and talents into new harness. He was wanted in fire management. He was wanted for training the next generation. He was headed that direction, and simultaneously mapping out a return to school, perhaps a quest for a doctorate, but this time in fire, in the very business that had commanded his life.

And this last season, this summer of 1990, had brought him to this place. To sobbing in the ashes. To being fooled, for the briefest hopeful moment, into thinking that there was life in the yellow-shirted man he found there in the ashes in Walk Moore Canyon. "I rolled him over. I put my cheek right up to his nose and his mouth to see if there was any air. A tear rolled off my eye and fell on his cheek. I saw it, I thought it was his tear, and for just a fleeting second I thought that this guy was alive. And then it settled on me. I was in a canyon with a bunch of dead people."

At the outset, the Dude Fire had gleamed with the facets that had kept Gleason in the game for so long. Big fire. Problem fire. Nothing easy. And with it came a cross-section of grunts, the gritty groundpounders who do the hard work of forest fire. There was a tough Navajo crew. An Arizona prison crew from Perryville. And hotshot outfits from around the West. Bulldozer jockeys and engine crews, too. Gleason's kind of people.

Beneath the battlements of the sweeping Mogollon Rim, outside the Arizona town of Payson, Gleason's Zig Zag crew had joined the others on the line. The fire was pushing toward Bonita Estates, one in the archipelago of island subdivisions tucked into the forests and brushlands of the rural West, dictating tactics and limiting options when fire sprouts in the forest around them. Gleason and the others were denied the luxury of choosing where to make a stand; some developer had determined years ago that they would make it in the bottom of Walk Moore Canyon, between the fire and a cluster of four dozen homes.

So the crews had lined out along the bottom of the canyon, first the Navajos, then the Perryville inmates, then the hotshot crews, one after another. They had worked along a bulldozer line gouged the length of the canyon, improving it and burning out patches as the main fire came down off the slopes. They had fought it through the long hot afternoon of a day when the thermometer went to 122 degrees Fahrenheit in Phoenix. They worked it as the temperature climbed and the humidity fell, and it had gone sour on them. It had sent a plume laddering into the sky, then countered it with a cascade of downburst winds that produced, in moments, a firestorm that avalanched down the canyon side.

At the low end of the canyon, the fire had come hardest at the Indians and the inmates. Gleason had always admired the sixth-sense sort of savvy he saw in Native American firefighters. He would learn later, and not be surprised, that the Navajos had sensed the blowup first and had triggered the sprint that saved most of those who survived. The fire had split the line, and Gleason and all the hotshots lost sight of the others. As the crews fell back, Gleason and two other hotshot bosses had charged down the canyon, toward the place where they had last seen the prison firefighters.

An inmate, horribly burned and barely coherent, had come stumbling out of the smoke and fire. Flames too intense to be approached were still wrapped around him, and the hotshot bosses had screamed, "Move, move, move!" until he broke free. Gleason would learn later that his name was Geoffrey Hatch. The fire was roaring toward them, and farther down the canyon it was vaulting across the area where the inmates had been working. Already it was racing upslope on the opposite side, a towering wall of fire preparing to devour the houses. Gleason had headed down the canyon toward it, looking for more of the inmates. But the other crew bosses, fearing for his life, had persuaded him to stop.

A stretcher and firefighter medics had arrived. With the fire pursuing them, Gleason and the others had packed Hatch up the canyon at a run. They had clambered up a slope and into the cluster of houses, knowing that somewhere beyond them all the other hotshots had found refuge in a cleared safety zone where fire had passed earlier. In the lower end of the neighborhood, houses had begun torching off. In the stretcher crew there was talk of being overrun, of deploying shelters and riding it out. "There was a moment there, where I was ready to tell them all to take off and leave me with Hatch," Gleason would say later. "I had a shelter and there might have been room for both of us. Whatever happened next would be between me and Hatch and God."

Then they had heard the other crews calling to them. They had grabbed the stretcher and, with homes and vehicles burning around them, and propane tanks exploding, had made a last uphill push through heavy brush. At the top was the burned-over clearing where two hundred firefighters had clustered. For more than half an hour they had ridden it out there, had cleared a spot and talked a helicopter down through the smoke to fly Hatch to a hospital. Then Gleason had told the other 'shot superintendents that he was going back into the canyon.

And now he was there, stumbling through the ashes, looking ahead, finding the man half in, half out of a crumpled fire shelter. "Somewhere in there, I called my foreman on the radio," he said. "I told him I was all right, but I was just crippled. I didn't know if I could move. I fall down. I'm just down there in the ashes. I don't know if it's five minutes or fifteen. I wept. I love fire. I like lightin' it. I like fightin' it. And I'm there with this guy, and this was not what I had signed up for. I'm trying to tell myself that this part doesn't exist, that I had seen Hatch before and that was as bad as it could get."

But now, sobbing over the dead man and watching his own tear trickle down the face below him, he knew otherwise. Rising to his feet, he went stumbling through the ashes, finding another body, and then another, and then another. There were six in all, five male inmates and a woman who was one of their supervisors. Gleason had talked with some of them only a few hours earlier. He would end his day bagging their bodies. For the next day or two, the crew bosses from around the West, the old hands he had known through so many Western fires, would talk him through it all. He would weep often. He and the others would have their sessions with the critical incident stress counselors. And at week's end, he and the Zig Zag Hotshots would be three thousand miles away, battling a conflagration that roared across Alaska's tundra.

■ ■ ■

Death is not commonplace in the summer battles of the West. It comes, sometimes in horrendous numbers—seventy-five firefighters in the Northern Rockies fires of 1910, twenty-five in the Griffith Park Fire of 1933, fifteen in the Rattlesnake Fire of 1953, a dozen in the Loop Fire of 1966, fourteen at South Canyon in 1994. But more often, across thousands of fires large and small, the West loses six or seven firefighters a season. And some years, none at all. Still, risk defines experience. And the knowledge that the ultimate price is sometimes exacted on the fire lines stands always in the background, a defining shadow for those who speak of forest fire as the moral equivalent of war.

South Canyon, near Glenwood Springs, Colorado, was a small fire that exploded in moments to become a huge and historic one. It delivered the largest set of firefighter fatalities in more than forty years and shook the wildland fire community to its foundations. In a summer in which new fire starts seemed always to exceed available crews and resources, the fire sprang from a lightning bolt that nailed the mountain's flank in early July. Smoldering small and innocuous in oak brush on the steep, dry slope, the fire was monitored but not fought for several days because larger Colorado fires were threatening homes and resources were in short supply. It was still small, about thirty acres, when firefighters got to it on July 5. The following day, when it had swelled to fifty acres, a reinforced contingent of forty-nine smokejumpers, hotshots, helitack firefighters, and BLM and Forest Service groundpounders took it on.

In late afternoon, with the fire still growing, a cold front with stiff winds blew down on nearby Storm King Mountain. It triggered a blowup that sent flames hooking beneath the firefighters on a steep canyon slope cloaked in brushy Gambel oak. Within moments, a wall of flame three hundred feet tall and a quarter-mile wide funneled up the canyon.

Nine members of Oregon's Prineville Hotshots and three Forest Service smokejumpers—from McCall, Idaho, and Missoula, Montana—were caught in the fire's path on a section of steep upslope. For crucial moments, they had not been able to see the approaching fire. Too late, they sensed their predicament. Too late, the found themselves in the race that could not be won. The fire rocketed twelve hundred feet in two minutes. It overran them as they sprinted and tried to deploy fire shelters in the final, heartbreakingly steep stretch below the ridgetop. Nearby, the flame front cascaded over an adjoining ridgeline and chased down two firefighters from a BLM helitack crew that was based in Grand Junction, Colorado. Fleeing the fire, they died when a steep rocky chute, fifty feet deep, cut off their escape route

As always, the tragedy was followed by an investigation. It concluded much like investigations of other fatal and near-fatal wildland fire incidents. The rules of engagement for wildland fire are simple and broad. Organized as ten Standard Fire Orders and eighteen "Watch-Out" situations, they are, in effect, a safety code. But veteran firefighters can debate like Torah scholars

Above: After long hours of digging
in Idaho's Boise National Forest,
the Mormon Lake Hotshots of Arizona
sleep in the dirt of the fire line they've created.
On big forest fires where hotshots can be asked
to work fifty hours of grueling manual labor at a stretch,
sleep becomes the most precious commodity.

■ ■ ■

Left: Like a sprinter with a flaming baton,
Tony Sanchez, a squad boss on Arizona's Payson Hotshots,
wields a fusee to create a burned-out black zone
that will halt approaching flames
driven by forty-mile-per-hour winds.

■ ■ ■

Above right: Only two days after six firefighters died
at Arizona's Dude fire, two members
of Arizona's Prescott Hotshots receive intravenous fluids
after being overcome by heat and smoke at the same fire.
They were caught in a brief fire flare-up
on a hundred-degree Arizona day.

■ ■ ■

Bottom right: In the aftermath of a fire blowup
that killed six firefighters in Arizona's 1990 Dude Fire,
Prescott Hotshot K.C. Yowell comforts crewmate Steve Emery.
As fire roared around them, the Prescott crew
rode out the incident in a burned-over clearing.

over precisely how the rules should be applied in given tactical situations. So, like all of the world's fundamental codes, from the Ten Commandments to the Bill of Rights, the simple precepts become the mother of debate, and interpretation goes on forever. The difficulty is in the details. Will this chosen escape route actually work if the fire blows up? In tough, uneven terrain, how many lookouts must you post to be certain that you really know what the fire is doing? And how do you come to terms with risk, how do you strike the balance that resolves the counterpoised yin and yang of Fire Order No. 1, "Fight fire aggressively but safely?"

Indeed, the veterans say, when fire is roaring on the mountainside there are few certainties about the application of a set of precepts that were, after all, written at a flat desktop. But always there's one: A death on the fire lines inevitably will be followed by the official conclusion that one or more of the rules was breached. And for the most part, the firefighters do not disagree. Drawn broadly enough to cover every forest fire situation, the rules tighten inexorably when hindsight focuses on tragedy. There is something in them to cover every disaster, too.

So it was at South Canyon. The report found that electing to build fire line downhill had been too dangerous for the circumstances, that designated safety zones were too difficult to reach from the slope, that the support system had not relayed a forecast for high winds of a prediction on fire behavior. As with other fatal fires, the investigators, old fire hands all, focused not on blame but on lessons to be learned. And they departed from the chapter and verse of the fire orders to take on a more intangible topic. In their report and in subsequent public appearances, the panel of experts talked about the can-do attitude of firefighters, who sometimes seem impervious to messages of caution. "The can-do attitude is a positive attribute that needs to be balanced with a concern for safety," said Mark Reimers, a deputy Forest Service chief and one of the fire investigators.

And therein, he defined the central anxiety of every fire commander and crew boss. At some level, those who step onto seasonal fire crews are almost all seekers of risk, different from those cautionary souls who grew up never climbing trees and always staying in the crosswalks. Fresh from high school, or perhaps a year or two into college, they hire on, thinking mostly of work in the outdoors, a physical challenge. At that point, it is to most of them an adventure not much more hazardous than trying out for the basketball team. But in their first weeks, they learn of injury and death. The awareness of danger is hammered into them by their trainers, safety-conscious old hands who may remember too well being in some fire camp swept by word of a death on the line. So those who stay, and who come back for another season, and another, and another—they have learned about the risk. It becomes a reason, one among many, why they return.

Danger is no looming daily presence. Not at all. Because, as a paramilitary venture, forest fire fighting can droop with routines any GI would recognize. It can deliver moments, days, even weeks, of stultifying boredom and teeth-grinding frustration. It offers mindless times of hurry-up-and-wait. It serves up occasions when an order to march down the mountain is followed immediately by an order to march back up. It mixes racehorse action with plodding bureaucracy and layered regulation.

But in the background, risk is ever-present. The possibility of one of those defining events that can become a setpiece in a life's memories hangs as near as the next shift on the line. Sooner or later, those who stay on will have their moment of epiphany, their day when they beat fire by the narrowest of margins. And the possibility alone imparts to the work an aura of excitement and a veneer of the heroic that offsets bad food, long shifts, scant sleep, aching muscles, and endless days of monotonous mop-up. Risk. Few forest firefighters strut about it, few of them talk about it at all. They joke, in fact, about the line they have all used: "It's not dangerous, Mom." And yet, that denial may be the reason so many find it so difficult to make others understand why they glory in dirty, mindless, menial, dirt-throwing labor, the sort of work that most of them would never embrace if risk were not part of the equation.

Kim Maynard, who went on to become a smokejumper, was a rookie Forest Service groundpounder in Washington state. Her baptism came at age nineteen in the Olympic National Forest. "It was a big fire, crowning out," she said. "Incredible. We got there at night, did everything wrong. We had to dig line down to a main trail. We were throwing tree trunks and dirt. The fire was coming after us. It was a race. We whipped it, then crashed in the salal bushes and slept for a while, then got up and fought it some more. It was one of those dramatic events in your life. And I just said that this was it. I loved it. This was the life for me."

For many, the isolated anonymity of the work, the French Foreign Legion feel of it all, becomes one of the attractions. Frequently the summer's posting will be to a remote ranger district or engine station in some hamlet on the fringe of a

■ ■ ■

Right: With a professional river guide as their skipper, a crew is ferried across Idaho's Payette River en route to a remote forest fire. In roadless sections of the West's national forests and wilderness areas, amphibious operations often become part of the fire battle plan.

Above: In a flag-draped casket delivered by an ancient smokejumper aircraft, Doug Dunbar, a Prinesville Hotshot who died in 1994 at the South Canyon Fire in Colorado, comes home to Oregon.

Above: Stirring up a blizzard in mid-summer, a firefighter at the Yellowstone National Park fires of 1988 uses soapy foam to coat trees and brush near park structures. Foam engine crews were credited with savingmany of the park's historic buildings

forest or mountain range. Faraway families and friends will never see what they do and will understand it only imperfectly. And in the firefighters' most challenging moments, when they stop the dragon on some lonely ridgeline, the world seldom will know.

"You go out for five days and you're working nineteen or twenty hours a day, just killing yourself," said Dave Gilbert, an Alaska helitack foreman who began as a ground-level firefighter. "You've been having this amazing adventure. And you come back to town and nothing's changed. Cars are still driving down the street. People don't look at you twice. You've had this intense experience. Some part of you thinks you're a hero, and nobody even notices."

The seasonals who march off to battle wildland fire usually find their way into the work between the ages of eighteen and twenty-two. In Western small towns and on college campuses the grapevine carries word that firefighting offers hard work but big money, that it is perhaps the best-paying summer job around. A few tendrils of the grapevine twine eastward, and snare a smattering of students from universities as distant as Harvard and Miami.

Those who come to wildland fire have heard in some vague way of the possibility of excitement and even a bit of travel. They know, or they will learn soon after they sign on, that the amounts of work, money, excitement, and travel will hinge upon how busy a fire season they've drawn. Soon enough they will come to the view that always seems paradoxical, if not perverse, to outsiders: A good season comes with an abundance of fire; a bad season is spent twiddling thumbs and talking about good seasons. They become not so different from all of society's other specialists whose callings depend upon calamity. Like emergency room surgeons and fighter pilots, they wish no ill upon anyone, but they know that using their skills to the fullest depends upon something going seriously awry somewhere.

By dint of its sheer size and the number of seasonal fire jobs it funds, the Forest Service stands as the most common port of entry for newcomers. The service is the historic model for all of the West's wildland fire agencies, so the first-year experiences rookies encounter there will be much the same as those dealt out in other federal and state operations A scant few of the novices, with good physical qualifications and perhaps a broad background of outdoor experience, will make it onto an elite hotshot crew or into a helitack operation even without previous work in fire. But that is uncommon. More often they'll be assigned to a ranger district on some national forest. Typically, depending on local climate and the duration of the fire season, they'll be offered from three to six months of work.

In the world of wildland fire, the seasonal Type II crew is the basic combat unit. Ranking below the Type I, or hotshot units, the Type II crew is an infantry platoon of twenty foot soldiers, armed with shovels, pulaskis, and chainsaws. The men and women in its ranks are generalists. They become the wide, deep base of the manpower pyramid for wildland fire. In the timber-rich regions of the Pacific Northwest, many local Forest Service ranger districts have carried a standard Type II fire crew of seasonal combatants. On a conflagration that draws firefighting resources from around the West, the Type II grunts and groundpounders will easily constitute the greatest number of bodies on the fire lines, though they will seldom draw the most difficult assignments.

Though the seasonal Type II crews are the foundation of the fire-fighting force, extreme fire years such as 1988 or 1994 deliver another version of the Type II outfit to the fire lines. In those seasons agency regulars—the full-time clerks, wildlife biologists, and recreations specialists—are formed into emergency crews. The practice survives as a vestige of the day when the land agencies operated on the principle that every employee was a potential firefighter. That philosophy eroded as the agencies grew, created departments far removed from forestry, and took on sociologists, anthropologists, and engineers with job descriptions that decidedly did not include fire. But, even in the 1990s, the land agencies still train many of their full-timers as firefighters, though they are called to the lines only in those horrendous seasons when smoke seems to rise on every horizon.

While it is trained as an operational hand crew for fire line construction, the typical seasonal Type II outfit will spend most of each fire season sweating over local project work—clearing brush, building trails, maintaining campgrounds. Often the work will include prescribed fire, deliberate burning of sections of land to remove excessive dead fuel or invading plant species. In Forest Service districts with small budgets, perhaps only a half dozen seasonals will be scattered over several different summer jobs. But they usually are melded into an emergency plan that will let them combine into a twenty-person crew with seasonals or full-timers from neighboring districts or even from other agencies. All the seasonal groundpounders will be trained in fire, prepared to chase minor smokes in their own territory, or, with luck, to be dispatched to some distant campaign fire. Some of the rookies will land on engine crews, usually contingents of three to six firefighters. In the Bureau of Land Management, and in many of the state agencies, the preponderance of summer fire jobs are engine jobs. The rookies will be introduced to the squat, powerful mountain fire engines, or brush rigs, favored by Western wildfire agencies, and they will begin learning the complexities of pumps and hose lays.

■ ■ ■

Fire training is a ritual of spring in the West. In the past, fire bosses at local ranger districts would train their rookies with either a few days of classes or a gradual acclimatization spread over the early weeks of the fire season. Typically, the instruction concentrated on the rudiments of tactics, fire behavior, weather, topography, tool use, and line-building skills, all with a heavy emphasis on safety. But large rookie camps, where several agencies bring their recruits together for a week of intensive training, have become common since the mid-1980s.

Perhaps the best of the West's rookie camps comes off on the Yakama Reservation in central Washington. Every season, about 185 rookie firefighters from the Forest Service, the BLM, Washington's Department of Natural Resources, and the federal Bureau of Indian Affairs gather there. The Yakama Indian Nation maintains America's only reservation where public access is barred, so the trainees rank as honored guests of the tribe. Tribal elders who fought fire in their youth give formal welcomes and speak poetically of how Mother Earth needs firefighters to protect her forests.

After the welcome, the rookies are hauled deep into the Cascade Mountains to a secluded tribal retreat, a collection of teepees, cabins, classrooms, and a dining hall. Formed into training crews, they mix class time and field work for the next week, learning to dig line, run portable gasoline-powered pumps and analyze fire safety situations. In the evenings, they field teams that compete in relay races built around fire skills. Before the week is out, a small piece of the reservation is set ablaze and the rookies face live fire. On their last night in camp, the tribe fetes them with a traditional Northwest Indian salmon bake.

Because of the thousands of firefighters who have bought into the seasonal lifestyle and choose to come back year after year, rookies will be a distinct minority on virtually every crew. Whatever its size and assignment, each crew will have at least a boss with significant fire experience. The typical twenty-person hand crew will be led by a superintendent and two or three squad leaders, all with multiple years of wildland fire experience. Often one or more of the crew leaders will be a full-time land agency employee. At remote districts, crews may be housed in barracks.

Variations on the Forest Service themes for hand crews and engine crews play out around the West, whether the unit in question is a state forestry department engine crew in Oregon or a National Park Service hotshot crew in Colorado. The twenty-person hand crew is the standard configuration for every federal agency in wildland fire. With some of the Western state agencies, the typical crew size is sixteen or seventeen, often because the lesser number works best with the type of vehicle preferred for crew transport. Engine crews range from two to six members. They include scores of county-based wildfire crews. Those crews, often volunteers in local fire districts, stand as the main line of wildfire defense in such states as Wyoming and Colorado.

In a broad sense, the mix of experience levels and the training regimen for the government crews are similar for seasonal fire crews assembled by private industry. At some level, such private fire crews always have been part of the West's wildland fire battles. The tradition dates to the era when sawmill gangs and logging crews rolled into action at the first sign of smoke. On private timberlands in the mountain West, fire crews hired by timber firms and privately funded forest protection associations have never stopped being the first line of defense. Once, huge sections of the backcountry West were protected by such associations, which were funded by the private timber owners.

Later, much of that fire protection responsibility was handed to state government, a step that literally created several state forestry departments in the West. In some locales, the private associations have remained strong. In central Oregon, the Walker Range Fire Patrol, responsible for protecting two hundred thousand acres, each summer adds thirty-five seasonal firefighters to its small core of five full-timers. In Idaho, the Southern Idaho Timber Protective Association and the Clearwater-Potlatch Timber Protective Association, which together defend 1.3 million acres of forest land, add seventy-five firefighters to the minimum crews they maintain in the winter. The associations field a mix of hand crews, engines, and bulldozers.

Logging outfits and timber companies still send their own workers into battle, too. In the timber regions of the West, few big fires are fought without squads of local loggers who range the most hazardous sections of the fire lines, dropping precarious, fiery snags with monstrous chainsaws. The logging outfits are dovetailed into the fire-fighting system with preseason contracts signed with the state and federal agencies. The contracts resolve in advance questions of pay, hours, and travel, so that the timber-falling crews, bulldozers, and other heavy equipment can be mobilized on short notice. The tradition of dropping everything to pitch in on a fire has eroded in some logging companies, but it remains strong with most.

Les Shank, a veteran Washington logger, has rolled his six-employee outfit and its equipment onto fires for decades. "I believe in it," he said. "These days not everybody does, but I do. You never make as much money fighting fire as you do logging. But these mountains and these woods are my living. I sign an equipment contract for fire every year. No matter what we're doing, if they want it, all they have to do is call."

In the mid-1980s, as budgetary cuts hit the government land agencies, private crews fielded by forestry contractors began emerging as a significant fire-fighting force. Hired by the federal and state agencies, they showed up in increasing numbers at bit Western fires on public lands. In the timber-rich sections of the West, particularly Montana, Idaho, Washington, and Oregon, private forestry contractors specialize in tree planting, thinning and stream enhancement projects on public and private land. In summer, they contract with government agencies to provide hand and engine crews on a call-up basis. In a big fire year, the companies may provide up to five thousand firefighters. Some of the contractors, such as Inland Forest Management of Sandpoint, Idaho, primarily provide engines. Others, such as Grayback Forestry of Merlin, Oregon, can field a half-dozen or more twenty-person hand crews in a typical season. In 1994, with the wildland fire system stretched to its limits, many of the contractors were recruiting, training, and deploying additional crews in midseason. Some of the private crews run heavily to year-round forestry workers, some are collections of Hispanic workers who mix agriculture and forestry work, and many are the familiar blend of students, adventurers and perennial fire bums .

"We get our share of the kind of people who just want to fight fire for the summer," said Mike Wheelock, president of Grayback. "They're not interested in anything else. They want to fight fire for a few months and then go skiing or head to Mexico." The larger forestry companies often have managers and crew leaders with extensive government fire-fighting experience. Wheelock, an ex-hotshot and smokejumper, is typical.

In Arizona, Rural/Metro Corporation contracts year-round as the local structural fire department for Scottsdale and about twenty other Arizona cities and rural fire districts. Beyond protecting homes and businesses, the company also takes on wildland fire and activates its own force of seasonals. Lou Jekel, an attorney who is the corporation's wildland fire director, stepped into the fire world as a college student and never stepped out. He smiles memory's smile when he talks of the seasonals who come back year after year to work for his company. "We call them annual reserves and they're on our list all year for whatever we might need. But, for them, it's the wildland season that's the reason they stick around. It's what they wait for."

Like recruit Marines, new seasonal firefighters are indoctrinated on the rituals, traditions, and hazards of their corps. They hear stories of big fires, monumental snafus, unforgettable road trips. A crew scrapbook, or a wall plastered with pictures and news clippings, provides illustration. Their assignment may be in a spot that serves up glimpses of a hotshot crew or a smokejumper base. Or older firefighters will roll out stories of those upper echelons of the wildland fire game.

The rookies will hear tales of exhaustion, of dropping and sleeping in the ashes, of fire shifts that ran to thirty, forty, even fifty hours. They will learn where danger lurks—in fire-weakened trees that fall like silent scythes and kill firefighters every year, in boulders that come rocketing down slopes after fire loosens the roots and earth that held them in place, in stumps that burn as pits deep into the ground and become thousand-degree crucibles waiting for the unwary. The newcomers will learn, too, that some firefighters bounce around the West like saddle-tramp cowhands, jumping from crew to crew and agency to agency over the years. Very likely, their crew boss and some of the veterans in their outfit will have worked fire in two or three states.

In the timber regions of the West, professional loggers are always called to battle in big forest fires, where their skills are needed to drop fiery snags. Oregon loggers Bob Gardener and Larry Ashcroft felled a giant danger tree at the Warner Creek Fire in 1991.

■ ■ ■

Terry Grogan, for example. Tough and leathery, still fighting fire in his late forties, Grogan's past ranges over years as a logger, cab driver, tugboat deckhand, and bartender. He took the helm of a seasonal Type II fire crew in Washington's Wenatchee National Forest in the late 1980s. In seventeen years of fire chasing, he worked for both the Forest Service and the Bureau of Land Management. He spent a season in Alaska, did some helitack work and fought fire throughout the West. In slow moments he can spellbind his crew with tales such as the account of a season when fire took him from the Arctic Circle to the Mexican border. Around the West, hundreds of veterans like him become mahatmas of fire, elders who pass down to rookies the oral traditions of a small subculture. For the crew bosses, creating that sense of group, of inclusion, is as important as the day's lesson on fire behavior.

"The new person on a crew is usually just awestruck the first time I take them up against a big fire," Grogan said. "They say, 'My God, how are we ever going to stop anything like that? You guys are crazy.' Then they get a bit of experience and learn to trust the people they're with. I see it year after year. In the good years, a fire crew becomes a family. People who have nothing in common come together as a team. They share the adrenaline rushes and the excitement and the camaraderie. It's why I stay."

On the federal crews, rookies most often will begin with a lowly U.S. Civil Service GS-2 rating, earning less than seven dollars an hour and working forty hours a week. Two or three years of experience may bump them a couple of GS ratings higher on the pay schedule. But fire pushes them all into overtime and hazard pay categories, which can increase their base pay rate by seventy-five percent. In 1994, a GS-4 working a big fire bust on overtime and hazard pay earned over fourteen dollars an hour, with meals and sleeping bag provided. In a season with long-running fires, eighty-hour weeks, and uninterrupted work stints of up to twenty-one days, a groundpounder or an engine firefighter on a federal crew may earn eight to twelve thousand dollars.

But by the time they have cashed a few fire paychecks, new firefighters have begun to hear of the earnings of some of the fire specialists. Helitack and hotshot crews see much more fire. They sometimes roll up weeks of a hundred hours, all on hazard pay. In huge fire seasons, they may work six hundred to eight hundred hours of overtime and pull down more than fifteen thousand dollars.

Smokejumpers usually have Civil Service ratings of GS-6 and higher. Along with some senior hotshots, helicopter firefighters and Type II crew bosses, they sometimes earn placement in special permanent-seasonal categories which provide annual reemployment rights, fringe benefits, and upward movement to higher steps on the federal pay schedule. A hundred-hour fire week for such a veteran can be worth over seventeen hundred dollars. On occasion, jumpers have twenty-five-thousand-dollar and even thirty-thousand-dollar seasons. In general, seasonal firefighters on the state crews earn less than their counterparts on the federal

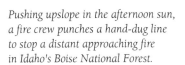

Pushing upslope in the afternoon sun, a fire crew punches a hand-dug line to stop a distant approaching fire in Idaho's Boise National Forest.

agencies' Type II crews or engine outfits. However, the pay schedules of the California Department of Forestry and the Alaska Department of Natural Resources, though structured differently, compare favorably.

■ ■ ■

Hank DeBruin remembers the drums. DeBruin rose to become the national director of fire management for the Forest Service. Before he went to Washington, D.C. to fight political fires, he fought real ones around the West. He is something of an oral historian of the post–World War II years, when the scope and complexity and technology of wildland fire fighting expanded exponentially. As a young Turk, he was part of the movement that ushered out the thinking of the 1930s and crafted the wildfire system that operates in the West of the 1990s. To his core, he is a modernizer. But still, he remembers the Zuni drumming.

"The Zunis. God, how I loved having them on a fire," he said. "They were the best. They had a unity. I didn't have to worry about one of them running and starting a panic. A fire blowup is so chaotic, so crazy. You have to hunker down, stay with it, think it through. The Zunis always had that ability. And they simply loved to fight fire, these small, wiry people who could work right under the fire, right up against it, and never complain. And then, at night in camp, they'd build a fire. And the drumming would start and the chanting, and the hair would just stand up on the back of your neck. Wonderful stuff."

Few big fires in the West are fought without Indian help. The Zunis, a Southwest Indian tribe, are still on the line every season. So are thousands of other Native Americans—Crow, Blackfoot, Apache, Shoshone, Athabascan, Quinalt, Navajo, Warm Springs, Arapaho, Hopi, Ute, Gros Ventre, Mandan, Eskimo, Macah, Sioux. Pulled into the national mobilization network, native fire crews travel vast distances. Athabascans from Alaska's Yukon River battle California chaparral blazes in the hills around Malibu. Navajo from the Arizona desert fight fire in Oregon's tall timber. Sometimes when crew members communicate by radio with their tribesmen, the rest of the fire line listens in puzzlement as the airwaves fill with the sounds of the Crow language or some Eskimo dialect.

In forty-five years, fire fighting has become the new warrior tradition in many tribes. Fire, with its challenge, its paychecks, and its macho tradition, provides an invading enemy, a journey to be taken, a war to fight, booty to carry home, stories to tell. "Fighting fire is a respected thing in our village," said Darrell Franks, an Athabascan in the Alaskan hamlet of Minto. "We are maybe two hundred fifty people in the whole village and thirty of us are firefighters. You grow up with it."

On some reservations, the entire population turns out to see its firefighters off to battle. In the Southwest, tribal medicine men sometimes come to bless the warriors before they board the bus. "In the tribe, fire is an important job," said Randy Pretty-on-Top, a Crow from Montana. "It's like being a warrior again. The younger generation knows fire as part of growing up on the reservation. The fathers and grandfathers did it, and they'll do it, too. Fire is something you're supposed to do when you're growing up."

Tribal leaders around the West know fire fighting as an economic force in their communities. They religiously track each season's fire payroll and are quick to complain if a neighboring reservation garners more call-ups. In Alaska, where unemployment in the villages runs at eighty-five percent, fire provides the *only* cash income for many natives. A slow fire season is economic disaster. "In the good seasons, you can be out fifty or sixty days," said Roy Charlie, an Athabascan crew boss in Minto. "You could make fifteen thousand in a good summer, and that is a very large amount of money in the village."

A Native American fire telegraph spans the West, an invisible network that threads from one reservation to the next. Mysterious in its workings, dazzling in its speed, it recalls the drum messages of earlier centuries. Let a big fire erupt anywhere in the West and, on reservations a thousand miles away, even before the fire has made the national newscasts, Indian firefighters will begin gathering at fire headquarters. With packs ready and canteens full, they will sleep through the night in their cars to avoid missing a call to arms. "I don't know how they know" said Bob Jacob, BIA fire management officer at Wyoming's Wind River Reservation. "But they know. They find out long before we get the word. And they start showing up, sitting outside, just waiting, before we've ever put out a call."

In the game, they are all known as emergency firefighters, or EFFs. Around the West, the federal and state agencies cooperate in running the EFF corps, a network of thousands of on-call firefighters. The emergency troops do not hold continuous seasonal positions, like the firefighters who hire onto on the regular state and federal crews. Instead, the fire agencies train and certify emergency firefighters and their crew leaders each spring, then activate them as needed and assemble them into twenty-person crews. At many reservations, the crews are filled on a first-come, first-taken basis when a call-up occurs. But in some Alaska villages, the economic benefits of fire fighting are so profound that a standard of one crew member per family is imposed. Even then, villages sometimes rattle with political battles over the question of favoritism in fire assignments.

The roots of the emergency firefighter program lie in the Indian tribes and in the Hispanic community. Many of the reservations still run EFF crews that are effectively limited to tribal members. Other emergency firefighter crews ostensibly are open to non-Indians and non-Hispanics. But overall, the EFF system remains distinctively ethnic. Only a small percentage of its firefighters are Anglos—white Americans of European heritage. "Natives are the majority on Alaska crews," said Dave Dash, operations chief for the BLM's Alaska Fire Service. "But we see all the possible mixes, even a few EFF crews that have no natives at all. I was on a fire once with a crew of Yupik Eskimos from a remote village. They were an excellent crew, but they barely spoke English. And their leader was a black guy. I don't know how they communicated with each other. I don't know why he lived in their village. I don't have any idea how he got there. But I know he must have showed them something, because the villages elect their crew bosses."

The Mescalero Apaches began it all. In 1948, facing dismal economic conditions on their New Mexico reservation, officials of the tribe created a fire crew. Within five years, the Mescalero Red Hats were in demand far beyond the borders of their state. That success ultimately led to creation of the Southwest Fire Fighters, a multitribe, multiagency network that trains more than twelve hundred emergency firefighters, mostly Native American, augmented by a few Hispanic-American fire crews. Coordinated by the Bureau of Indian Affairs, the Southwest organization became the model for others, including Alaska's EFF network, the Rocky Mountain Indian Firefighters, the Montana Indian Firefighters and several smaller operations. All told, the system can produce nearly seven thousand emergency firefighters on demand.

It is a system that sometimes demands much from them, including the willingness to be scooped up on short notice and set down in the middle of a running battle a thousand miles away. Don Mitchell, a Wyoming Shoshone, was delivered in that fashion to the long-running Southern Oregon fires of 1987. Day after punishing day, he and his Shoshone and Arapaho crewmates—Sho-Raps, in the lexicon of firefighting—trekked six miles into rugged mountains of the Siskiyou National Forest, fought fire until twilight, and hiked out. In the middle of that campaign, fire roared out of a canyon, growling and snapping like a rogue bear. As the Sho-Raps beat a retreat toward a burned out zone, four-engine retardant planes dared low passes in curdling smoke, and worked to buy them time to reach safety. Mitchell stepped atop a huge, ancient stump to get a better view of the terrain.

Sometimes, fire burns underground. It fingers into a crack in a stump, then eats downward, burning out the root wad. On the outside, the stump can look charred but solid. But it may be only a facade, a lid as fragile as a pastry shell over a burned-

out pit perhaps five or six feet deep. Inside that earthen oven, the walls will glow red, and temperatures may climb above a thousand degrees.

When Mitchell stepped to the top of the stump, it crumpled beneath him and he went down into a searing blast furnace. "It was deep enough that if I went in with both legs, I never would have gotten out," he said. "It was one leg all the way to my crotch, and I was by myself. I came out as fast as I could. I blew out my knee, tore my groin, and got some burns. It took five crews to pack me out of the mountains. That night the surgeons did the job on my knee."

Beyond the reservations, the Snake River Valley Firefighters rank as the EFF system's largest non-Indian component. The network of about a thousand fire-trained Hispanics is clustered in a rich agricultural region on the Oregon-Idaho border. For generations the valley lured Hispanic farm workers. Now its towns have permanent Mexican-American communities, which swell each year with an influx of migrant workers. In 1963, the BLM began tapping the Hispanic labor pool and organizing fire crews to fight the desert and range fires of the Intermountain Region. Like the Mescalero Red Hats, the Snake River crews established themselves locally, then became certified for call-up on the big Western fires.

"We are the best mop-up crews in the country," said Ambrosio Vasquez, who followed a brother and a sister onto the fire lines. "No matter how solid an EFF crew is, you're going to get used for a lot of mop-up. But sometimes we get more action. In the big Yellowstone fire in 1988, we were doing lots of backburning and cutting line right next to the fire." A firefighter on a Snake River crew can earn as much as a thousand dollars a week during a call-up, far more than the pay for topping onions or harvesting potatoes. And that has become an agricultural fact of life in the valley. Hired as day laborers in the fields, workers with firefighting certification are certain to drop their hoes and opt for the big money whenever a fire call-up comes.

Almost uniformly, EFF crews are drawn from rural communities of low-income Americans of color. Alcohol and drug problems, anchored on an intractable bedrock of poverty, have been a fixture on reservations and in Alaska's native villages for generations. They are no less a problem in some segments of the migrant farm worker population. Inevitably the ripples of those problems touch fire crews. The presence of drugs or alcohol in a fire setting will net a firefighter or an entire crew an immediate trip home. Peer pressure from crew members who do not want their fire paychecks jeopardized, drug education efforts by fire managers, and screening of would-be firefighters have helped reduce the problem. The fire line delivers lessons;

tribal and village elders use fire crews to underscore their arguments that jobs would solve many reservation problems. All of them point to men and women in their communities who annually go off the bottle or give up drugs during fire season, so that they can be eligible for crew work.

Though it is seldom acknowledged officially, some EFF crews and even entire reservation programs become *persona non grata* for failures of crew discipline on fire assignments. The fire grapevine spreads the word like quicksilver, and call-ups simply stop. The Sho-Rap fire crews from Wind River have drawn high praise for their work through the 1980s and 1990s. But it was a different story in the 1970s. "There were some disciplin-

. . .

Far from home, a crew of Hopi Indian firefighters from the Southwest march through a Montana fire camp. Indian crews regularly are flown great distances to fight fire around the west.

ary problems, drinking problems, things like that," said Jacob, the reservation's fire management officer. "Some Sho-Raps got blackballed off a California fire in 1972 and the word spread. The program fell apart. It took years for it to come back together."

Jennie Joe, an anthropologist, and Dorothy Lonewolf Miller, a sociologist, are Native Americans and faculty members at the University of Arizona. For years they have researched the world of Indian firefighters. Their work extends from Alaska to the Southwest. "Fire fighting is now engrained in tribal culture," Miller said. "You go outside, accomplish something, and bring home money and honor. You can do something good in the context of the reservation. You are a warrior. You do not have to give up being native to be a firefighter."

But the two researchers decry many aspects of the EFF operation. "If you look at fire camps, they're segregated," Joe said. "The bosses, the overhead people, are in one section. It's military. It's officers' camp. And if an Indian who happens to be a crew boss shows up in officers' camp, people treat him like he doesn't belong there." Joe and Miller argue that wildland fire operates on an employment caste system that holds Native Americans to the role of on-call firefighters, and denies them access to regular seasonal crews and to elite, high-paying hotshot and smokejumper jobs, or fire management roles. But they also acknowledge a hiring difficulty that even the most aggressively affirmative fire managers encounter regularly: Many Indians raised in the traditional reservation or village culture are so uncomfortable being away for extended periods that a six-month seasonal job seems an untenable eternity.

Peter Solomon, a veteran Athabascan firefighter, tugs against the pull of the village. "It is more difficult for the people who live the strong native lifestyle to take jobs and be away for a long time," he said. "We see it often, even on fires. If an EFF crew is away from their village for two or three weeks, nothing is more important than getting home. For the jobs that take more time, we have the most luck with those who have more education and have done some traveling." Solomon builds bridges. Hired by the Alaska Fire Service, he teaches white fire managers about native culture. Trekking from village to village, he recruits natives for the six-month seasonal fire jobs that pay better than EFF work. An Alaska Fire Service training crew now helps a few natives each year make the transition from the villages to the bustling fire center at Fairbanks. Native graduates of that crew are showing up in the ranks of the BLM's two Alaska hotshot crews and the Alaska smokejumpers.

A few EFF crews have evolved without Native American or Hispanic roots. Around posh Santa Barbara, California, college students are trained as emergency firefighters with on-call arrangements not all that different from the poorest reserva-

Battling against a forty-mile-per-hour wind, Turner Brooks of the Arizona's Fort Apache Hotshots sprints to spread a burnout fire down an Idaho ridgeline.

■ ■ ■

tions. But the most unlikely crew in the world of wildland fire is the South Central Panthers, recruited from the mean inner city streets of Los Angeles. Street gang members fill its ranks. Formed in 1993, the crew is a by-product of the disorder that swept the South Central neighborhood after the verdicts from the controversial trial in which police officers were acquitted in the beating of Rodney King, a black Los Angeles resident. In the aftermath, government and private industry rushed to create jobs in the social powder keg of South Central. Efforts to sculpt truces among warring street gangs were part of the campaign. The Forest Service suggested creating a wildland fire crew from the inner city. Ron Lamount, a community activist in South Central, began recruiting on the streets.

Structurally, the fire crew created in South Central differed little from an EFF crew in Alaska or Arizona. Firefighters would be trained in advance, then called into action when wildland fire struck in the hills of Southern California. But practical differences loomed large. Most of the thirty-seven recruits brought aboard by Lamount had spent their entire lives on asphalt. Though a few had fought fire as prison inmates, most had no concept of tool use, had never held a job, and could barely imagine working in an outdoor environment. Those who joined the crew—black gang members from the Crips, Bloods, and Blackstone Rangers, plus a smattering of Hispanics and Cambodians—pledged to set aside all gang and ethnic rivalries. But skeptics within the gangs opposed the idea and refused to certify the neutrality of any piece of neighborhood turf for training. Ultimately the training was moved to the Angeles National Forest.

The Panthers proved themselves in the fire season of 1993, including the huge October fires that swept through the Los Angeles basin. They reaped substantial publicity, including national television exposure. And, in retrospect, they learned to laugh at the spectacle they were at the beginning, streetwise tough guys looking over their shoulders and worrying about spiders and snakes as they bedded down in the boondocks. The Forest Service expects to expand the concept to additional urban crews.

"In the beginning, we had brothers who could barely stand to sleep outdoors," said Hashim Abdullah, a former Blood who was on the line in that inaugural season. "They couldn't stand to be out of that South Central environment. They thought they were so tough, but when the bus was going up those little mountain roads all they could think about was falling off. We had all these people who had been killing each other on the streets. They all came together, and it worked. Being on fire is a serious thing, and people just forgot all of that other stuff. We had Crips and Bloods working and sweating right next to each other. We actually did it."

■ ■ ■

The flame front, a wall towering higher than a seven-story building, roared out of the pines and curled over the truck at seventy miles an hour. In that first wave, the crew that huddled inside the six-man cab saw the windows become an incandescent panorama of orange, as if the sun itself had dipped to touch the earth and inhaled them into its corona. Fire wrapped around the truck, and the temperature inside the cab soared toward three hundred degrees. The tires burst instantly into flame, the gaskets around the inside of the doors glowed red briefly and were gone, the windshield cracked into a spider web tracery, the smell of burning rubber and plastic rolled through the cab, and the front grille melted and ran down across the bumper, like a waxworks display tossed onto a griddle. The cap on the gasoline tank blew and more fire spewed from the opening. The radiant heat sent the men in the truck clawing into each other's laps or diving for the floor. For ten minutes the five of them endured, their throats constricting in the heat, wondering if suffocation would take them before the flames. And then, inside the cab, upholstery began to burn around them.

Like foot-slogging infantrymen deriding the artillery corps as it rolls by in its trucks, true groundpounders sometimes snicker at engine work. Real firefighters walk, they say. The fire grapevine says engine work is safer, easier, not quite so grueling as trekking mountains and hand-digging fire line by the mile. But it has its moments. Dave McMaster, a Forest Service foreman on an engine in Northern California, was there that day the Crank Fire rolled over two engines from the Forest Service and one from the California Department of Forestry. Trapped in a small clearing with a hand crew of California prison inmates, McMaster saw the downburst winds of a thunder cell lash a slow-moving fire into a galloping blaze. "Just instantly we had winds of forty miles an hour and hundred-foot flame lengths," he said. "We knew we were caught. It happened in ten seconds. The three of us running the engines made a decision. We

thought we could hold out and save everybody in the clearing. I knew I couldn't let things break down with my crew. If one person tweaked and started to run it was going to be all over."

In the postage-stamp-size clearing, surrounded by downed trees and limbs, the engine crews rode out a long, brutal first wave of flame in their cabs, an accepted last-ditch safety practice. The inmates took to their fire shelters. As the interiors of the trucks ignited, those inside the cabs retreated. They deployed shelters in the tiny space at the center of the circle of blazing vehicles. But the heat from the burning trucks soon made the position untenable. For thirty-five tense minutes those on the outside of the flames thought all twenty-four firefighters had been lost. Then they saw them, a ghostly single file marching out of the flames and smoke, with foil shelters draped like capes over their heads and shoulders. No one said a word about engine work being easy.

The wildland fire engines favored around the West are close-coupled and powerful. They range from four-wheel-drive pickup trucks with hundred-gallon auxiliary tanks mounted in their beds to one-hundred-thousand-dollar diesel workhorses that pack two thousand gallons of water and a mile of hose. Many of them can generate foam, a soapy surfactant which can be used to coat ground fuels and buildings in the face of approaching fire. The incongruous effect looks like nothing so much as a winter wonderland poised against a wall of flame. But in the confrontation it is the flame that melts. In 1988, scores of historic structures at Yellowstone National Park survived because engine crews blanketed them in foam as fire roared down upon them.

The West's largest collection of brush engines roams California. Its core is a fleet fielded by the California Department of Forestry. Immense stretches of road-accessible forests and brushlands, as well as tens of thousands of rural and suburban homes, fall in CDF's bailiwick. Other off-road engines ply the Golden State behind the logos of the Forest Service, the BLM, large county fire operations in places such as Los Angeles and Santa Barbara counties, and scores of smaller local departments where firefighters are trained to fight wildland fire, as well as structural blazes. In the huge fire busts that bedevil California even more often than earthquakes, the engines and their crews range hundreds of miles, a benign blitzkrieg rolling to the rescue of besieged communities.

More than any other group of wildland firefighters, California engine crews know about the business of triage, deciding which houses will burn when saving every house is not possible. In October 1992, a fire erupted in the Eldorado National Forest in Eastern California. Before it was done it would claim two tanker pilots' lives, sixty-two homes and twenty-five thousand acres of timber. The losses would total 245 million dollars. The arsonist who triggered it would elude capture. Along Highway 50, the road that connects Sacramento and Lake Tahoe, triage was the order of the day.

"It was guerrilla fighting, house to house," said Eric Jack, foreman of a CDF brush engine from the Highway 50 community of Camino. "We were trying to stay ahead, trying to make a difference. We'd knock the fire down at one place, then run to another and hit it. We had to make choices. You'd come to these places that had firewood stacked against the house and the brush not cut back at all and the fire coming right at it. There was no way. When he had a chance, the owner hadn't done anything to help himself or to help us. And you'd just drive on to another place. You had to make those decisions. Sometimes it was, 'Is my life worth this guy's house?' Or you'd look at some houses and you'd make up your mind—this one can be saved and that one can't. In a while, you'd look back, and the one you passed up would be burning."

On big fires, engine crews and groundpounders often work in tandem, and it is not the engine outfits that draw the heavy digging work. But on small, initial-attack fires, the engine troops are full-service firefighters, trained in pick-and-shovel fire fighting. When terrain is too rough or too steep to be reached by the engine, the hand tools come out of the truck, and the crew goes after fire the hard way. Engine crews often set their trucks up as stationary pumpers, drawing water from streams or from larger water tank trucks. In those circumstances they may extend hose for a mile or more. "The hose lays are so tough," said Constance Collier, who works on a CDF engine crew at Porterville. "You have to perform. You make these trips up and down the hill, over and over and over, like a mule. You pack two hundred feet of hose and all the fittings on every trip."

In the vastness of the interior West, the region east of the Sierras and the Cascades, engine crews often stand as the first line of defense. Much of the territory is desert and rangeland, the province of the BLM or of state fire operations such as the Nevada Division of Forestry. Throughout the open country, firefighters face a mix of natural and humanmade hazards. The region runs to light, fast-burning fuels—grasses, brush, and pinyon-juniper woodlands far different from the timber types of mountain zones. To the north, much of the intermountain region is feathered with cheatgrass, a fine-stemmed annual that sprouts thick and dense in spring, then dries in summer heat. "When it gets going, it just races," said Bill Casey, who manages BLM fire operations at Boise. "We've had trucks on gravel roads pacing cheatgrass fires, and we've seen it go forty miles an hour. It's nothing to see it take a thousand acres every twelve or fifteen minutes. They're not hard to put out, but they're very hard to catch."

Typically the desert and rangeland outfits put engines on each flank of the fire and work until they pinch it off at the head. Because the land does not carry the same high value as mountain timber stands, they have the luxury of letting fire run toward a convenient natural barrier or to a road, a strategic spot where setting a countering fire can produce a quick stop. In Arizona and New Mexico, desert fires often are given their head until they reach pinyon-juniper woodlands, where they slow down and become manageable. Desert brush in the Southwestern states can erupt in thick, galloping walls of flame that cover ground faster than a fleeing truck. Other worries come with the territory. After more than a century of human exploitation, much of the desert is a wasteland of mine shafts, wellheads, coal seams, bulldozed pits, and illegally dumped wastes.

"This country's real deceiving," said Allan Wyngart, an ex-hotshot who now runs BLM engine crews in New Mexico. "The fuels aren't heavy, but they're flashy. They can get up and going and catch you off guard. It can get real intense out there in a truck. All of a sudden, you've got flames twenty feet high and deep enough that you're not going to drive through them. And the fire's not the worst of it. When you get into old oil fields you can hit all sorts of problems, gases that are real toxic and highly flammable, just deadly. Or you can have a roaring fire that burns down on a natural gas pumping station out on the pipeline. Things like that keep engine work interesting."

■ ■ ■

Stephen Youhouse raced down a tunnel of flame. Tools and packs were scattered behind him, tossed helter-skelter in a moment suddenly become desperate. The fiery pipe, a horizontal vortex of fire, had shaped itself in an instant as a wall of flame rose out of the brush of Utah's Antelope Island, arched over Youhouse and the other men in yellow shirts, then bent down to catch new fuel on the opposite side. Now, with fire overhead and an arm's length away on each side, the men sprinted for the tunnel's end, hurtling back down the thin line they had dug, each aware that he must not stumble, must not fall. It was not thirty yards long, this cylinder of fire that roared like a jet engine, but it seemed a mile, and every stride of it would be etched in memory.

They would make it to the end. They would escape. They would laugh and break out cigarettes and talk their macho talk and joke about scorched eyebrows and mustaches. They would share the telling of it with their captors, the guards who also wore the yellow shirts and carried firefighting tools. They would take the tale back to prison and play it over for men like themselves—petty thieves, armed robbers, murderers. And later, best

Trained and equipped for wildland fire, a rural department moves in on a galloping sagebrush blaze in Benton County, Washington. Across the West, more and more local fire departments are widening their focus to join federal and state agencies in battles against wildland fire.

■ ■ ■

of all, they would tell it again during weekend visiting, and they would be heroes to the women and children in their lives. "It was like being in a wave, like a surfer in the tube," Youhouse said. "It was incredible."

Since the 1940s, prisoners have fought fire in the West. They came to it in great numbers when World War II siphoned away the abundant bodies of the Civilian Conservation Corps. Old men and teenage boys and 4-Fs and even the West's first female crews were not enough to fill the void, so state fire bosses began showing up at penitentiary gates, begging wardens to loan them prisoners. Now, among the Western states, only Alaska, Colorado, and New Mexico do not send inmates off to fight fire. California and Nevada even put juvenile offenders on the fire lines.

Among all the inmate firefighting operations of the West, none is quite like Utah's. In Utah, inmates with gasoline credit cards in their pockets drive engines and even take

them to fires in distant states, without guards in the cabs. In Utah, alone in the West, an inmate crew is recognized as a hotshot outfit, good enough to take on the worst of fire. And in Utah, in a program that stokes itself on pride and a sense of elitism, the guards assigned to fire crews train and work as firefighters beside the inmates. "If you didn't, you'd never hear the end of it," said Derk Penrod, one of the tool-wielding corrections officers who, like the prisoners themselves, are volunteers for the program.

The Utah inmates call themselves the Flame-in-Go's. In the fire camps of the West their crew T-shirts are trading stock without equal. The Flame-in-Go's were born as an on-call, EFF sort of program in 1978, promoted by Utah corrections and forestry officials. At first, it was only a matter of training a handful of prisoners as firefighters, then letting them sit in their cells until there was a fire. But the concept evolved into an outside-the-walls conservation honor camp for inmates nearing release.

Within a few years of their inception, the Flame-in-Go's were a recognized wildfire operation, with a twenty-man crew viewed around the northern Rockies as a legitimate Type II outfit, and a strike team of engines operated by inmates. Though a guard or two always traveled with the firefighters, no attempt was made to put one in each vehicle.

The Flame-in-Go's routinely journey to distant states. On fires, the Utah prisoners, unlike most other inmate firefighters, may be given individual or small-group assignments without supervision. The program has never had an inmate walkaway incident during a fire trip. Privileges for Flame-in-Go's inmates include weekend home visits. Pay rates of over five dollars an hour make fire fighting one of Utah's most lucrative inmate jobs.

The Flame-in-Go's operation stretched toward its zenith after an inmate smitten with the fire game announced to Glenn Beagle, the program's director and champion, that he would gladly pass up release to a halfway house if only the prison had a hotshot crew. By the 1990s, the Flame-in-Go's were sixty-five strong, with a lineup that included the new hotshot crew, the Type II crew, and a six-engine strike team. Technically hotshot crews are considered national firefighting resources and are fielded only by federal agencies. But, in fire camps from California to Montana, federal fire bosses routinely pay the Flame-in-Go's varsity crew the honor of putting it on the assignment board with other 'shot units.

More important, perhaps, those other units seem to view the Flame-in-Go's program's top crew the same way. "When we get to the big fire camps, there's always a lot of handshaking and people saying, 'Good to see you again,'" said Jeremy Wil-son, an inmate squad boss on the hotshot crew. "And the people who are seeing us in action for the first time can't believe it when they find out we're an inmate crew." In 1993, federal wildfire officials agreed to review a proposal to give the Flame-in-Go's Hotshots full national status.

When fires are not burning, the Flame-in-Go's take on conservation project work around their state. Because many of those jobs fall in remote locations, the crews sleep two hundred nights a year in tents. State and local parks and wildlife programs, as well as some nonprofit institutions, are the beneficiaries of their work. In conservative Utah, the idea of prisoners volunteering for a community service program and periodically braving fire goes over well; the annual Flame-in-Go's awards banquet always attracts television cameras and a collection of civic dignitaries.

In other states, the West's inmate firefighter programs have organizational profiles that are much larger, but less elite and decidedly more restrictive than Utah's hand-picked, carefully structured operation. Though the inmates in the other programs may occasionally cross a state line to fight a fire near the border, they do not range far afield. They almost always are kept in groups, with omnipresent supervision. Just as in Utah, the other inmate fire operations most often are crafted around conservation camps. Most of the camps are remote, minimum security facilities, accepting inmates scheduled for release within two to three years. Typically the inmates have served most of their time in a conventional penitentiary, then been chosen for assignment to a camp toward the end of their sentence. Sex offenders, arsonists, and those considered escape risks are screened out. Motivation, willingness to work, and ability to pass a basic physical fitness test weigh heavily in placement decisions.

In the dirt of a bulldozer trail, a California inmate crew breaks for lunch. California fields nearly five thousand adult and juvenile inmate firefighters and moves them around the state to large fires.

At most of the camps, the inmates receive a minimal rate of pay, as low as twenty-five cents an hour for routine work, and a premium rate, seldom more than two dollars an hour, for fire duty. Because the conservation camp crews do low-cost work projects that benefit local communities, they often bask in public approval. They even inherit some of the mantle of esteem that Westerners drape over those who fight forest fire. In Nevada, legislative attempts to scale back funding for the conservation-firefighting program have been buried in grassroots groundswells of protest from rural towns.

As eclectic collections of personalities, inmate crews yield nothing to other fire outfits. The Flame-in-Go's hotshot crew that went to the field in 1993 styled itself the "jock and the junkies," because its manpower complement ranged from a clean-cut, handsome college football quarterback to a collection of tattooed and streetwise drug dealers. California inmate crews regularly mix ex-bankers and defrocked lawyers with drug dealers, murderers, and inner-city gang members. One California crew was home to an inmate firefighter who had embezzled more than four million dollars. At some level, the crew bosses find, all of them seem to respond to the challenge.

Howard Carr, a California building contractor in his forties, stepped outside the business world and tried bank robbery. Midway through his five-year sentence, he was placed on a California inmate fire crew near San Luis Obispo. "I did everything I could to get out of it. But after I'd been in the camp for a while, there was nothing else I wanted to do. Looking at it from the outside, you see all the work. I never thought that at my age I could get in shape to do that work or run the mile in the time they say you have to run it. I told them they were crazy. But I did it. I'll be out of here before too long. But I'll remember fire fighting all my life. I'll remember it like I remember Vietnam."

Most often, an inmate crew goes off to battle a big fire with two sets of supervisors—guards from the state's corrections department and fire-trained leaders from the forestry department. The forestry supervisors function as fire crew bosses. The corrections officers, who may not even go to the fire lines, assume custody when the troops return to fire camp. If the fire assignment is small and local, with no likelihood of an overnight stay, the crew may travel without guards. Some states eliminate the dual staffing altogether by training corrections officers as fire crew bosses.

In states such as Oregon and Washington, inmate crews are a relatively small part of the overall firefighting resource. But in fire-prone California, where the inmate program is large, the budgetary implications of doing without it are beyond consideration. So, in many minds, are the tactical implications,

because the prison crews are the force that the engine-based California Department of Forestry must rely upon when miles of hand line are needed. "In CDF, we like to think we put out fires with all of our engines and our air tankers," said Deen Oehl, who flies one of those CDF tankers. "The truth is that most California fires are put out by prisoners." Of the six thousand or so inmate firefighters in the West, nearly five thousand are in California. Various classes of offenders, including juveniles and women, are apportioned through forty conservation camps and a few county programs. All are trained as fire line hand crews.

As the face of American crime has changed, so has the effectiveness of inmate firefighters. Uniformly, the supervisors of prison crews complain of inmates, particularly those from urban areas, who know nothing of work. "You get all these people who come into the system through drugs and gangs," said Tom Reavis, a CDF fire captain who looks like a roundup trail boss, talks like John Wayne, and began running youth offender crews in 1965. "They're not people who were temporarily out of a job and robbed a gas station. They've never had a job. Not once. They've never even carried out the garbage. They've never been in the woods, they've never been off pavement. What we have to offer them is a whole lot different. And yet they actually learn to do a decent job on fire. And they get the same adrenaline squirt from it that everybody else does. I think it makes a difference in some lives."

Indeed. Around the West, most states report that the rate of re-imprisonment for fire crew inmates is decidedly lower than for the general prison population, at least partly because the selection process delivers to the crews inmates with some prospect for rehabilitation. But fire makes a difference in other inmate lives, too, including those who ride the cycle of repeat offenses. "You get the career criminals who really like fire work," said George Biddle, a CDF captain who runs inmate crews. "Every time they're back in prison they ask for it. They'll send a letter through the system, telling their old fire captain that they're back and they're available. And some of them are such good firefighters that the captains will go up and talk to the assignment people, just to make sure they get the guy back onto their crew. We had one guy who liked fire fighting so much that, whenever he was released, he always got himself back into the system inside of two months. When they finally disqualified him medically for fighting fire, he never committed another crime."

■ ■ ■

Brett Bower and the Santa Barbara Hotshots were having an easy day of it. On a steep slope of juniper and grass near the

Southern California hamlet of Cuyama, the sixteen firefighters were corralling a fire that crept slowly downhill. The 'shots assessed the fuel at a modest quarter-ton per acre. Wind and weather were working for them. The flames licked no more than a foot high as the crew bent to the task of chinking in line below, then setting off modest burnouts to stop the oncoming fire in its tracks. Elsewhere on the slope, a unit of helicopter firefighters had another burnout operation going.

But overhead, the heat and smoke from the fires were mingling, creating a microclimatic change above the hills and building a smoke column that spiked upward. And then, unannounced and unexpected, a small thunder cell rolled over the fire. Its winds cascaded downward. Just twenty feet in front of Bower and his crewmates, the creeping fire flashed instantly into an eight-foot wall of flame, growing in height and depth as it came, pushing downward faster than they could run. The hotshots had no choice.

"There was no time to think, no time to pull shelters," Bower recalled. "It was coming too fast. There was only one thing to do. We ran uphill, straight into the fire. Our only chance was to get behind it, get into the black. I looked for an opening that you can get sometimes between the mass flame front and the thermal pulse. It was like a dream. A little window opened, and I went right through it. But the other people, most of them went right into the fire. They pushed right through and came out on the other side. And then we were in the black. We had guys who had inhaled that superheated air as they went through. They had singed their lungs and were having problems. We were in the black, but we were in a whirlwind that was following the fire, just hot red embers filling the air all around us and going down our shirts. I lost part of my mustache. We sent four people to the hospital. And then the rest of us we went back to work."

Hotshots play with big fire and thrive in a world where the reward for hard work is more hard work. Less glorified than smokejumpers, less visible than helitack crews and engine outfits, they are the gritty, soot-faced endurance runners of the world of wildland fire. Knowledge of fire in all its nuances is their specialty, coupled with a capacity to deliver day after day of grueling manual labor. Sometimes, in the heat of battles such as the Southern California fires of 1993, they pull unbroken work shifts that run for fifty hours or more. "When all the rules about work shifts get bent, it's always the hotshots who take the brunt of it," said Steve Raddatz, who heads a national fire command team based in Idaho.

Until 1994, hotshots had always endured an undeserved sort of anonymity. The high-profile glamour job in fire fighting is smokejumping, the stuff of movies and television documentaries. Jumpers and 'shots spend a lot of time needling each other. But privately they will admit it is a dialogue based on mutual respect, one tough outfit conceding nothing to the other. Somehow, though, jumpers garnered the acclaim of the public while hotshots settled for the esteem of the fire community. To those outsiders who asked, hotshots were forever awkwardly explaining the prime role they play in wildland fire, wishing that someone else would do it for them. But then came the deaths of nine Oregon hotshots on Colorado's Storm King Mountain, and the world learned about another class of firefighters. Newspapers, television, and magazines told the story of the shock troops of wildland fire. At a price they would never have chosen to pay, the hotshots of the West suddenly found themselves understood.

In fire parlance, hotshots are a national resource, known technically as interagency hotshot crews. In the mid-1990s they are all federal crews. The Southern California county hotshot crews, such as the unit Bower served with in the late '80s, have been budgeted out of existence. But some state forestry departments have begun to express interest in creating their own elite 'shot operations. Meanwhile, the federal crews go to battle organized in the standard configuration of twenty-member units. They are based most often in ruralish, out-of-the-way places— Zig Zag in Oregon, San Carlos in New Mexico, Hungry Horse in Montana. Like fires, they sometimes come with colorful names, such as Midnight Suns, Smokey Bear, Chief Mountain. Though they may be stationed at a BLM district, Indian reservation, national forest, or national park, they belong to the system, not to their host unit.

When fire bosses order up manpower for the big blazes, hotshot crews top their lists. When big fire beckons, 'shots head for airports with their packs and tools, or pile into bulky crew carriers and drive through the night to be on the lines at morning. Smelling of smoke, sweat, gasoline, liniment, and chewing tobacco, the crew rigs are rolling locker rooms, reverberating with music from up-tempo tapes, and awash in magazines, soft drink cans, backpacks, candy wrappers, elastic bandages, sleeping bags, dirty T-shirts, grimy baseball caps, and sack-lunch leftovers. The mix of passengers may range from forty-year-old hippies to earnest young college students. Because the federal agencies, especially the Forest Service, are aggressively affirmative in their hiring practices, 'shot crews almost always are a tapestry of race and gender. The common threads are peak physical condition, an addiction to excitement, and an individualistic sort of competitive edge found most often on asphalt basketball courts.

"Other people see us as adrenaline junkies," said Holly Maloney, a former University of Montana track athlete and a squad boss on Montana's Lolo Hotshots. "It's true. I know I am. There's no denying it. But it's so interesting on the hotshots. We

have a team concept, and yet, within the team, there's a constant struggle to make a name for yourself and to establish your position. You must create a place and a role within that group. It never goes away. When you're a hotshot, you have to prove yourself every single day. The people around me expect that, and they know I expect that of them."

The hotshot concept, the idea of an elite, highly trained crew of specialists to take on major fires, has evolved steadily since the early 1950s. The number of crews rose steadily in the eighties, especially in the ranks of the Bureau of Indian Affairs, which responded to tribal pressures for better paying fire jobs and recruited from the EFF ranks to create five Native American hotshot units in New Mexico, Arizona, Oregon and Montana. Based on reservations, the Indian 'shot crews have proved attractive to young firefighters who want a permanent seasonal job, but do not want to abandon the tribal setting. The Mescalero Apaches, the ancestors of all Indian fire fighting, field one of those crews. When the Mescalero Hotshots set up in distant fire camps, an artist on the crew will draw on traditional imagery for a hand-painted sign that will mark their sleeping area. The signs, looking like nothing so much as warriors' shields, are always brought home. Like talismans in some ancient war lodge, they hang on the walls of the crew's reservation headquarters.

In the tradition of their tribe, the Mescalero Hotshots are serious runners. As a crew, they regularly reel off jaunts of up to ten miles, all of it above seven thousand feet elevation. Each year they sponsor an invitational mountain run for teams of wildland firefighters in the Southwest. The run's trophy and the right to host the event the following year go to the winner. But the Mescalero team has never been beaten; the trophy has never left the reservation.

In 1988, the Mescaleros volunteered for a punishing assignment on a Utah fire deep in a canyon. The terrain had already been ruled too steep for climbing, and dozens of other crews had been held off of it. The Mescaleros were helicoptered two thousand feet to the bottom, with the understanding that they would need to be flown out at day's end. Under punishing heat, they worked in the depths all day. In the early evening, as the fire's management team stood at the canyon edge and prepared to dispatch the helicopter, the Mescaleros hiked over the rim, carrying their gear. "They told us that they knew we couldn't climb out of there," said Leo LaPaz, the Mescalero crew boss. "We had all day to think about it."

■ ■ ■

Left: Calculating the risks, a weary crew of hotshots sets flames loose to counter an approaching forest fire at Idaho's Dunnigan Creek in 1992.

Hotshot crews attract people for the long haul. Those who move up from the ranks of Type II crews or find their way in from other fronts of the fire game usually have discovered something they like, and are looking for more. Many will stay five years, a few a decade or longer, admitting that their life's plan has been altered by the experience. But the typical 'shot crew also makes room each summer for a few pure rookies, newcomers who have never seen a forest fire. For some, the effect is profound.

Carl Bianco ran with the Hollywood crowd. With Latin good looks and a muscular body chiseled from year-round weightlifting, he strutted with the Chippendales, the most famous of the male dancing groups that play night clubs and show up on national television. Family money made life easy and pleasant. He drove fine cars, sported a flashy wardrobe, dated starlets and was a regular on the glitzy club circuit. Then his mother's booming Los Angeles real estate business fell on a year or so of hard times, and he went looking for work.

Almost by accident, Bianco wound up in the early 1990s with the Dalton Hotshots on the Angeles National Forest. Within a year, he had the fire disease. He turned down an Asian tour with the Chippendales, because he didn't want to miss a fire season. His family's fortunes rebounded, but he never went back to his old haunts. Or to his old girlfriends; instead, he fell into a steady relationship with an athletic girl-next-door type on the fire crew. He was offered an executive spot in real estate but passed it up. When Bianco tells his story it is laced with a certain wonderment at watching himself make the choices he has made.

"I cannot even explain to people what this is like or why it's so important to me," he said. "If someone really wants to know, I tell them about the Cienega Fire. We got helicoptered onto a ridge. I was on the last load and the pilot didn't want to let us off because the flame was just right there. We finally talked him into landing. He just barely touched and we were out. He took off and the flames came shooting over the top, way up in the sky, and the smoke was rolling over us. And they gave me the saw that day. And they're yelling, 'Bianco, over here. Sawyer! Sawyer!' And I'm running down the ridge past the hot shovels, and it's like combat, just like combat. I remember my heart pounding and I'm sawing and people yelling and the fire's just going crazy, roaring all around us. It would beat us back and then we'd go in again, just right on top of it. That day was my eye-opener. I knew I was in a different life."

CHAPTER 5

The Jumpers

EVAN KELLEY FERMENTED IN A HIGH BUREAUCRATIC DUDGEON on that July day in 1935. He was a staunch follower of the traditional mores of the U.S. Forest Service, a tough old fire officer who certainly had not risen to the position of regional forester in Missoula, Montana, by indulging in foolishness, or by tolerating it in others. But foolishness had bubbled up from the ranks. It was afoot on his turf. And he was about to nip it in the bud. Never mind that his superiors in Washington, D.C., seemed to be intrigued by this cockamamie idea that had wafted out of the pipe dreams of younger fire managers in the Northern Rockies. He would set matters right. So Kelley fired off a stiff letter to Forest Service headquarters.

"I will remind you that you wrote some time ago about J. B. Bruce's scheme of dropping men from airplanes for firefighting. Pearson of Region Four was a party to the scheme," he wrote. "I am willing to take a chance on most any kind of a proposition that promises better action on fires, but I hesitate very much to go into the kind of thing that Bruce proposes. In the first place, the best information I can get from experienced fliers is that all parachute jumpers are more or less crazy—just a little bit unbalanced, otherwise they wouldn't be engaged in such a hazardous undertaking; accordingly, I discount materially the practicability of Bruce's ideas... If the Washington Office wishes to carry on further experimentation in this line, it is my request that you assign this project to other quarters."

Five years later, a smokejumper base operated in the heart of Kelley's territory, sending firefighters off to be dropped along the spine of the Rockies. The scheme hatched over Kelley's objections would foreshadow creation of the U.S. Army's airborne paratrooper units for the looming battles of World War II. Over the next half century, Missoula, the command post of Kelley's region, would become the repository for the traditions of the subculture of "more or less crazy" adventurers who leap from airplanes to tackle fire. Kelley would live to see a smokejumper museum built in Missoula. Later, a smokejumper oral history and research collection would be established in the city at the University of Montana. Filmmakers, authors, journalists, and foreign tourists would troop to Missoula for a sampling of the jumper mystique.

The mystique feeds upon itself. With prickly individuality and irrepressible irreverence as hallmarks, the smokejumpers are a small and elite corps, seldom numbering more than five hundred in any fire season. In the world of wildland fire, no outfit is as conscious of its own tradition as the smokejumpers. Jumpers track their history with zeal. Their archives detail the seasons, jumps, fires, transfers, and injuries of every smokejumper who ever stepped out an airplane door.

Above: Somewhere over Oregon's Cascade Mountains, Gene Minnich, a Forest Service smokejumper, contemplates the task ahead. Jumper flights, buffeted by quixotic winds from mountain ridges, are often so bumpy and uncomfortable that stepping into the air comes as welcome relief.

▪ ▪ ▪

Left: Numbering just over four hundred strong, smokejumpers from the Forest Service and the Bureau of Land Management chase the most remote forest and range fires from nine bases scattered around the West.

The walls of the jump bases of the West are hung heavily with photographs and talismans of jumpers past and fire seasons past, like the trophy rooms of Ivy League universities.

Some minor rivalry intrudes between the jumpers of the federal Bureau of Land Management and the Forest Service, the two agencies that parachute firefighters into Western skies. BLM jumpers and Forest Service jumpers, for example, use different types of parachutes, with each group adamant about the superiority of its own equipment. The Forest Service, which began jumping fires in 1940, has seniority. The BLM, which put jumpers in the sky in 1959, is fond of noting that its physical qualification standards require a few more pushups and pullups, and a faster time in the mile and a half run. But the two groups jump together on joint operations so often that they are effectively one fraternity. Their pedigrees commingle. Scores of jumpers, for reasons related less to logic than to wanderlust and the peculiarities of the jumper psyche, have spent time under the parachute canopies of first one agency, then the other.

Around the West, regiments of seasonal groundpounding firefighters aspire to be jumpers. They nurse that ambition even as they grow weary of hearing the recurrent question that assumes smokejumpers are the *only* firefighters, and of parroting the answer they loathe: "Yes, I fight forest fires. No, I don't jump out of airplanes." Beyond Missoula, smokejumper bases dot the northern reaches of the West—at Redding in California, at Redmond in Oregon, at Winthrop in Washington, at West Yellowstone in Montana, at Fairbanks in Alaska, and at Boise, McCall, and Grangeville in Idaho. Though Evan Kelley would have shuddered at the thought in 1935, smokejumping has become both proven firefighting tool and gleaming public relations icon for the BLM and the Forest Service.

To this day, jumping has its detractors in the politics of wildland fire. It has never shaken the image of heels-dug-in resistance that was its stance in the early 1980s, when the first female candidates stepped into jumper bases, braved a chilly reception, and changed the boys' club forever. And it confronts a new generation of critics, fond of helicopters and armed with calculators and spreadsheets, insistently asking whether smokejumping in the 1990s is more romantic than practical. But political realists don't expect firefighters to stop dropping out of Western skies. They know that in the fusty, bureaucratic world of governmental land management, few programs have comparable cachet and public appeal.

■ ■ ■

They gather in the spring, from Mazatlan and Sun Valley, from Nepal and Thailand, from Harvard and Stanford, from ships at sea and cabins in the mountains. They walk away from the games and classrooms and jobs of winter and return, often with creaking knees, suspect backs, and nagging consciences. One of these years it will be time to grow up. Parents, spouses, mortgage holders, doctoral thesis advisers, divorce lawyers, and other champions of conventional responsibility continually find new ways to ask how much longer this can go on. The answer is always some version of, "One more season."

More than any other group in wildland fire, smokejumpers have elevated the seasonal firefighter's lifestyle to an art form. Over a bit more than five decades, they transformed what was once a summer job for college students into a pursuit that, for an ever larger number, consumes much of an adult lifetime. The average age at smokejumper bases around the West approaches thirty-five. The few students in the ranks are likely to be closing in on master's degrees or doctorates. Some years at some bases, there are no rookie classes at all. Here and there parachute canopies blossom each summer over active smokejumpers who will never see forty-five again, or fifty again.

"Sometimes I go around to schools and do the smokejumper talk," said Jack Seagraves, who jumps for the Forest Service at McCall. "I tell the kids, 'You want to be a smokejumper? Get a college education.' It's the truth. Almost every rookie we get is already done with college. The rest of the world looks down on the people who do this for so long. They say things about getting on with your life. They think that anybody who does this beyond his college years has to have something wrong with him. But it's a subculture. A true subculture."

Who should know better than the man who escaped its clutches only to surrender again? Seagraves jumped at McCall in the early 1960s. He was a college student from Oregon, paying for his education by fighting fire, typical of the jumpers of that era. He took his last step out the airplane door in 1965, then dutifully finished dental school. A few years later he was running a successful family dental practice in Coeur d'Alene, Idaho, chasing plaque and fathoming root canals. Then, at the age of forty-five, he went to a jumper reunion at his old base. Beer and memories flowed. Seagraves decided that he wouldn't be going back to dentistry. He spent six grueling months beating his middle-aged body back into shape, readying himself for tests that would make no allowance for age. He requalified as a smokejumper in 1988. In 1994, at the age of fifty-two, he was still jumping. He never returned to his profession. Smokejumping, six months a year, became his life.

While jumpers are older and better educated on the average, they are not slavish about it. Despite the jumpers with master's degrees in molecular biology and English literature, and the jumpers who read *The New Yorker* in planes en route to fires, there are still many who are classic, close-to-the-land Westerners. Indians jump in summer and go back to the reservation, small-town carpenters jump in summer and go back to their tools. Willie Lowden, a Forest Service jumper in Redmond, Oregon, is a logger, like generations of his family before him. For twenty years he has lived his own version of the two-season lifestyle, accepting both its drawbacks and its rewards. In summers, he saves trees from fire; in winter, he cuts them for market. "I got out of the Navy when I was young," he said. "Went to work in the plywood mill. Hated it. Couldn't handle it. Got out of plywood and went into jumping. My brother had done jumping for a couple of years. He got out of jumping and went into plywood. He's still there. Spent his life there. He's got benefits and something for his old age. But I've had more fun than he ever will."

Jumpers are not charged with fighting conflagrations. They are airborne smokechasers, initial attack specialists commissioned to run down small fires in the backcountry and prevent them from becoming big ones. A classic successful mission is one where two jumpers leap into remote country and spend a day or two holding to three acres a fire that had the potential to go to thirty thousand. The ideal is not always realized, of course. Some fires are detected too late or grow too fast, so any jumper with a few years of experience has met big fire. The most famous tragedy in modern forest fire history, Montana's Mann Gulch Fire of 1949, was small and tame at the outset; but it transmogrified itself into a man-eater, raced up a hillside faster than the fastest runner, and killed thirteen smokejumpers. In Alaska, smokejumpers can face enormous fires, tundra-gobbling monsters whose diets are measured in the hundreds of thousands of acres.

The jumpers, more than any other group of wildland firefighters, work in wilderness settings. Like commandos operating behind enemy lines, smokejumpers go to battle in roadless outback regions and sustain themselves with what they pack on their backs. For them, life offers no fire camps with showers, no hot meals from caterers, no daily truck rides to the fire line. They go out of the plane with two days of provisions. If their fire runs longer, they will be resupplied by cargo drops— although some of the best jumper tales come from those fires where a weather change made it necessary for two days of rations to stretch for a week. Almost every year some jump crew in the Northern Rockies will drop onto a high elevation fire in a heat wave, run afoul of the weather gods, and hike out through three inches of August snow.

Perhaps because they spend so much time chasing small fires, jumpers' favorite tales tend not to be stories of four-hundred-foot flames and hairsbreadth escapes. Most of them, even the ones involving serious injury or serious scares, are told with a fillip of humor. A jumper is expected to get a laugh or two out of the story of his broken leg, and to make others laugh about it as well. Those who are paid for jumping out of airplanes and experiencing wilderness regions that few humans see usually manage to tell stories with the moral that getting there is much of the fun. Few tales are treasured more than ones where the wilderness experience turns bizarre. Like the bear in Lynn Flock's tent.

Flock, the training supervisor at the Bureau of Land Management's jumper base in Boise, met the bear during a fire in Alaska. Six jumpers had whipped a tundra fire during the night. A light rain fell as they finished. So, in the jumper fashion, they used cargo parachutes to build hootches, rude tents for a few hours of sleep until a helicopter arrived. In the early morning, Flock and jumper Rich Halligan were awakened by a noise outside their tent. "I looked up and saw this big black bear claw through the material of our tent and stick his head inside," Flock said. "It got us fairly excited. I sat up in my sleeping bag. Rich sat up. The bear looked at us. He looked down. Then he took a big bite of my sleeping bag right where my feet had been. That didn't work for him, so he grabbed the sleeping bag and started pulling me out through the hole in the tent. I kind of lifted myself up and let the sleeping bag slip off. The bear pulled it about halfway out, then got bored and went over to another hootch."

The bear climbed atop the next tent and broke its spruce ridgepole. The tent's occupant woke up screaming and looking at claws in his bedroom. Meanwhile, Flock and Halligan were trying to scurry into clothes. In the process, Flock's head was bumping against the side of the tent. The bear, perhaps deciding that he had been mistaken to leave a prospective meal so soon, returned and swatted Flock on the head. "One of us yelled," Flock said. "I've always thought it was Rich, but he swears it was me." Halligan charged out the side of the tent, ran into a tree, and broke his nose. The bear sauntered off a short distance, sat on his haunches, and regarded with contentment the spectacle of half-dressed macho smokejumpers running in circles in the rain. A couple of them fired up chain saws in hope that the noise would drive their visitor away. But the bear only sat and watched, like a pleased child at a circus. Then a barefoot jumper ignited a fusee, and began waving it in the air, screaming at the bear. His screams escalated when hot drippings from the flare fell onto his feet. In desperation, he tossed the fusee at the bear. Slowly, and with dignity perfectly intact, the bear turned and ambled away.

*Above: Rigged, ready, and numbered, smokejumpers'
parachutes await a fire dispatch at the Forest Service
Aerial Fire Depot in Missoula, Montana.*

■ ■ ■

*Right: Hung up in a tall snag, a smokejumper must make a
rope descent, hoping that the collapsed parachute does not pull
free and drop him to the ground. Later, the tree will have
to be scaled with climbing spurs and rigging,
and the chute retrieved.*

*Above: Parachutes, especially free-falling cargo
parachutes, can hang up regularly in trees,
so smokejumpers, like this group practicing at Missoula,
Montana, must master the high-climbing skills
that are the traditional domain of loggers
and electric utility line workers.*

■ ■ ■

*Right: Perhaps more than any other aspect of wildland
fire fighting, smokejumping hinges on partnership
and mutual trust, reflected as BLM jumpers in Boise,
Idaho methodically work their way through the ritual
of pre-jump "buddy checks" of equipment and fittings.*

■ ■ ■

For all the aura of risk that pulsates around the business of chasing fires by jumping out of airplanes, the jumping part of smokejumping is relatively safe. Smokejumpers have died on the ground, fighting fire. They have died in plane crashes, en route to fires. But, in over a half century of jumping, only three have died in jumping accidents. ""Everybody likes to brag about the job, to be proud of being a jumper," said Tom Cook, who entered jumping with the Forest Service at Missoula at the age of thirty-six. "It definitely carries some mystique. But it's no longer that ridiculous to jump out of an airplane and into a forest. A tremendous amount of time, energy and money has been put into the safety aspect of everything that surrounds smokejumping. It is so much safer now. You no longer land like a four-hundred-pound box of rocks."

Still, the injuries come, and they are sometimes horrendous: fractures, blown-out knees, concussions. Hard landings, spawned by aberrant winds or "down air," take their toll in the immediate, traumatic sense and in the longer, cumulative sense. Recreational skydivers choose landings in soft, flat meadows; smokejumpers, their destination determined by the vagaries of fire, go into tall trees and onto rocky slopes. Jumpers often are injured in falls after their parachutes snag in the upper reaches of trees. Every jumper carries a long rope and "letdown" hardware for rappelling out of trees. The process depends upon a firmly anchored parachute. "Of all the things you can encounter, hanging up in a tree is one of the scariest," said Margo Freeman, a Forest Service jumper in Oregon. "You're way up high and you're not sure if your parachute is going to hold, or if it's going to let you fall." When a collapsed chute slides out of a towering tree, a jumper can drop like a stone for a hundred feet.

But it was a small tree that got Gary Dunning. Out on Alaska's tundra, the black spruce are mostly small. They range over thousands of square miles and seldom stand above thirty feet. They are spindly-limbed and skinny; if they were Christmas trees they would be the ones still unsold on Christmas Eve. When big Alaska fire is up and rolling, it marches through thousands of acres of black spruce. Their thin, fire-hardened skeletons stand for years as the greenery returns around them. On the Fourth of July in 1986, Dunning and a partner were the first two jumpers out of the plane on a tundra fire northeast of Fort Yukon. The winds swirled and eddied as they went down, and the two jumpers were separated. Dunning caught down air and lost all capacity to steer his chute. Descending fast and straight, he knew a hard landing awaited. Beneath him, coming up at twenty-two feet per second, he saw a bristling, blackened stand of fifteen-foot spruce that had burned three or four years

earlier. Then he was in it, and he heard the noise and felt the impact and the pain.

In a sitting position, Dunning looked out over the top of the trees. Strangely, the ground was still more than a dozen feet below. His legs protruded to the front. His parachute was draped over a snag behind him. And emerging through his right thigh, protruding upward in his lap, was the twelve-inch tip of a spruce tree. He had landed squarely atop the tree. Like a lance, the blackened treetop, two inches in diameter, had pierced the canvas of his jump suit, gone into the back of his thigh and emerged through the front. Impaled and alone, he perched between sky and earth, holding fast to the pointed top, bending over it so that he would not tumble backward, and looking out over miles of roadless Alaska. He knew that other jumpers would be descending. He yelled and yelled. The wind scattered his words like chaff. The tree swayed.

For ten minutes, perhaps more, Dunning sat in the treetop. No one had seen him drift into the trees. Jumpers always regroup after landing. When he did not show up, they would search. But he had no sense of how far away they were, how long it would take them to find him. He had been trained as a paramedic, and the things he knew frightened him. The pain after the initial impact was bearable, like a deep thigh bruise. And there was no blood around the wound. But Dunning was not certain what that meant. When he had first seen the spike protruding through his leg he thought that surely it must have severed his femoral artery. And from his training he knew that, even though he saw no blood, accident patients sometimes died when ruptured femoral arteries bled internally into the tissues of the thigh.

He felt himself growing woozy and shocky. Though he had no escape plan, it was time to do something. He took off his helmet and his gloves and tossed them down. He reached to his shoulder and unfastened one of the Capewell connectors that attached his parachute to his jump harness. The lines on that side fell away easily. But on the opposite shoulder, the lines were in tension, and when he let the connector go, the release spun him slightly. He heard the tree break beneath him. Then he was falling, hurtling to the ground, with a two-foot section of wood protruding from his leg, front and back.

They found him there, still conscious. The word went down the line that Dunning had been impaled on a stob—woods slang for a chunk of limb. Radio messages flew. Half the crew went off to a small clearing and began enlarging it as helicopter landing zone. Kim Maynard, a Forest Service jumper from Missoula, was one of the first medical technicians to reach him. "It was the worst spot, the worst possible spot," she said. "A thicket, just a mess. We couldn't believe what we were seeing. There he was with this huge stob through his leg and he was still conscious, still able to talk to us. We put him in a tent and carried it by the corners. We had to maneuver through all the trees and people were stumbling. Every move just hurt him like crazy."

Dunning was two hundred miles from the medical help he needed, and the solution was pure Alaska. A helicopter to an airstrip. Then a plane to Fairbanks. From treetop to operating room took three and a half hours. But the surgery that followed went well. Deep inside his thigh, next to the wood, the doctors found the femoral artery intact. By September, Dunning was running. He jumped again the next season. In 1993, he closed out his career at age fifty-three. For a jumper, a good story is worth a good reminder. The stob is mounted on a plaque in his home.

■ ■ ■

The tough truth about smokejumping is that the hard part is not jumping but walking out. Jumpers, as few as two or as many as twenty, will parachute to a remote fire, assess the situation, and then radio for cargo drops of equipment and camp supplies. But, with the exception of a small amount of burnable trash, everything that comes down must come out. And it comes out on the backs of smokejumpers. For that reason, jumpers will sometimes call for the drop of an old-fashioned "misery whip," a twin-handled crosscut saw. It strains backs and raises blisters, but it is far lighter to bring home than a chain saw.

When the last ember is cool, the jump crew divides up the equipment. Each load starts with the seventy pounds of parachute, jumpsuit, and personal gear. Then the firefighting tools and camp equipment are added to the cavernous packout bags. On a big fire, the freight may include chain saws and gasoline-powered pumps. The weight is divided evenly, and every jumper—whether she is five-one and weighs 120 or he is six foot and weighs 190—saddles up with a pack that will go 100 pounds, or perhaps as much as 130.

Female jumpers sometimes pack the equivalent of their own body weight, and in training the packout accounts for more washouts of women recruits than any other factor. Still, plenty of them have showed they can handle the load. "I came out in the rain once with a pack that went one hundred twenty pounds," said Leslie Anderson, one of the first female jumpers at Missoula. "Four miles, all uphill. I weighed just a little more than the pack. On packouts, you go at your own pace. Every packout I ever did, I made a point of finishing in the front half of the crew."

With luck, a packout is downhill on an established forest trail and no longer than four or five miles. But sometimes it is a cross-country slog through spongy, energy-sapping tundra, or a trek over brushy, pathless mountain ridges. Epic packouts of twenty miles or more were common in the decades before helicopters were as near as a radio call, and before logging roads laced the backcountry. Even then, jumpers often took their heavy loads to a trailhead and waited for a pack string of Forest Service mules, just as they now take them to a helicopter landing spot. "The toughest packout I ever had was three and a half miles, right over a mountain in Washington," said Ted Mason, who continued to jump with the BLM at Boise after completing a master's in business administration in 1993. "About half the trip was straight uphill. I weigh one hundred seventy-five. We always weigh the packs when we get back. Mine went one hundred forty seven pounds. That was a tough one."

In an average fire season, the jumpers of the West will make up to twenty-five hundred fire jumps, and the individual seasonal jumper will head out the airplane door and into battle about ten times. The full-timers, the handful of jumpers who fill the overhead positions at each jump base, will jump less, splitting their time between the joy of fire fighting and the drudgery of administration. But, at every base, everyone jumps, everyone fights fire, and everyone—even the jump base manager—must pass the physical training minimums each year.

The jumper contingents at the West's nine bases vary from a high of seventy at McCall to a low of fifteen at West Yellowstone. Jumpers are regularly shifted between bases, and across agency lines, as the fire season peak moves from region to region. A force of BLM and Forest Service "boosters" go north to the BLM base at Fairbanks almost every year for Alaska's early fire season. Most years, some Alaska jumpers come south in late summer. Auxiliary jumper bases, at such locations as Grand Junction in Colorado, Silver City in New Mexico, and La Grande in Oregon, get a plane and a temporary squad of jumpers when local fire conditions warrant.

At their bases, smokejumpers go on an assignment board in a rotation. When a fire is reported, the jumpers at the top of the board make the flight, and they are usually airborne in less than ten minutes. On the tarmac and en route in the airplane, they religiously check each other's harness and fittings. The size of the fire determines the number of jumpers who actually go out the airplane door, but it is always at least two. Most fires are small and are extinguished within a few days. The ones that get away and grow to be project fires often are turned over to other firefighters—frequently to hotshot crews—so that smokejumpers can return to base and be available for dispatch on new fires, which are always considered the highest priority. In Alaska, however, jumpers are more likely to stay with big fires. As native crews and other resources arrive, the original jump group may break up and assume command roles in the extended attack.

No jumper expects to be on fires for every working hour of every summer. So each jumper has a ground-level job. Many of those jobs are in the parachute loft. Every smokejumper base has one, a big sprawling room where parachutes are inspected and repacked. Virtually every jumper qualifies on the sewing machine. Many become experts who prefer to spend their non-fire time working in the loft. Jumpers do not make their own parachutes. But they do make the complex and heavy jumpsuits, along with an array of packs, rigging, and specialty items that make life easier in the air and on the ground. The most talented of the warriors of needle and thread are certified to do large-scale repairs of damaged parachutes.

Some jumpers, especially in Alaska, work in paracargo, handling a large measure of the logistics needed to support ground operations in roadless backcountry. They have standard packaging and parachute setups for chainsaws, hand tools, food, fresh water, rescue gear, and fuel. The Alaska jumpers who become paracargo specialists log hundreds of air hours "kicking cargo" when tundra fires turn into long-running campaigns, and thousands of firefighters—jumpers, native crews, and visiting troops from the Lower 48—need to be re-supplied. Most jumper bases run an active visitor program, with assigned jumpers ready to give tours whenever a carload of tourists stops. At Missoula and McCall, designated jumpers work as archivists, maintaining extensive photo collections, oral histories, clipping files, individual jumper histories, and other documentation of their jump centers' pasts. Often those with degrees or professional skills get ground jobs that tap their expertise—an exercise physiologist writes a conditioning manual, a videographer packages a training film, a carpenter builds storage cabinets.

Steve Nemore, operations chief for the BLM's Boise Smokejumpers, briefs a helmeted and masked firefighter as their plane approaches a drop zone. On every jump, a senior jumper such as Nemore serves as spotter—picking the landing zone, checking winds and signaling jumpers out the door.

■ ■ ■

The making of smokejumpers begins in spring. It starts in early May in Alaska, where all BLM rookies are trained and where drying tundra can bring fire before the month is out. At the Forest Service bases in the Lower 48, most rookies report in June. As a requirement, the candidates arrive with forest fire experience. They've worked fire as part of a Type II crew on some Forest Service District or on an engine crew with the BLM. They've done big fire with a hotshot crew somewhere in the West or flown with a helitack squad. Most, while they have the adventurer's soul, have never parachuted before.

Thousands of inquiries cascade into jumper bases each winter. Just a few years ago, when the jump force ran heavily to college students, a base could lose twenty-five percent or more of its contingent in a year. In that era, rookie classes at individual bases sometimes welcomed thirty or more recruits. Now, in some years, the rookie count for all the jump bases in the West may be fewer than thirty. "It is nothing for us to have two hundred qualified applicants just for the five or six positions we may have open," said Steve Nemore, operations director at the BLM's Boise jump base. "The ones we pick, it's interesting to watch them. I think they're afraid when they walk in the door. They've heard a lot. They have qualifications or they wouldn't be here. But the fear they have is the fear of failure. They want to do it. But they're afraid for themselves. Can they do it?"

At whatever base they begin, they face a month of hell. In some classes, half may wash out, a few on the first day. Though the regimen varies slightly from one jumper base to the next, the rookies will share similar ordeals. Their first week runs heavily to physical training, interspersed with classroom sessions on first aid, fire-fighting tactics, and introductory parachute nomenclature.

Though jumper bosses would like something tougher, they tolerate a federally mandated physical performance standard that applies to a variety of government jobs with heavy physical demands—seven pull-ups, twenty-five push-ups, forty sit-ups, and a mile and a half run in eleven minutes. While that is posted as the official hiring criterion, rookies in training often are worked much harder. Like a Marine drill sergeant, a jump trainer may order fifty push-ups for errors, real or imagined. Over the course of a day, he may ask for it again and again, and rookies go to their bunks at night rubber-armed. Recruits who train in Alaska learn about the "BLM standard," which demands ten pull-ups, thirty-five push-ups, sixty sit-ups, and a much faster mile and a half of nine minutes, thirty seconds. Though it has no legal standing, the BLM standard comes with the freight of esprit de corps and peer pressure. No rookie wants to fail it. Few do.

By the second week, the rookies are dealing with strange mockups of airplane fuselages and tall pole assemblies that seem to have more lines and rigging than a schooner. They begin at ground level with hours of parachute landing falls, tuck-and-roll drills designed to save ankles and knees. They move on to practice jumps while hooked to overhead cables that simulate a short fall and the sensation of a parachute opening. On the training towers, they drill in the exit techniques required by the variety of aircraft they will use. They learn to launch from the standing and sitting positions, to deal with malfunctions, to handle descents on the letdown rope. More running, more push-ups, more classroom time accompanies all of it.

And they begin to climb trees. Because a fact of the jumping life is this: If you hang up in a tree, you will use your letdown rope to get to ground and to the fire as quickly as possible, but then you must come back after the fire is out and retrieve your parachute. And that can mean a trip up a pine or fir that may tower as high as two hundred feet. Jumpers learn to use the climbing spurs and rigging that are the tools of loggers. It is difficult work, digging in the spurs, flipping up the sling rope encircling a trunk that may be five feet in diameter, switching to an alternate sling to get past protruding limbs.

Many jumpers, rookies and veterans alike, find climbing far more frightening than the thought of stepping out of an airplane at fifteen hundred feet. "It's literally true that we've had more people quit during training because of tree climbing than because of fear of jumping out of airplanes," said Mike Fitzpatrick, who heads the training section at the Forest Ser-

vice jump base in Redmond, Oregon. "I hate it myself. It's absolutely the worst part of jumping. When I have to do it, I've got such a death grip on the rope that by the time I get up into the tree my forearms are just wasted."

Along the way in training, the rookies meet the jumpsuit. Cumbersome and heavy, the suit looks not so different from the outfits jumpers wore in the early 1940s. But it reflects half a century of design evolution and thousands of detail improvements, often as a result of specific jumper mishaps. The leather football helmets of early jumpers have yielded to motorcycle helmets, with a face mask of heavy wire mesh. The canvas-colored suit is worn over the standard firefighter's yellow shirt and green pants. The suit is made now of Kevlar, the high-technology material favored for bullet-proof vests; Gary Dunning's landing in the spruce tree is one of the reasons for that change.

The suit hangs on a rack. The pants legs zip up the inseam, so that a jumper can back up to the rack, don the heavy jacket, then zip into the pants and pull heavy suspenders up over the jacket. The suit is armored at key points with pads to protect the spine, crotch, elbows, and knees. Much of the protective material built into the suit is borrowed and adapted from several contact sports. The suit's seat is laughably misshapen, with stuffing ample enough to stir envy in a circus clown. The jacket's collar rises stiff and elegant around the neck and ears, a medieval sort of ruff that provides protection when a jumper goes crashing through the upper limbs of tall trees. Two spacious leg pockets carry essential gear; one holds the 150-foot letdown rope and the other a packout bag. It will unfold to accommodate the suit and vast amounts of other gear when the jumper hits the trail after a fire. Built into the suit are the attachment rings a jumper will need to hook into the rope for a letdown from a tree.

The rookies feel as burdened as a knight in armor the first time they don the suit. Then come the parachutes and their harness, the main worn on the back and the reserve on the stomach. And finally, the heavy personal gear bag, slung in front from the waist like a bulky apron and left to bounce off the thighs. All told, the outfit is seventy pounds of canvas, hardware, plastic, steel, aluminum, straps, buckles, nylon, rigging, connectors and gear. The rookies' first attempts at walking in their new vestments are straddle-legged studies in klutziness, and they learn one of jumping's dark secrets. No matter how dashing and daring the image, no matter how great the ease with which they will fly through the air, no matter how heroically they will perform on the fire, jumpers making that brief walk from the equipment rack to the airplane door are ugly ducklings not yet become swans. They look like nothing so much as a troupe of Michelin men waddling through thick mud.

Left: Like this Montana duo, smokejumpers usually take to the air in "sticks" of two. When conditions are right, they may descend close enough to talk on the way down and land within a few feet of each other.

■ ■ ■

Below: With his tiny initial drogue chute just beginning to deploy, a Bureau of Land Management smokejumper plummets toward an Idaho forest. Jumpers, an elite corps of four hundred highly trained firefighters, are specialists in remote backcountry fires.

■ ■ ■

Below right: Commitment takes many forms, but few last longer than the tatooed emblem of the Forest Service smokejumpers—an evergreen tree on a set of parachute wings.

■ ■ ■

Right: Smokejumper and sawyer Mark Wright, a high school special education teacher in his off-seasons, works to drop a dangerous and fire-weakened snag that could broadcast wind-borne sparks and start additional fires if left standing.

waited, hot and uncomfortable, until the fire burned itself out around them and moved on. They were uninjured. Big Ernie had smiled.

Big Ernie is the god of smokejumpers, a cousin perhaps to Coyote, the trickster of Indian legend, or to the Fates of Greek mythology, who spun the thread of human destiny and, armed with shears, cut it off when they pleased. Big Ernie is the keeper of jumper karma. He lives in the smoke of big fire, in the roar of jump plane engines, in the air where parachutes float and even, some say, in the jump assignment roster, where his capricious touch controls the bestowing of Soft Landings, Big Overtime, and Easy Packouts. He giveth and he taketh away, and the minds of mere humans, or even smokejumpers, will never fathom when he will do which. Around a thousand jumper campfires they tell tales of Big Ernie. He is the cause of woe, he is the cause of happiness, and he will always get you in the end. Sometimes he appears in strange costume at rookie initiations, like the personification of Neptune who comes aboard to inaugurate new sailors when a ship crosses the equator. Dressed in a black robe and carrying a spruce bough, Big Ernie always stops by when the BLM rookies at Fairbanks are welcomed to the fold.

The god of smokejumpers has no church and no priests. But the chronicler of his enigmatic ways is Murray Taylor, a jumper and writer who works earnestly at codifying the theology of Big Ernie. "To be a smokejumper, you must be brave and you must do things absolutely right," Taylor said. "Guys jump a forty-acre fire over the Bitterroots with hundred-foot flames, and they're packing an old knee injury, but they do it. They have confidence. They carry rabbit's feet. Some cross themselves discreetly before they jump. They knock on wood. But most of all they believe in Big Ernie. All jumpers talk earnestly about the deals they've gotten or the deals they're going to get. Big Ernie controls your deals, good or bad. Smart jumpers know never to figure your angles too tight, or Big Ernie will get you. He will let you get out there on a fire, miles out there, get beat up by nature, let you call in retardant planes and use everything you have. He'll let you expend all your resources, let fire come toward your camp, and then, in the end, he'll send some rain to knock your fire down. Big Ernie is a jokester."

But his followers march their own curious paths, too. Invented fun is a jumper hallmark. At McCall a few decades back, a contingent of Idaho jumpers wanted to attend the annual season-end party of the Missoula jumpers, a wild affair known for attracting young women from all over Western Montana. The McCall jumpers took a collection to cover aviation gas and quietly persuaded the contract pilots of a DC-3 jump plane at McCall to make a clandestine flight to Montana. They loaded a

keg of beer aboard the plane. When they arrived in Missoula, they found that the Montana jumpers had been dispatched to a big fire bust in Utah. So the Idaho delegation took over the Montana party, with its liquor, food, and women.

The party broke up in the small hours of the morning, and the Idaho plane roared out of Missoula. Meanwhile, the McCall base had received a dispatch for the same fire that had pulled in the Missoula jumpers. Then the McCall brass discovered that their plane and many of their jumpers were missing. The managers scrambled to put together a groundpounder crew of the remaining jumpers and dispatched them by bus to catch a commercial flight for Utah. When the plane arrived from Missoula at 7 A.M., the brass was waiting, and they were not happy. A jumper who survived the ensuing confrontation recalls, "The guys who organized the whole thing were hiding under chairs. The only thing that saved us was that they had so many fires going they couldn't can us all."

Other extracurriculars were more serious. As early as the 1950s, jumpers would sometimes note that committed colleagues, firefighters considered likely to stay with the game for years, would simply not show up for several seasons. Rumors abounded, tales of shadowy connections with the Central Intelligence Agency and adventures in faraway places. Over the years many of the rumors crystallized into fact through disclosure by the federal government, and through the research of Professor William Leary, a University of Georgia historian who specializes in intelligence history.

In the 1950s, smokejumpers were recruited by the CIA as parachute operations specialists and cargo handlers for missions where agents or supplies were dropped in clandestine operations. The jumpers, known first as "parachute dispatch officers" and later as "cargo kickers," participated in scores of missions over China and Tibet. Later, some smokejumpers helped train Cuban paratroopers for the Bay of Pigs invasion in 1961. They worked most often with Air America, a cargo hauler that has since been officially revealed as one of several CIA airlines used for covert operations. In the Vietnam War era, Air America supplied guerrillas in Cambodia, Laos, and Vietnam with arms, ammunition, and supplies.

Leary estimates that over a hundred jumpers served with the CIA between 1950 and 1974, when the federal government grounded Air America. "The CIA wanted people who knew air cargo operations, who were well educated and who had a sense of adventure," Leary said. "In the smokejumper program they found exactly the right place to look." Some of the jumpers became permanent CIA operatives and stayed until retirement. One, Jerry Daniels, went from fighting fires at Missoula to serving as the CIA's chief of air operations at Long Tien, Laos. Three

In the high elevations of the Northern Rockies, rapidly changing weather catches a few smokejumpers every year. In Glacier National Park, five miles south of the Canadian border, a crew of smokejumpers endures five inches of August snow.

◼ ◼ ◼

former smokejumpers, John Lewis, Darrell Eubanks, and David Bevan died when an Air America plane was shot down in northern Laos in 1961. The contributions of the jumpers, pilots, and others who had served in the Air America era were publicly acknowledged in 1989 with dedication of a memorial in Dallas, Texas. The names of Lewis, Eubanks, and Bevan are listed on the memorial. Former CIA director William Colby spoke at the dedication, and a tribute from President Ronald Reagan was read.

Dale Carlson, a McCall jumper from the early 1960s, never signed with the CIA. But he left jumping one year, went home, and was jilted by the love of his life. He took his heartbreak and did what a couple of other jumpers had done, signed on as a mercenary in the Rhodesian Civil War. "When that first rocket round went over, I decided I didn't love her that much," said Carlson, now an artist in Oregon. "But it was too late. I was stuck for two years."

In many ways, the smokejumper corps has cultivated that sort of larger-than-life image, and it may be forever defined not only by what it does on fires, but by what it does off of them. It seems true even within the jumper ranks; nearly all jumpers with more than a couple of years experience say that the draw is not the fire and not the jumping but, rather, the richly variegated assemblage of humanity that finds its way to the work.

Ted Mason, the MBA who jumps from the Boise base, sat once in a campfire circle at the center of a thousand square miles of Alaska tundra. "There were eight of us on this fire. We'd finished it and were sitting around, waiting for a helicopter ride the next day. I was the youngest by far. Most of them

were in their forties and there were a couple of fifty-year-olds, real old-time Alaska jumpers. It was such a scene. We were miles from anywhere. Everybody was filthy, black soot all over their faces, because there are no showers on Alaska fires. The dirtiest collection of people I'd ever seen in my life, and I was one of them."

Around the fire, bits of biography and life history began to flow. Mason watched and listened, fascinated at a tableau that was a cross between a tea party and a locker room. In the eight, he tallied nine bachelor's degrees and three master's degrees. One jumper was fluent in French and Spanish, another in German. Several had traveled the world. "It was just a phenomenal group of people, sitting out there at the end of the earth, in the most remote place you can imagine. In the middle of all the stories, a guy pulls a book out of his pack. And another one of these filthy jumpers looks over at him and says, 'Is that *Immortal Poems*'? The guy with the book says that it is. And the filthy jumper asks him if Andrew Marvell's work is in the book. While the guy with the book is looking, everybody is quiet, and before he's ever found it, the jumper starts reciting Marvell from memory, '*To His Coy Mistress*. Had we but world enough, and time…'." For Mason that moment—the wilderness, the fire, the eclectic collection of humanity and something as unexpected as seventeenth century poetry—defined the jumping experience.

Others put it differently. In 1993, on the chalkboard of the ready room at Fairbanks, someone wrote, "We really *are* fire gods." Over the summer, more than a hundred jumpers passed the board. None saw any reason to erase it.

CHAPTER 6

The Air Tankers

GARY NAGEL HAD THE DC-6 LINED UP ON FINAL when the word changed. Through the afternoon's heat, he had been working a stubborn fire on a timbered ridge twenty miles out of Santa Rosa. He had measured his way down the ridge, extending the thin red line of retardant a quarter of a mile eastward with each sortie. On long, thundering passes, the four-engine DC-6 had skimmed the treetops at fifty feet. Below, the fire gnawed its way up the ridge's south face, exhaling billows of smoke five thousand feet into a blue California sky. Nagel had caught glimpses of the ground firefighters and their engines, laboring up the roads along the ridge and moving in to pick up the fire. And he'd seen that the retardant line was working, slowing the fire, giving the ground crews a shot at corralling it.

Nagel and his copilot, Ted Bell, had been on the fire for a little more than an hour. They made their runs down the ridge and winged quickly back to the airfield tanker base, where the ground crew, sweating in retardant-soaked coveralls, would race to pump in another twenty-five hundred gallons of red muck. Then it was up in the air again, picking up orders from Blaine Moore, the Forest Service air attack coordinator. Moore, riding as a passenger in a small plane circling high overhead, was a flying air traffic controller and fire boss, running the air operation and using his radio and his vantage point to steer the ground crews into action. In his spare moments, Moore unlimbered a camera to record the action below. As tanker operations go, this was an easy day. Chasing fire along ridgelines seldom demands as much as chasing it deep into the canyons. There would be other days for flying the canyons. This was a day for working on top.

With a lifetime of passenger service behind it, the DC-6 was a flying cavern. Behind the cockpit, the cabin had been stripped of every seat, restroom, luggage rack, reading light, and passenger amenity. Riveted onto the ship's underbelly, the protruding paunch of the retardant tank made the old plane look more like a pelican, less like an eagle. Beneath the floor ran the valving and controls that actuated the six clamshell doors along the tank's bottom. Whatever milk runs it had known during its first life with United Airlines, the red-striped DC-6 was a ten-thousand-horsepower warship now, born again as a low altitude bomber and sent off to find adventure in its old age. In Nagel, sitting at the controls and wearing his customary sunglasses, it even had an old Air Force bomber pilot.

On Moore's word, Nagel and Bell set off down the ridge. Below them, the ribbon of red retardant draped through a ridgetop meadow and over trees and brush just ahead of the fire's advancing front. Feeding power and flap settings to Bell over the radio, Nagel began bringing the plane on line over the stripe. He was

Above: With two engines gone, the windshield blown out of its cockpit and a landing gear door flying through the air, a crippled DC-6 tanker piloted by Gary Nagel struggles to stay aloft after plowing into a towering tree on a fire near Santa Rosa, California.

■ ■ ■

Left: Against a sky clotted with smoke, a lone air tanker dispenses a cloud of retardant in the path of approaching fire.

on final approach now, dropping and slowing, lining up as if he were making a landing at some familiar airport. He would come to minimum altitude, punch off the drop doors with the button beneath his left thumb on the steering yoke, and extend the line. Then Moore's voice crackled on the radio. He'd been watching the fire's progress, noting its behavior on the far flank. It looked as if they'd headed it now, he was saying. Instead of stretching the retardant line straight ahead, could Nagel bend it—throw a sharp turn and head the line to the south? Nagel understood. They'd caught the fire's front. Now it was time to turn the corner and seal the flank. His reply was quick. No problem.

It was Nagel's practice to do a reconnaissance flyover on any new course assignment. Go around once, take a look at the new target, then come back and do the drop. But here, on the ridgeline, it seemed unnecessary. He'd already brought the plane down low. He was coming up on the new line. The territory was familiar. He rolled the DC-6 into the sort of tight, banked turn it had never known in its passenger days. Coming out of the turn, he dropped toward the treetops and brought the plane in on the new line. Just in time to start the drop. No waste motion. Nagel thumbed the button on the steering yoke and felt the first three drop doors open. He knew that he'd caught the end of the line, that the red ribbon would have a ninety-degree bend the next time he saw it. A second later he punched off the final three doors. And then the DC-6 plunged into the smoke.

In his circling of the fire, Moore, the air attack boss, had noticed a patriarchal pine that towered above all others on the ridge, a stalagmite of green needling into the sky. A survivor, most likely, of fires or logging that had cleared the ridge in some earlier time. It stood now just against the roiling smoke that climbed from the ridge, like an evergreen bough nailed to the side of a cloud. Nagel was approaching from somewhere behind it.

Federal air tanker safety regulations say that pilots of retardant bombers will not fly in smoke. Routinely they will fly around towering smoke columns, like small boys romping around the legs of tall uncles. They will work in conditions where visibility skitters near the legal minimum. But they will not, the regulations declare, fly into the sort of smoke that drapes the windshield like a coat of gray paint. Every tanker pilot does it, of course, though not always deliberately. Fire creates its own wind patterns. Smoke floods and ebbs on a choreography all its own. For a plane winging through a forest fire's atmospheric mosaic at over a hundred miles an hour, minimum visibility can become zero visibility in an instant. The experience usually is fleeting, over as quickly as it began, like passing through a tunnel on a speeding train. Hold the course or climb a bit. Pop out on the other side.

Nagel flies in the smoke now. Moving fast. Visibility near zero. Gray, gray, gray against the windshield. Surfing through an acrid cloud, red retardant streaming out the open drop doors. Beside him, Bell, locked on the instruments, jacks the power settings to maximum for the climb out. Nagel looking up now from watching the ground and punching off the load. Leaning to his right to throw the flaps to twenty degrees. Shifting from action to reaction. Windshield gray, gray, now thinning slightly, coming out. Suddenly green, green, green, a wall of green. At 125 miles an hour the plane hits the pine seventy feet below its top.

In that second, Nagel's world detonates. Sensations and pain and demands avalanche upon him. The plane takes the tree head-on, dead center on the fuselage. Up ahead of Nagel's feet, the ship's nose cone disappears. The front landing gear doors and other chunks of forward hardware rip away, spinning toward the ground. The windshield panel directly before him implodes, its shrapnel ricocheting off his sunglasses, nibbling into his face. The window opening is small, barely two feet wide, but through it, as if fed by some giant mechanical chipping machine, rushes a cataract of limbs, needles, pitch, branches, bark, pine cones, wood chunks. A firewood-sized billet rockets past Nagel's head, crunches the bulkhead behind him and caroms forward to take out gauges on the instrument panel. The DC-6 suddenly loses power.

But somehow they are still flying. At over a hundred miles an hour, the wind screams through the missing window. Nagel and Bell sit hip-deep in a sea of greenery and debris that overflows from the cockpit into the cabin behind them. Splintery ingots of wood are scattered through the pile. Every one of them has come past Nagel's head. Because he was leaning to the side at the instant of impact, not a one has hit him. Bell clutches his eyes. The wind and airborne detritus have spun his contact lenses up and back, behind his eyelids. He is effectively blind. The DC-6 is dropping now. At Nagel's knee, a hulking wood chunk has wedged the throttle levers closed. Frantically he digs through needles and branches, claws the two foot chunk out, shoves the throttles forward. Engines two and three, the powerplants nearest the fuselage, are knocked out, clogged with debris. But one and four respond. Crippled but not felled, the DC-6 claws upward.

The wind knifing through the window is brutal, but when Nagel sees the alternative he is grateful. In front of Bell, the right windshield panel is a gummy, opaque pastiche of pine pitch and needles. Bell gropes and finds the microphone. Nagel tends to a hundred details, reads his remaining instruments, tries to make sense of the chaos. Bell raises Moore on the radio and transmits the vital information: They've hit a tree, two engines gone, two responding, trying to fly it back to Santa Rosa.

Moore watches them go, limping off toward the south. He radios the tower.

The crash trucks waited as they landed. Despite the damage, the landing gear deployed and locked normally. The ground crew gaped, and not just at the plane's battered nose and missing windshield. When the DC-6 struck the pine, the tree's top had snapped off and whipped down the side of the airplane. The base lodged at the root of the wing and the treetop laid down, paralleling the fuselage. When Nagel brought the plane into Santa Rosa it was carrying a forty-foot Christmas tree, like a ladder slung on the side of a truck. At the hospital, the doctors dug the glass out of Nagel's face and extricated the contact lenses from Bell's eyes. Nagel was cleared to go. His DC-6 would need some work before it fought again. But fire season was on. Nagel caught a ride going north. The next day he was in Oregon, flying another plane on another fire.

■ ■ ■

Only sixteen years after Wilbur and Orville Wright swooped the sands of Kitty Hawk, aviation and forest fire met. They were made for each other. For more than seventy years the battle against wildland fire has been an air war. If there is a single image that centers the public eye on the summer battles of the West it is the picture of giant, aging aircraft performing like tiny stunt planes. Wheeling and roaring in the sky, they dare impossibly deep dives into smoky canyons, trailing their red plumes of retardant like matador's capes.

But fifty-year-old warbirds on bombing missions over the Malibu hills are only a facet of the world of fire aviation. The numbers add up quickly. A fleet of fifty of the big retardant tanker planes. More than 250 helicopters, from flitting two-seat gnats to twin-rotor behemoths the size of boxcars. Spotter planes that patrol Western forests and rangelands at the peak of the fire season. Helitack crews and rappel outfits that descend from the sky to take on fire. Lead planes that guide the lumbering tankers down into the fire's maw. Air attack command ships that circle high overhead as eyes and ears for air and ground operations. Doorless planes that usher smokejumpers into the sky. In some regions, fire was never battled on any significant scale until flight made it possible. "In Alaska," said Frenchie Malotte, who heads wildland fire operations for his state, "we use airplanes the way people in the Lower 48 use pickup trucks."

Aviation began lifting itself out of the barnstorming realm in World War I. British, French, German, Italian, and American pilots catapulted the military role of aircraft from flimsy reconnaissance kite to aerial warship. Still, the performance and the sheer bravado of those daring young men in their flying machines did not convince all the doubters. In the decades after the war, the military establishment, barely sixty years removed from the era of muzzle-loader warfare, earnestly debated the military future of the airplane. But out West, the lessons of war were not lost on the forest fire community, which had its own campaigns to fight. So it was that America's military aviators, uncertain of their future, were most receptive to a request that arrived at the headquarters of the fledgling Army Air Service in 1919. The Forest Service, plagued with the perennial problem of detecting fire starts in vast unroaded areas of the West, was curious. Would the Army consider flying fire patrol over Western forests, providing the information that would permit rapid dispatch of ground firefighters?

It would. It assigned to the task Major Henry "Hap" Arnold, an Army pilot who had fought in France. Arnold, who would go on to command US air operations in World War II, took to the task with verve. His leather-jacketed fliers and their open-cockpit biplanes were welcomed around the West. Foresters clamored to have planes assigned to their regions. Citizen volunteers built airstrips. The pilots performed their mission with spectacular results, repeatedly giving firefighters the early start that prevented small fires from becoming conflagrations. Their success came in spite of the fact that they worked that first year without radios. Instead, they resorted to bombing forest ranger stations with messages in tin cans. The Forest Service experiments attracted the attention of Los Angeles County officials. Soon, they were using manned gas dirigibles to patrol Southern California mountains.

The Army, which caught over fifteen hundred fires a season, had pulled out of the patrol program by 1926. But, for the forest fire community, the aviation genie was out of the bottle. Forest Service experiments with aircraft paralleled the military experience in World War I: The initial role of eye in the sky mushroomed to the concept of air-to-ground delivery and attack. In the mid-1920s, mail, food, and supplies were free-dropped without parachutes to fire camps. Experiments with water and chemical drops to combat fire began with the military planes and continued after the Forest Service switched to contracting with private pilots. By the 1930s, fire officers in the Northern Rockies had introduced parachutes for cargo drops. It was a step that led inevitably to the firefighters-in-the-sky thinking that created the smokejumper corps, despite official skepticism.

For more than three decades, while fire spotting, cargo dropping, and smokejumping progressed, the idea of directly fighting fire with airplanes wore the cloak of mad science. In some of the experiments, water was dropped in wooden barrels

A ramp worker at an air tanker retardant base in Bettles Field, Alaska wears the messy frosting of his trade. During a big, long-running forest fire, ramp crews will pump tens of thousands of gallons of retardant into the bellies of air tankers.

■ ■ ■

that shattered on impact, with minimal results. Exploratory efforts ranged through foams, chemical retardants, gaseous extinguishing agents, and aerial bombs that combined explosives and liquids. A decade or more was wasted on the concept of bomb packages because the physics department at the University of California issued a report that proved "conclusively" that liquids broadcast from airplanes would not reach the ground. That misconception didn't die until after World War II, when scores of veterans could attest that fuel and water ballast jettisoned from large planes was often felt at ground level.

Some of those veterans were pilots, farm boys who had marched off to war and returned with combat aviation records and dreams of civilian careers in the cockpit. They were available. So were hundreds of military aircraft that began reaching the surplus market in the 1950s. A scattering of those pilots and planes became crop dusters, winging just above the corn and cotton rows, and proving daily that air-dropped liquids would reach the ground. By 1956, the crop dusters were being dragooned to fight fires. In national forests in California they went winging through mountain canyons with 120-gallon payloads of water. A year later, California's state forestry department took to the air with its own fleet of seven aircraft.

Over a decade, the air tanker concept simply exploded around the West. Soon single-engine torpedo bombers were supplanted by multi-engine warships that had flown missions over Berlin and Guadalcanal and Tokyo. In the planes' belly tanks, water was replaced by borate, a chemical fire retardant that could slow fire's advance and give ground crews the opportunity to collar runaway blazes. The preferred tactic of laying retardant just ahead of the fire, not on it, evolved. Borate proved to be a potent soil sterilant, effective on fires but bad for the forest. Eventually it would be replaced with kinder compounds built around fertilizer components that promoted regrowth after fire had passed.

Chasing fire forty miles above the Arctic Circle, a hulking C-130 military transport reborn as an air tanker in the fleet of Oregon's Butler Aviation deftly spreads retardant over a stand of black spruce.

• • •

As ever larger airplanes were converted to fire bombers, payloads climbed to two thousand, three thousand, even four thousand gallons. Most of the big planes were flown by small operators rooted in agricultural flying. Scattered around the West, they were shadetree geniuses, spiritual cousins of every bush pilot who ever kept an old plane flying with baling wire and ingenuity. Through an odd mix of competition and collegiality—battling for Forest Service contracts while they swapped parts and ideas—they evolved a complex technology of tanks, drop doors, and controls.

"We had so much to learn," said Cal Butler, founder of Butler Aviation and an Oregon pioneer in air tankers in those heady days of the late nineteen fifties. "We had to learn how to actually hit a fire, which was not as easy as it seemed. We had to learn about fire behavior. We had to learn what the airplanes would do. I had some friends who were new in the business. They finished tanking up a B-Twenty-Five one day and wanted

to see how it would do on a drop. So one of the partners sat his brand new pickup truck in the middle of the runway for a target. The B-Twenty-Five came over low and fast and let go a whole load of water at once. When that pickup got done rolling over and over there was nothing left of it. It was just destroyed."

Other parts of the learning curve were steep and tragic. A hundred new contractors scrabbled for a place in a business where there was no experience, where the safety margins were being plucked off the tree of theory. Simple lessons, such as the concept that the ideal drop speed was very slow, somewhere near 120 miles an hour, were learned the hard way. The mortality rate was horrific. Dozens of Western fires were punctuated with piles of mangled aluminum. For the big retardant tankers, the mortality rate some years ran at thirty percent.

Dale Newton, the president of Aero Union Corporation of Chico, California, one of the West's largest tanker operations, flew fire missions then. "The first year that I flew the B-Twenty-Five, they lost seven of them. Seven in one year," he said. "There was a whole raft of B-Twenty-Fives being flown by guys who didn't have the slightest idea what the mission was. They'd fly up canyons and expect the airplane to get them out, and it wouldn't do it. A couple of guys went down with just plain old engine failures. One guy exceeded the red line of the airplane in trying to be a hero and dive down into a hole to make a drop. He dropped at something like three hundred and sixty-five miles an hour. The airplane just came apart. When you drop a big load of liquid at that speed, for just an instant it's a protruding glob that's part of the airplane. It blocks the normal flow of air. All of a sudden there's a big low pressure area behind it and the tail sucks down. It's like grabbing the yoke and throwing the nose straight up at three hundred and sixty-five miles an hour. The wings take a big bite, the structural loads go out of sight and the wings come off. It happened more than once."

For many in that era, it was a hairsbreadth existence. But they sculpted a risk ethic that, even in a new era of tighter safety standards, still defines a job that is one of the most dangerous in America. Caught once in vicious turbulence off a roaring fire, Cal Butler took a B-17—the hulking Flying Fortress of World War II fame—through a narrow basalt canyon with one wing pointing to high noon and the other straight at the ground. Looking out the top of his cockpit, he could see cold, black rock directly overhead. At Lakeview, Oregon, in the early 1960s a B-25 tanker pilot hit the end of the runway short of the airspeed he needed to get aloft. The copilot cranked up the landing gear as the airstrip disappeared, and, without ever touching the ground, they mowed through a hundred yards of low sagebrush before lumbering into the sky. Bill Rosenbaum, a legendary tanker contractor from the 1950s, once had three engines condemned in a preseason inspection of his small stable of B-26s. He steam-cleaned the powerplants to make them look new, then swapped the nose cases for replacements with different serial numbers. With that cosmetic change and a bit of creative work in his maintenance logbook, he flew the season.

It was all part of the hubris of fire flying. "In the beginning, there was something strange about most tanker pilots," said Gene Powers, a tanker pioneer in Wyoming. "You'd get a guy with such incredible skill and expertise that you knew he had to be goofy in some other way, maybe flawed from chasing women or drinking whiskey. If he was that good and wasn't flawed, he wouldn't be flying tankers—he'd get a real job."

■ ■ ■

In the summer battles of the West, most of the big retardant bombers fly for the federal agencies. But California has its own fleet, and a few other states field one or two ships. The larger ships are provided by a dozen or so contract companies, from Hawkins & Powers in Greybull, Wyoming, to Hemet Valley Flying Service in California. Although California's twin-engine tanker planes fly with only a contract pilot, the big four-engine tankers take to the air with a crew of two. The copilots are understudies who set flaps, tend power settings, monitor air speed, and wait for the day when they will get their own ship. The real work is done by the captains. It is hands-on, seat-of-the-pants aviation, combat flying in a peacetime setting, low-altitude work that treats big old transports and retired airliners as if they were Piper Cubs.

Tanker pilots play for high stakes, with sobering odds. Of the fifty or so retardant planes in service, at least one goes down almost every season. Survivors are rare. From retardant bomber flying's inception in 1956 through 1994, a hundred tanker and lead plane pilots died in action, an average of more than two a year. In 1994, the worst season for firefighter fatalities in sixty years, two tanker planes went down; a pilot and copilot died in Montana when their converted navy subchaser struck a mountain, and a three-man flight crew died in southern California when a huge C-130 tanker went down. "Beginning pilots, when they first start taking lessons, are taught realms of flight to avoid at all costs," Nagel said. "The biggest one is that you can fly low or you can fly slow, but you never fly low and slow at the same time. Never. And that's what tanker flying is all about—taking big airplanes and flying low and slow. Even combat pilots don't do that. They train for high and fast. And then, on top of low and slow, tankers work with tight confines, low visibility, high wind loading, and engine speeds that are always behind the power curve. Everything you've been taught not to do, you do as a tanker pilot."

Typically the pilots who come to tanker work have flown for the military or the airlines, or both. They are a singular breed, most commonly fliers who stumbled into aviation at an early age and never outgrew a boyish certainty that flying should contain large measures of excitement. "So many of them have been combat pilots at some point in life," said Wes Shook, a Forest Service air operations coordinator in Goleta, California. "This is the last place, the last chance that they get to use the things that they were taught." A few who do the work are barely thirty and have, in fact, never seen military service. Others are past sixty and have been to war more than once. Flight uniforms and gold braid and the politesse of passenger announcements over the intercom hold no attraction for them; jeans and cowboy boots and endless hours of flying stories are the more likely combination.

For all of them, flying giant planes just off the treetops is addicting. Jan Reifenberg, a Notre Dame graduate and a former

Vietnam pilot, admits to the addiction. Even the business of leaving eight feet of the wing of a DC-7 tanker on a Washington state mountainside did not deliver the cure. "I've done the point A to point B flying in four-engine jets all over the world," he said. "That was interesting for a while. But there's not much flying to it. Basically the airplane flies itself on autopilot. If you want, it will even land itself. I didn't want a lifetime of that. What I do now is really flying." If the pilots of retardant bombers share a virtue, it is an odd ability to couple infinite patience with instant action, to tolerate week upon week of thumb twiddling in airport ready rooms in exchange for the opportunity to indulge themselves in a brand of flying that is like no other.

"Tanker pilots are all individualistic, opinionated people who have enormous egos when it comes to their flying ability," said Charlotte Larson, the Forest Service overseer of tanker aviation. "The good ones are really good at being in idle, just being calm and collected while they're waiting and waiting and waiting. They don't get frustrated. They don't lose tempers. And when the bell goes off, they get the shot of adrenaline and they're ready to go to work right now." The tanker fleet is no less colorful than its pilots. It is not quite the home for antique aircraft that it was in the years before 1980, but some World War II ships still fly off to battle fire and so do some former passenger planes with pedigrees that go back to the 1940s. The most romantic of the remaining warbirds are the PB4Y2s, four-engine patrol bombers flown by Hawkins & Powers and still capable of stirring memories of every World War II aviation movie ever made.

World War II amphibious planes, modified so that they could scoop loads of water while skimming along rivers or lakes, once were common in the Western tanker fleet. In the West, only one amphibious warbird still flies fire duty, under contract to the state of Washington. An ex-Navy PBY, it has a boat-shaped hull and retractable landing wheels, and can set down on land or water. But across the years many of the amphibious PBYs have come to grief when they hit water with the landing gear door for the nose wheel only partially closed. With the hull's lines broken by the open gear door, the impact of a water landing ripped the planes open and sent them plummeting nose-first for the bottom.

Eric Johnson pilots the Washington PBY. At other times in life, he flew crop dusters, battered his body as a human guinea pig on experimental Navy deceleration sleds, and took his chances on rodeo broncos. On a summer day in 1992, Johnson and his copilot, Monnie Overson, were flying the Klickitat Fire in southern Washington. For seven hours they had endured hammering rides as they scooped water from the choppy surface of the Columbia River. At day's end they headed for a nearby Oregon airfield. Johnson activated the landing gear. But the gear

doors beneath the cockpit had been bent by the river's waves. The doors opened three inches and jammed. They would not open fully. They would not close. Neither a water landing or an airport landing was possible.

In the gathering darkness, with fuel running low, Johnson climbed out of the pilot's seat and left Overson to handle the flying. Tinkering with hydraulic valves in the plane's belly did no good. Measures less scientific seemed in order. In the back of the plane, Johnson found a heavy steel pry bar, about four feet long. He brought it into the cockpit, and stared for a moment at a small glass window in the floor, an inspection port to permit the pilot to check the landing gear. Johnson took the bar and broke the glass. He jammed the bar through the hole and, like a farmer tackling an old hay baler, began prying on the landing gear. For forty-five minutes Overson flew circles in the darkness, while Johnson beat and pushed and pulled on the bar. In the end, in the tight confines of the cockpit, Johnson was standing on the bar, jumping up and down on it. Finally, he hit upon the idea of synchronizing his jumps with Overson's attempt to activate the landing gear switch. And the doors swung shut.

They had exchanged one peril for another. The landing gear was up and they were committed to a water landing at night, something neither had ever done. In the darkness they could not even locate the river precisely. Spending his precious fuel, Johnson turned north for Kennewick, Washington, searching for a river in the night and wondering how he would land if he did not know whether the water was ten feet below him, or a hundred feet. Air traffic controllers told him of a stretch of the river defined by a bridge and by the lights of homes and businesses along the shore. He came into Kennewick, cleared the bridge, and let the plane settle into the darkness as he eyed the lights on shore. The touchdown was perfect. When they pulled the PBY to its mooring for the night, its fuel tank held a teacup of gasoline.

As romantic as the old warships are, most of the tanker fleet of the 1990s is postwar aircraft, much of it built after 1955. Military aircraft, especially Navy submarine patrol planes that were designed with low-and-slow capability, and C-130 transports with enormous payloads, remain the backbone of tanker aviation. Many of the older tankers are airborne hot rods, refitted with powerful turbine engines in place of their original reciprocating-piston powerplants. The tanker companies keep their aging planes flying by scavenging the world for planes and parts. "It takes three old planes to keep one running," Gene Powers said.

Except for the very largest of helicopters, air tankers are the most expensive firefighting resource. The cost of having the airplanes manned and ready for fire is a weighty chunk of budgetary freight. A tanker may fly only 150 hours a year; the contract

Left: Pilot Dennis Lynch pulls an A-20 attack bomber of World War II vintage from a thick cloud of smoke in the 1988 fires of Yellowstone National Park.

■ ■ ■

Below: Laying his payload at the toes of a desert fire in Arizona, Aero Union pilot Bill Waldman skims above a strand of saguaro cactus. A precise drop can slow a fire's rate of spread and make it possible for ground crews to stop its advance.

■ ■ ■

Right: In an impossibly steep dive, veteran tanker pilot Laddie Lash takes an ancient DC-7 after a stubborn fire deep in a canyon on Oregon's Warm Springs Indian Reservation. During an afternoon that still is recounted by the old hands of Pacific Northwest fire, Lash returned to make the same dive over and over.

rates hinge on the considerable cost of maintaining a specialized aircraft that has no other function. In season, every contract tanker is in paid standby status six days a week, though there is no pay if the plane is down with a mechanical problem. A four-engine tanker costs as much as twenty-seven-hundred dollars a day sitting on the ground with its crew ready to fly. When the big planes fly, they inhale up to eight hundred gallons of fuel an hour. In action, their flight pay rate ranges up to three thousand dollars an hour.

With rare exceptions, the bombers do not put out fires single-handedly. Except in the thickest and most expensive concentrations, the red soup they spread in a narrow line on the earth usually will not stop a fire in its tracks. But it can turn a raging monster into a merely annoying vicious dog, a problem that can be handled. On the ground, fire crews cannot work directly against twelve-foot flames. But if a load of retardant knocks those flames down to four feet, the troops can pull up their bandannas, strap on their goggles, and move in. For other situations, retardant reinforces fire lines constructed ahead of an advancing blaze, either by slowing the fire just as it approaches the line or by dampening fuels downwind from the line and reducing the possibility of wind-blown spot fires.

On initial attack of a fire, the big tankers may operate solo, with the pilot choosing where and how to lay a line of retardant. But if a fire is big, other aircraft arrive. An air attack boss will sit high overhead as a passenger in a small plane, spending hours orbiting in a tight, right-hand circle and working like a casino blackjack dealer to slide competing aircraft into the fire airspace.

Wes Shook, the Goleta air operations specialist, flies as an air attack boss. "The most effective way is to let a tanker in, then let a helicopter in to drop a bucket," he said. "On some Southern California fires, there are more media ships than fire aircraft. We try to find ways to let them get in and do their work, too. In between, I may tell the people on the ground where they need to burn out, where the fire is making a run and might be a safety problem. You're just going all the time, working with five radio frequencies, and things coming at you right and left. You may have six tankers stacked up in orbit, waiting to come down and make their runs. Four hours of it is about all that your head and your stomach can take. I've come back with a blister on my thumb from pushing the microphone button."

On Forest Service fires, the big tankers will be shepherded on their runs by lead planes, usually fast, small twin-engine ships. The tanker pilots are contract workers, employees of the companies that own the aircraft; the lead plane pilots are on the federal payroll. The lead pilots, in effect, stand as both guides and airborne purchasing agents, deciding where retardant should go and at what concentrations it should be dropped. On Alaska

fires, the Bureau of Land Management's Alaska Fire Service combines the roles of lead plane and air attack boss in a single two-seat aircraft.

The relationship between tanker pilots and lead plane pilots is as delicate as a cobweb, and sometimes as sticky. Almost uniformly, tanker pilots confess to significant, even monumental, quotients of ego; lead plane pilots, flying their small planes, must tell the big ships what to do. In the typical situation, a lead plane will fly a deep canyon route while the tanker circles overhead. When the small plane emerges, its pilot will brief the tanker pilot on such details as the drop zone, wind currents, visibility, and the best escape route. But the small plane, much more maneuverable than the large one, is a swallow suggesting tactics to an albatross. When he wheels to follow the swallow back into the canyon, the albatross must decide if he is willing to bet his life on what he has just heard.

"When you fly the lead, you have to fly your little plane as if you were flying a big one," said Kathy Allred, who, like her husband, Bill, is a Forest Service lead pilot at Albuquerque. "You have to think like you're in a DC-4 or a C-130. You have to know how that plane performs, how much altitude it can give away and still climb out of the hole where you're taking it. You watch for turbulence and sinkholes in the air. You have to build trust. When you're flying with a tanker pilot you've worked a lot with before, it's just cool as hell. You're playing off each other and understanding what's going on without really talking about it. There's almost no talk on the radio. When the trust is there, they just follow you right in."

Sometimes, however, trust is slow in coming. In the 1970s, most lead plane pilots were ex-tanker pilots. With some older tanker pilots, it remains a sore point that now they most often follow the lead of pilots who have never flown anything larger than a light twin-engine plane. "I think we've lost some new, young tanker pilots because they followed lead planes where they shouldn't have," said Jack Dyer, a tanker pilot in his sixties and a veteran of Alaska fires. "New pilots think they can't ever back away. And some old dog like me will just look at a situation and say, 'No, I'm not gonna do that.'" Still, even old tanker pilots admit there are young lead pilots they trust, but it is a trust that has been dearly earned.

Most tanker planes are equipped with a series of six to sixteen belly doors that let off portions of their load. In the early days of tanker flying, the pilot triggered the doors manually, in a sequence that would allow the plane to spread retardant in a line as long as two thousand feet. The new generation of tankers come equipped with intervalometers, programmable devices that enable a pilot to preset a door sequence. By punching in the number of doors and the time interval between openings, the pilot can achieve any one of eight coverage concentrations that the lead plane pilot or the air attack boss might order. Punching the yoke button once triggers the sequence.

There remains only the quintessential problem of knowing when to punch the button. "It's what tanker flying is all about, but you can't tell someone how to do it," said Matt Ziomek, who owns a DC-4 and flies under contract for the state of Alaska. "It's like hunting and shooting at a duck on the wing. You have to lead the duck. How much? How do you tell someone how to lead a duck?"

In fire season, retardant planes fly from about forty-five bases in the West. Most are small-town fields, like the airstrips in Palmer, Alaska, and LaGrande, Oregon. But tankers also roar off the ground from large airports in the shadow of such cities as Denver, Phoenix, and Los Angeles. Some of the airports are homes to tankers of more than one stripe. At Hemet Valley airport in California, contract pilots from two different companies fly ships for the Forest Service and the California Department of Forestry.

The tanker bases usually are set at some far end of the airport. Always, there's a collection of storage tanks and piping where the red-orange retardant is mixed. Typically some old airport building provides a ready room where the pilots while away endless hours and days on standby, drinking coffee, reading aviation magazines and trading stories. In fire-active Southern California, tanker bases offer an additional amenity—bleachers. Because the spectacle of planes roaring off to battle, fire rising in nearby hills, and retardant ramp workers scrambling through fast reload sequences draws crowds, many of the bases have created spectator areas, with seating, picnic tables, and interpretive signs.

When a large fire erupts in a given locale, extra tankers from other bases are dispatched, and all of them reload at the nearest base. If a half-dozen tankers are flying out of a single airport, the action can be frenetic, comparable to watching take-offs and landings aboard an aircraft carrier in combat. Some planes are "hot-loaded," with one or more engines kept running while ramp workers scramble in the propeller backwash, wrestling heavy hoses and quick-release valves, looking like nothing so much as an Indianapolis 500 pit crew. When the drill goes smoothly, two thousand gallons will be pumped into the belly of an airplane in four minutes.

"It's hectic, just crazy sometimes," said Steve Barme, a seasonal ramp worker who makes the circuit of Western tanker bases. "We're in there in middle of the noise and the prop wash, and the pilots are always wanting to get back in the air just as quick as they can. The loose retardant that spills every time you disconnect a hose will get blown on you. Sometimes a hose will blow. We come out orange all over. But when it's really working, it's an amazing situation."

The Goleta bleacher crowd enjoyed its best show in 1992 when a fire erupted just off the end of the airport, which serves the Santa Barbara metropolitan area. With the airport closed to all other traffic, Jan Reifenberg, the contract pilot of a four-engine Orion tanker owned by Aero Union, was flying turnarounds that had him off the ground for scant minutes. He would send Tanker Number 27 screaming down the runway, lift up, retract the landing gear, immediately punch off his load and circle back for a landing. His passes were so low that the plane's backwash took out neighborhood telephone lines, but the fire was stopped short of homes and businesses that adjoined the airport.

■ ■ ■

The Moccasin Fire hurdled ridges near Sonora, California, on a hot August day in 1992. It had blown up, vaulted from the ground to the crowns of trees, and was running at flank speed. The bulldozer operators in its path, though going as fast as their clanking machines would travel, moved considerably slower. The group of them had been caught on the back side of a ridgeline, not far from its crest, when the Moccasin Fire blew. As they attempted to work their way out, the fire was on the ridge's opposite side, racing for the top, threatening to catch them like a flash flood spilling over the top of a dam. Overhead, Jim Dunn and a small squadron of pilots flying tankers for the Forest Service and the California Department of Forestry were about to set the rule book aside.

Individualists though they are, Dunn and other pilots of retardant bombers nonetheless get their marching orders from government agencies with thick safety manuals and firm operating procedures. Minimum altitude and visibility, maximum wind and drop speed, and a hundred other considerations are covered in print and underscored in annual training meetings. But, on occasion, the rules are bent. When houses lie in the immediate path of advancing flame, the rule about never dropping on structures may be broken. As a result, many Western homes which should have burned are still standing. And any rule becomes forgettable when a firefighter on the ground is in trouble.

A blowup such as the Moccasin Fire, with strong winds and towering flames, seldom is fought head-on. Ground crews and aircraft may worry its flanks, but good tactics and experienced leadership almost always will dictate that a runaway fire is waited out, until the cool of night or a weather change makes attack feasible. Even air-dropped retardant has little effectiveness against the head of a running crown fire. But the Moccasin Fire and the threatened bulldozer squad did not offer the luxury

Above: Climbing into the sun, a California Department of Forestry twin-engine tanker flown by Deen Oehl lets its retardant fly toward a fire near San Diego. The retardant dropped by tankers is fertilizer-based, and promotes post-fire regrowth.

■ ■ ■

Left: Plunging headlong into a cloud of smoke, an air tanker releases its retardant load on California's Powerhouse Fire. Fire aviation regulations forbid flying in heavy smoke, but there are few tanker pilots who have not done it.

■ ■ ■

Right: Battling to protect its roost, an Aero Union plane takes on a fire just off the end of the runway at an air tanker base in Goleta, California. Pilot Jan Reifenberg's passes on the 1992 fire were so low that the retardant drops took out neighborhood telephone lines, but the fire was stopped short of homes and businesses.

Left: A C-130, a former military transport plane, swoops low over a pair of groundpounding firefighters on an Alaska fire near Fort Yukon. Experienced ground firefighters sometimes provide radio direction for retardant drops.

■ ■ ■

of waiting. As two-hundred-foot flames crested the ridge, the tankers mounted a frontal attack. Down they went, salvoing off their loads into the teeth of the monster.

Dunn, the pilot of one of California's tankers, waited his turn in the stack of circling planes. He followed a federal ship down, and watched as the flames reached up and actually touched the plane. He heard the radio conversation that followed, the quaver in the voice of the circling air attack boss who, for the briefest instant, thought he had lost a ship. Dunn calculated as he threw his twin-engine S-2 into the dive for his run: If he did a sharp, banked turn just as he reached the fire, he could sling his load, pendulum it outward horizontally, so that it would hit the fire's base as he skirted beside the flames. He cranked up his speed for the maneuver. At 145 miles an hour, he tossed the S-2 on edge and began his turn. But big

fires, blowup fires, make their own weather and their own winds. The Moccasin fire, as it crested the ridge, was drawing in air like a tornado on a romp across a Midwest prairie. Dunn's plane was vacuumed into the heart of the fire. "I put it to max power, but it wasn't enough," he said. "The load was gone. The ship was lightened. Everything should have been working for me. But I didn't have the power to get out of it. I was on a ride that I couldn't change."

The plane disappeared into a skyscraper of flame. Inside the inferno, Dunn's windshield turned orange and he felt the flash of radiant heat. The S-2 had no air conditioning, and such cooling as it provided for its pilot came from a pair of air vents flanking the instrument panel. As Dunn watched, thirty-inch tongues of flame shot from the vents and licked the cockpit's interior around him. And then he was through. The heat was gone, but the windshield had not changed color. The fire's up-draft was so fierce that it had spit back much of the retardant thrown at it. Dunn's plane was coated with the load dropped by the ship that had preceded him. Peering through the muck, he made it to the airport, took on a fresh retardant load, had his windows cleaned and returned to the fray. The bulldozer operators made the most of the time the pilots bought. All of them escaped.

Death walks always around the edges of the tanker business, and makes it perhaps the tightest fraternity in the world of wildland fire. The community of pilots, ground workers, attack bosses and dispatchers is never morbid, and quick humor is its defining characteristic. But all those who work in it for any length of time have lost someone they know. Wanda Nagel thinks about it more than most. The wife of Gary Nagel, who brought the DC-6 home after taking on the tree at Santa Rosa, she flies a small air attack ship for the California Department of Forestry. Sometimes, with an air attack boss as her passenger, she circles above the fires where her husband dives low into the canyons.

"I don't mind flying with Gary on that kind of work, but watching him do it is very hard," she said. "There's a lot to think about in this business. I've had the experience of watching a friend die. I watched Roger Stark go in on the Railroad Flat Fire in nineteen ninety-two. He was killed. I was flying air attack up above that fire. To watch Gary make his run right after that was really difficult."

Tanker pilots are philosophers of risk, a mix of fatalists and optimists and realists. Some think often of grim possibility, and some never do. "I don't say it won't ever happen to me. That's a bad outlook. That's setting yourself up," said Gary Cockrell, a California pilot who flies a four-engine tanker on a federal contract. "You have to make yourself the best pilot you can be, and learn how to be cautious within the parameters of the job. I've thought about doing something else. I've had friends killed in the last few years. What are you going to do? No work in my life has ever been as fulfilling as this."

The only trait that seems shared by all of them is confidence in personal ability. Before the historic World War II raid on Tokyo, General Jimmy Doolittle assembled his pilots and estimated that fifty percent of them would not return. And each pilot is said to have looked at the man next to him, and thought, "You poor bastard." Tanker pilots would understand. Like combat pilots of every generation and every war, they live in a sort of reasoned, creative and self-serving denial. "It's not going to happen to you, it won't happen to you," said Gary Garrett, a pilot and co-owner of Ardco, an Arizona tanker outfit. "If you let it prey on your mind, you might as well not climb in the airplane. You have to believe in your ability and your airplane's ability."

The state of Alaska's tanker base at Palmer is run by Cheryl Wilcock. She is a firefighter, an ex-hotshot, married to a third generation firefighter. Over the years, pumping retardant and drinking coffee with tanker pilots, she has come to know them well. She has seen one ship crash. She listens and understands. "They don't talk about the danger," she said. "When there is an incident and one of them dies, they always say good things. They talk about what a good flier he was. One of the guys who was here for a season was one of those guys who never talked about it. But at the beginning of the season he gave me a letter to keep for his family, in case anything happened."

In the rituals of preseason briefings, tanker pilots are warned over and over about being drawn into the battlefield mentality, about letting the heat of the moment push them to unacceptable risk. It is not a war, they are told. No tree, no forest, is worth a pilot's life, they are told. Sometimes those admonitions come from Charlotte Larson, a former smokejumper pilot and lead plane pilot who now administers the Forest Service tanker program. But Larson flew as a lead pilot in the Oregon and California fires of 1987, a battle that went on for weeks, scourged six hundred thousand acres and choked three hundred miles of mountains with smoke so thick that cars drove with headlights at noon.

"We were taking off out of airports in Northern California on an instrument flight plan," she said. "We'd go out to a latitude-longitude coordinate, and start spiraling down through the smoke, just hoping that we weren't going to meet another plane or a helicopter or the ground. In the years since then, we sit around and shake our heads about nineteen eighty-seven. It's absolutely amazing to me that we didn't lose anybody. But the world was burning up. It was like being at war. On the ground, pilots stand around and say, 'They're just trees, they'll grow back.' But in eighty-seven, none of us listened to our own advice. We were all being nuts and trying to save the world."

Jack Dyer, the veteran Alaska pilot, had capped off an Air Force career before heading into twenty years of tanker flying. He has known the pilots who tried to save the world, and has been guilty himself a time or two. He wrestles regularly with the memories of tanker jockeys who ended their careers in a pile of metal. "I've got about a thousand hours of military combat time," he said. "But tanker flying is worse. It's unbelievable to me. I look up at the bulletin board in my office with all the pictures I've taken at different airports, and half of those guys are gone. It doesn't keep me from coming back, but to say it doesn't cross your mind would be some kind of goddamned lie. It crosses mine. Every September I say I'm never going to do it again. And every March, I show up."

CHAPTER 7

The Helicopters

I T WAS NOT BIEN HOA, South Vietnam, that place where Jerry Koschnick had flown all those missions all those years ago, that place where he had learned so much. No machine gun fire racketed up from the trees below, no enemy troops maneuvered in the shadows of the brush. But Koschnick could be forgiven for remembering. Because here, in central California in the 1990s, he was once again taking a helicopter—a very large helicopter—into a place where it was not meant to go. Near Tyler Meadows, outside of Kernville, Koschnick wheeled through the sky in a Chinook, a sixty-eight-hundred horsepower, twin-rotor giant, an airborne locomotive rushing to a piece of work that would require the finesse of a sports car.

On a hot August day, a pair of wind-driven lowland fires had burned together. On a front that ran for miles, the new alliance charged up mountain ridges into stands of pine and fir. The blowup, called the Stormy Fire, raced to seven thousand feet of elevation and overran a fire camp at Tyler Meadows. Most of the thousand firefighters posted there beat the fire out of camp. But more than sixty remained, mostly seasoned old hands and fire managers fighting a battle to save a portable kitchen and tons of equipment. In the firestorm that whirled around them, tents, sleeping bags and huge sections of trees climbed into the sky, passengers in a tornado of flame. The fire camp group had open space with which to work. They would survive.

But three miles away, where Koschnick was headed, more than a hundred firefighters who had been working on the lines were caught on a steep ridge with the fire front surging toward them. Eleven helicopters were working the fire. Nick Prodan, one of the fire operations officers on Stormy, was on the ridge with the firefighters. When the fire started its run, it fed itself on the upslope and gathered speed and size. Faced with the possibility of a massive entrapment of fire crews, Prodan had called for what would be the West's largest emergency evacuation of firefighters in a decade.

In the wildland fire game, helicopter operations endure hyperregulation, and even small infractions can generate paperwork that goes on for months. Many of the ships on the fire were certified only for carrying cargo and water buckets, not passengers. But the fire's air bosses shredded the rules, and dispensations rocketed down the chain of command. Even before the word came down, ships large and small were flocking to the ridge. Koschnick, who had flown helicopter gunships in Vietnam, was not the first to arrive. But he had a craft big enough to make a difference, a behemoth with a ten-ton payload. And in their rescuer, the firefighters had a pilot who had more Chinook stick time than any other flier in

Above: Clark Tiecke, a BLM helicopter operations manager at Oregon's Warner Creek fire, waits with Columbia Helicopter pilots Jon Baxter and Jerry Koschnick to see if the morning inversion will lift and permit the day's air battle to begin.

■ ■ ■

Left: Wheeling in a steep turn, a fire-fighting helicopter from the Los Angeles County Fire Department, spills water on a chaparral fire near Saugus, California.

the world. On oil field and construction jobs, Koschnick had ranged from New Guinea to Alaska. And now, looking at a landing zone barely adequate for the smaller choppers, he was being asked to thread one more needle.

"Things had gotten out of hand," Koschnick said. "They had little helicopters doing the best they could, but some of them could only take four or five people at a time. They had more firefighters than they could handle. We took two Chinooks in there that had everything stripped out of them—no seats, no seat belts, just the bare floor. Usually all that stuff is absolutely required. You just don't haul people without it. But you don't leave somebody standing on a mountain to burn up because you don't happen to have seat belts. So we hauled whoever we could cram in. It was like Vietnam all over again. We had thirty-five or forty people with all their packs and gear. They were just piled in. It was a mad scramble, but we got them out."

As the Chinooks climbed into the air, firefighters clung to the walls inside. When it was over and the hundred firefighters were on the ground, the fire's helicopter bosses called Lanny Allmaras, the national chief of helicopter operations for the Forest Service. They had confessions to make, and the list of their sins was long. "They told me they'd broken every damned rule in the book," Allmaras said. "And I told them they'd done exactly the right thing."

Just as the airplane had been a gift from World War I to the forest fire world, the helicopter was the bequest of World War II. Its development curve as a fire tool ascended quickly. By the mid-1950s, helicopters were transporting crews and equipment to fires, first in California and then around the West. Massive buckets that swung on long lines and that could drop water or retardant evolved in short order. One of the early improvements in technology was the addition of quick-release connections that enabled the pilot to dump both line and bucket if the rigging snagged in trees or if the helicopter lost power. Another was the creation of bulbous doors that enabled pilots to lean outward and see directly beneath their ships, so that retardant or water could be dropped with great precision. Los Angeles County sidestepped the dangling buckets by building tanks into helicopters, much like the retardant bombers. Ever-larger helicopters came on line each year, and payloads climbed accordingly.

Like the innovators who developed the fixed-wing air tankers before them, the devotees of helicopters in fire fighting had their own odd experiments. One of those innovations was the only scheme that ever sent firefighters jumping out of aircraft *without* parachutes. The brushjumpers, or helijumpers, leaped into the short blue yonder for just a few years in Southern California and the Southwest. Outfitted in heavy, protective smokejumper clothing and wire-masked helmets, they were dispatched to brushy deserts and chaparral mountain slopes where helicopter landings

were not possible. From heights as great as twenty feet they plunged downward. On the ground, they could handle a small fire, or clear a landing spot so more troops could be brought in to battle a large one. But it was audacious work, with a high injury rate. Gradually a network of permanent helicopter landing spots evolved. The brushjumpers were retired.

Other experiments were more successful. The 1950s saw the birth of helicopter attack teams for fire fighting. Usually groups of seasonal firefighters stationed with a helicopter at some outlying camp, they quickly became known as helitack crews and developed an array of skills built around the capabilities of their whirlybirds. As ships grew larger, so did the attack crews. Some operations would cram as many as a dozen groundpounders into a helicopter and whisk them to fires in minutes. Though air tanker planes would increasingly become a federal resource, available on call to states and local jurisdictions, the distribution of helicopters was more democratic. State forestry departments and even some counties with large wildland fire responsibilities bought or contracted helicopters.

Helicopters, although they were not used to drop smokejumpers, brought change to parachute fire fighting. The ships became the prime means for bringing smokejumpers out of the wilderness after fires. But jumpers and helitack firefighters developed an early and bristly sense of political turf over the question of who would fight the remote wilderness fires. Jumpers saw the irony: The rotary-wing aircraft that brought some critics to question the very existence of smokejumping were the same aircraft that made grueling twenty-mile packouts mostly a thing of memory for smokejumpers. The helicopter firefighters, for their part, never quite shook the conviction that no matter how well they performed, no matter how many fires they caught and killed, smokejumping would always remain the public relations darling of the Forest Service and the Bureau of Land Management.

Allmaras, the Forest Service's national chief of helicopter operations, also oversees the airplane side of smokejumping operations. Like a parent stepping into an argument between quarrelsome siblings, he sometimes shakes his head over the persistence of the debate. "No matter how hard you try, those two groups are after each other all the time," he said. "If you look at it honestly, they complement each other and, if they're used correctly, that's how it should work. The smokejumpers shouldn't worry. The helicopters are never going to replace them. And there are always going to be places where you can't send the smokejumpers, but a helicopter can get in."

The helicopter, of course, had been only a technological novelty at the end of World War II. It upgraded its credentials in Korea, bringing in the wounded for medical treatment at MASH units. But Vietnam was the helicopter war, and the 1970s were the beginning of a vastly expanded role for the helicopter in wildland fire. The war, which had begun in the mid-1960s, shipped home a stock of trained and experienced pilots at the same time that national and regional political processes were funding forest fire operations like never before. In the forests of the West, helicopter operations hatched like dragonflies in spring. Nowhere was that more true than in the Pacific Northwest, where a large commercial helicopter fleet built around the logging industry made seasonal contract ships readily available for fire fighting and helitack crews. "It was just a great time," said Wes Lematta, founder of Columbia Helicopters in Oregon and one of the pioneers of airborne fire fighting. "It was always exciting and we were learning things as went. There were all of these times when you'd be camped in some pasture with your ship, waiting to get out the next morning and get back on the fires."

In that same era, the idea of delivering helicopter firefighters directly from the air blossomed. At Chelan in Washington and Redmond in Oregon, some Forest Service innovators picked up an experimental program that had ended abruptly after a critical injury in Alaska. With hardware and techniques stolen from the worlds of rock climbing and skyscraper window washing, they created rappel crews of firefighters who descended from the helicopters on long ropes. Soon, rappel crews were coming out of the sky, zipping down the ropes all over the West.

■ ■ ■

In late July of 1989, fire hit Idaho like Hannibal coming over the Alps. The Payette National Forest alone had 248 fires in a single day. The neighboring private timber fire district of the Southern Idaho Timber Protective Association had another sixty. Adjacent national forests and BLM territory had more fires. Within days, sixty-five hundred firefighters, a squadron of retardant planes and seventy helicopters were in action. It was the sort of conflagration that, like the sweeping Idaho fires of the early twentieth century, emptied sawmills and brought every logging crew within miles into action at a run.

The region's helicopter crews were plunged into a marathon. "What you usually do with multiple starts is fly them and try to decide which one has the most potential to be a large fire," said Glenn Johnston, a helitack foreman for the Payette Forest. "But this was like nothing we'd seen before. On that day you could see thirty or forty smokes in one canyon. Just too many. Sometimes we left them alone for days, because they weren't doing anything. If something started running we'd ferry in some troops to see if they could pick it up. It went on for two and a half straight weeks. Every day we'd go out and just initial attack fires. Day after day after day. Those poor initial attack crews would come back in, and we'd give them a new food bag,

fill their canteens with water, throw them back in the 'copter, and take them out to another fire."

With that mob of small fires, the helicopter crews were doing what they did best, flitting from blaze to blaze like hummingbirds. But helicopter firefighters lead a bifurcated life. When fires are small and scattered, they are committed to initial attack. But big fire, the kind of fire that rolls over thousands of acres and chews through timber as if it were parsley, deals them other jobs. When big fire arrives, the helitackers and the rappellers are seldom found wielding tools on the line. They catch other jobs. They manage helibases at fire camps and remote landing spots deep in the forest. They rig ships for slinging cargo. They create new landing spots in the forest. They see that fire crews camped in the backcountry get timely deliveries of food and fresh water. They become, in effect, conductors, station agents, and baggage handlers for an airborne railroad that moves troops and supplies to the front.

In their workaday existence, helicopter fire crews most often are stationed at an airport, a remote Forest Service ranger district, a rural Bureau of Land Management post or the back lot of some state forestry complex. At some airports, arriving airline passengers can see the rappel crews practicing, making screaming, thirty-second descents down 250 feet of rope while a helicopter hovers overhead. The helicopter firefighters begin their training by soaking up all the basic skills given to groundpounder crews. Then they go on to learn about helicopter operations. Many of them move up to acquire credentials for managing helicopter landing spots or cargo operations. For those who moved into rappel operations, the training includes practice descents from towers. "It takes about a week to get someone to the point of rappelling from the helicopter," said Kyle Engstrom, the Chelan crew foreman who is the nation's senior rappel trainer. "We get a lot of physically active people, ski instructors and runners. It doesn't take that long to get them coming out of the helicopter. But we're always working on improvement. The proficiency rappels go on all season."

Though it is the flashiest program in helicopter fire fighting, helicopter rappelling nearly died in the 1980s. The Forest Service, which had fostered rappel crews, backed away from the concept for much of a decade. Rappel operations were shut down at most western bases. The helicopter congregation blamed smokejumper politics. Management countred by citing cost and safety concerns, particularly the vulnerability of rappellers dangling beneath smaller, single-engine helicopters that were common in the fleet in those years. Some on the fringes of the debate suggested that perhaps the rappellers had talked too often about squeezing out smokejumpers. "I remember the rappellers getting pumped up and seeing themselves as the ultimate replacement for smokejumpers," said Lloyd Duncan, a

Above: With its belly tank primed with a fresh load of water and fire closing in on its landing zone, a Los Angeles County helicopter lifts off to return to battle.

■ ■ ■

Right: At work just before dawn, a Columbia Helicopter maintenance team shares its outdoor garage with a herd of bison during the Yellowstone fires of 1988. Helicopter mechanics, with service trucks and a huge parts inventory, are part of every large fire operation.

Battling to keep flames from adding to the toll of 3,354 destroyed homes in the Oakland Hills Fires of 1991, helicopters flew dozens of water sorties from Briones Reservoir to protect a row of ridgetop houses near Grizzly Peak. The ships beat back fifty-foot flames that came within a hundred yards of the home at the canyon's edge.

veteran fire helicopter pilot who enthusiastically flies a rappel crew at Flaming Gorge in northeast Utah. "Smokejumping is a really sacred thing in the Forest Service. You never get to be one of the fire gods in Washington, D.C., unless you've been a smokejumper. It's a major ticket punch for your career. So you don't go around in the Forest Service talking about how you're going to replace smokejumpers. Some people had to learn that."

But the rappel operations survived their setback. With the concurrence of smokejumping fans in high places and with an increase in the fleet's contingent of larger, safer twin-engine ships, rappel crews once again began coming out of the sky in numbers in the late 1980s. The renaissance began in Arizona and New Mexico, and spread around the West. By converting existing helitack bases to rappel programs, the Forest Service created more than twenty rappel operations, with a corps of about two hundred trained firefighters. Meanwhile, the BLM launched three rappel operations of its own. The conversion is expected to continue until the majority of helicopter fire crews are rappel-trained.

Most of the pilots who fly rappel crews work for large and small Western helicopter companies, which contract for fire season assignments. Often the pilots are posted hundreds of miles from home. Typically they handle the same assignment year after year, an arrangement that fosters a tight sense of teamwork. The rappel pilots and their crews train constantly, operating on the principle that repetition breeds safety. The very early years of general fire fighting from helicopters were marred by injuries, death, and crashes. But, since it became fully operational in 1972, the rappel program has never had a fatality or a serious injury in delivering firefighters from air to ground.

Pilots who fly rappel ships accept the responsibility of human life dangling beneath their ships. Often they must thread needles, holding a solid hover position and centering the rappel ropes down past 150-foot trees to patches of forest floor not much larger than a good-sized living room. The greatest risk is tangling a rope and a jumper in a tree. "It's work that a lot of pilots don't want to do," said Bob Stucke, who works for Queen City Helicopters of Seattle and flies a rappel crew at Gila Center, New Mexico. "It's a specialty. The minute or so that they're on the rope, you are absolutely committed to being in one position. You have to hold the spot, no matter what. The absolute worst situation is to have people on the ropes and get a wind change."

In Vietnam, Duncan flew in operations that involved men on lines beneath the ship. In the military the pilot always had the mechanical capability, and the orders, to cut the line if trouble arose and a crash was imminent. The decision to sacrifice one or two lives to save several in the ship was difficult, but it was sometimes made. "In fire rappelling you fly without that option," Duncan said. "The spotters, the guys who work in the

back of the ship, carry a razor-edged rope cutter. And they're told in training that if the ship gets in trouble—if the lines are tied up in trees, if you're about to go down—they will have to respond to the pilot's order to cut the ropes. But think about Bill, the spotter, back there with his friends, Bob and Susan, on the ropes. In the military you might get the instant reaction to your order and the guy would cut the ropes. But I think that in our situation, where the crews are so tight and people know each other, he's never gonna cut his buddies lose. I think about that all the time when I fly rappellers."

Around the West, fire bosses view the helicopter as the tool of choice for scores of tasks in remote country. But in populous Southern California, flying urban wildfire specialists demonstrate every season that the tool works for them, too. In Los Angeles County, the helicopter attack teams are called fly crews. Some of the county helicopter bases from where they lift off to tackle chaparral fires in the San Gabriel Mountains are bedded in suburban neighborhoods. One, with the ruralish name of Camp Two, actually stands not far from the Rose Bowl, with pleasant homes on one flank and the famed NASA Jet Propulsion Laboratory on the other. The fly crews stand as the first line of defense against many of the brush fires that charge out of the mountains to plague Southern California's suburbs. Called fire suppression aides, the wildfire specialists on the crews often are college students taking fire science courses in local colleges and aiming for a full-time job with the county's structural fire operation.

Many of the metropolitan area's top high school athletes show up in the helicopter program after graduation. And some become so enamored of helicopters and wildland fire that they set aside the idea of riding shiny red fire trucks to urban house fires. The Los Angeles helicopter crews go to battle with a foreman and eight firefighters; when they're on the ground and taking on fire, their helicopters back them up with water drawn from hydrants, cisterns and reservoirs spotted in the mountains around the urban basin. Chaparral fires travel with racehorse speed and landing in their path is not work for the fainthearted. In 1993, two firefighters from a Los Angeles County helicopter crew, Arthur Ruezga and Christopher Herman, died when a small fire in the San Gabriels caught an updraft and rocketed up a narrow, rocky chute of dry chaparral. They were overrun barely a hundred yards from a suburban neighborhood with lush, watered lawns.

A typical federal or state helicopter crew in the rural West takes to the air at first report of fire. A helitack crew is landed as close to the fire as possible. Depending on the size of their ship, the helitack crews may go to battle with as many as ten firefighters or as few as two. A two-person detachment is common for remote lightning strikes that are caught early. Helitack

Above: Managing a helicopter landing zone, Clyde Whyte of Colorado's Mesa Verde helitack crew oversees the demobilization of an initial attack force of smokejumpers and the arrival of ground troops to replace them. On campaign fires, helicopter firefighters switch gears to become coordinators of helicopter operations.

■ ■ ■

Left: a mammoth Chinook from Oregon's Columbia Helicopters lifts off from a mountain pool with three thousand gallows of water for the fire line.

■ ■ ■

Right: Bound for the ground, a pair of Forest Service fire rappelers work their hardware and ropes in a 250-foot descent that takes less than thirty seconds.

crews, like smokejumpers, find that two firefighters can dispense with a two- or three-acre blaze if burning conditions are not extreme. The rappel crews operate on the same principles but usually drop no more than four firefighters at a time. However, they have no need for a helicopter landing zone. Their ropes can spot them onto the side of a steep ridge or into a tiny clearing in the forest.

On some lightning bursts, where nature has sprinkled fire randomly across the forest or desert, helicopters run like a commuter buses, dropping two firefighters here and four there, picking them up and moving them as needed. When crews are in place, the pilot lands, attaches the water bucket to his ship, finds a lake or a stream and swings back to help the groundpounders. The ship will dump water until nightfall, then fly off. The crews, which go in with equipment and provisions for two or three days, will stay. For the small fire starts, they count on a day or two of intense work, digging and burning out, often working well past dark. In the backcountry, they almost always spend one additional night after they think they've whipped a fire. A final perimeter patrol the following morning lets them leave with certainty that the job is done.

In Alaska's vast, roadless, tundra country, almost every fire involves placing or retrieving firefighters by helicopter. Smokejumpers who ride airplanes to fires most often ride helicopters home. Alaska helitack crew members regularly swing out of the initial attack role to take over supervision of native crews who have been flown to big fires. Then the fire world's penchant for conferring large responsibility on the young is very much in evidence. Dave Gilbert, now a helitack foreman for the state of Alaska, once found himself running a fire of three thousand acres with nearly a hundred native firefighters. At the time he was twenty-one, and looked sixteen. The experience provided lessons in both fire management and native humor. "Some of those village crew bosses were fifty years old," he said. "They did everything I asked. They were great. But instead of sector boss, they called me sector boy."

A virus of sorts pervades helicopter fire work, a passion that brings those who do it to talk endlessly about the dual attractions of flames and flying. Those who come to the work often are well-traveled, with experience on ground crews, engines or hotshot outfits. Kelly Martin trekked through most of those steps to a helitack job on a Payette National Forest helitack crew in Idaho. "I like the adrenaline and the challenge of going after fire this way," she said. "Fire to me is a living being. Sometimes people can control it. But there are other times when there's a wild card in there and you just don't know what's going to happen. For me that's the exciting part, the good part. Every assignment is different. This job is never mundane."

Tom Dean, who began his eighteen years of seasonal fire fighting in Washington, found his niche in helitack work in Alaska. His finance degree from Gonzaga University has been shelved. He is a musical composer with recording studio projects to keep him busy in winter and a fire traveler in summer. "Alaska is a wilderness state," he said. "That is the draw. People don't realize how vast and roadless this place is until they see it from the air. It just goes on forever. It's tremendously expensive for people who come up here and really want to see it. They wind up chartering airplanes and still only experience a tiny part of it. But we fly around over it all the time. We are always touring Alaska. The helicopter is our bus. Fire takes us all over this country."

For helicopter firefighters, 1994 was a grueling year. Two firefighters from a BLM rappel crew based at Grand Junction, Colorado, were among the fourteen who died in the fire on Storm King Mountain. A week later, a ship contracted by the Forest Service near Silver City, New Mexico, went down, killing the pilot and two firefighters. In Silver City, a place that counts itself among the fire towns of the West, a thousand people packed a football grandstand for a memorial service.

On big fires, many helicopter pilots don't fly firefighters at all. They pack only water or chemical retardant, making endless trips between the fire line and the nearest lake or stream. The largest helicopters are used solely for that work, and do no crew movements. Most of the firefighting helicopters fly with the mechanical buckets on the end of long lines. The few with integral water tanks grafted onto their underbellies dangle an intake tube that sucks up liquid like a milkshake straw. On some high mountain fires, where creeks are too shallow and too confined to dip a helicopter bucket or a tube, a ground crew will operate a portable pond—a canvas or metal tank filled by gasoline-powered pumps that move water from the stream to create a dipping reservoir for the helicopters. The dip tanks have other uses; on many fire crews, veterans consider any rookie's season incomplete without an involuntary swim in the tank. In the Southern California fires of 1993 some veteran helicopter pilots dipped from the ocean for the first time. In an only-in-California-scene, one squadron of large and small helicopters had to thread their buckets around surfers, while fires raged only two miles away.

■ ■ ■

When wildland firefighters of all stripes get into trouble it is often helicopters that save them. In the late 1980s a rookie California groundpounder became separated from his crew as fire enveloped a ridge. His long run down the ridgeline to safety was successful only because a trio of helicopters kept him in their sights, showering him with light rain for the distance. On Oregon's Paulina Lake Fire in 1988, a helicopter crashed after its water bucket swung up into the tail rotor. But another helicopter was overhead in moments, rappelling a medic down to aid the seriously injured pilot and oversee evacuation. In the era of interface fires, the ability of helicopters to make precision water drops has given them a hero's role. In scores of instances, individual homes have been saved because a water drop stopped an onrushing fire or doused a spot fire on wood-shingle roof.

However, helicopter work on the big fires usually is more ticklish than exciting. Typically the fixed-wing retardant tankers do the dramatic work during initial attack, swooping low over ridges and into canyons when the fire is in its early, racing stages. The helicopters find work at that juncture, too, but much of it is moving troops and cargo, serving as the pack mules of the fire operation. In Alaska, huge twin-rotor ships sometimes hook onto small bulldozers and haul them away, dangling like Christmas tree ornaments, to be used on fires in the backcountry. Helicopters truly earn their money when a fire settles into a long-running campaign, and they will still be working after the airplanes have gone home. Then, they will fly long, long days, moving vast quantities of water or retardant. Very often they'll work in tandem with the ground crews. A helicopter may be teamed with a single hotshot crew dealing with problem spots on one flank of the fire. As firefighters work the line, the ship may use its water to help contain a deliberate burnout, to make a pinpoint drop that will douse a flaming snag, or even, on request, to cool an overworked and overheated crew.

Not all the helicopters on big fires operate under government flag. The big timber companies of the West often own helicopter fleets, and are quick to put them into action when fire blooms in the forest. Very often they wind up working fire on public lands or even on the timberlands of their competitors. In all the timber companies, fire supersedes any other mission for the helicopters. "Everybody knows that fire is the highest priority," said Dale Dempsey, a helicopter pilot for Weyerhaeuser Company. "If I'm flying some company executives and there's a fire, they know they're going to get left right where they're at. I go get my bucket and go to work, and they figure out on their own how they're going to get home."

Depending on the size of the helicopter, the buckets swinging in the air pack as little as a hundred gallons or as much as three thousand. They swing on lines fifty to a hundred feet long, and flying them is not a simple task. The hardest work a helicopter can do is a straight vertical ascent under load. And yet, dipping from small streams or ponds walled in by canyons or surrounding trees, that is often exactly what they are required to do. Most often, the pilots will try to establish forward motion as soon as possible. Sometimes, they achieve the final few feet of clearance over trees or a canyon lip by throwing their ship into a turn, lifting the bucket by making it swing to the side, like a yo-yo on a string.

The state and federal wildfire agencies in the West contract for about 250 small and medium-sized helicopters every season. Virtually every one is assigned to a helitack or rappel crew. Scores of other helicopters, including the huge tandem-rotor ships, are signed to "call when needed" contracts, with pay rates negotiated before the beginning of the season. Those contracts are activated only for campaign fires. Typically the on-call ships will drop whatever commercial job they might be handling when they are summoned for a fire.

Pilots and crews for most of the West's big helicopter outfits lead a gypsy life. Many who work Western fire in the summer will be on jobs in Southeast Asia, Africa, or South America in winter. Picking up and moving a thousand miles for a fire is a routine as familiar as a run to the corner store. "You could be anywhere in the West when it happens, maybe on a logging project or a construction job," said Herb Edmonds, a Columbia crew chief who is a nursemaid for the largest helicopters. "Everything happens quick. When the call comes, you just drop whatever you're doing. You get a parts truck and some people headed for the fire on the ground. Then the ship takes off with just the pilots and the crew chief and a bucket and a few parts. And you know your life is going to be real crazy for a week or so."

The ships and pilots assigned to helitack and rappel jobs on full-season contracts do not come cheaply. The agencies pay a daily standby rate of five hundred to twenty-five hundred dollars, depending on the size of the aircraft. In addition, the meter rolls with an hourly charge of up to 850 dollars for flight time. The hulking twin-rotor helicopters—Vertols and Chinooks—are so expensive that they come on the payroll only when fire is raging. Their charges can run as high as seven thousand dollars an hour, but they are a resource like no other in the long, long days of putting a big fire to rest. "The operating costs seem enormous," said Allmaras, the chief of Forest Service helicopters. "The airplanes and the helicopters both have their niche. But when we get past initial attack, when we have time to get in and set up a portable retardant operation near the fire, we can do really well. If we can keep a round trip in the neighborhood of seven minutes, one of the big ships can outwork two or three large airplanes. And it can fly slower, it can get in closer, it can work with more accuracy. On a fire, that's what helicopters are about."

CHAPTER 8

The Fire Generals

AT MIDSTREAM IN THE ICY NORTH FORK OF THE PAYETTE RIVER, Bill Williams wondered what he would do even if he reached the old man. If the secret of command is to delegate wisely, well and often, how was it that Williams found himself in this place? Here he was, at forty-nine, the general in charge of an Idaho project fire, an up-from-the-ranks commander whose training and position should have had him running a briefing, interpreting a map or hammering out a battle plan with his operations chief. Instead, he was swimming through swift water in his heavy boots, racing flames to the opposite bank and puzzling over what he would do if he reached it.

Miles away in fire camp, his incident command team was tracking multiple blazes bearing down on the isolated mountain town of Lowman, an unincorporated shoestring community that stretched for three scenic miles along the river. Williams, whose team had taken over the fires only the night before, had opted for some ground-level reconnaissance that morning. In all the years he had been a Type I incident commander, seeing the terrain and getting a feel for the fire had been standard practice for him. The collection of four fires he had been handed was only going to grow worse. He had started the morning by getting the few fire crews he had into the field, and by ordering up more. While his command team was working out details of a night shift plan, he would learn the lay of the land he was defending, and take a look at the town that might be threatened.

So, on this late July day in 1989, with the nearest of the fires still two miles from town, he had spent the morning with Morris Huffman, the man in charge of the local Lowman Ranger District of the U.S. Forest Service. Huffman wanted to show him rural homes that might be endangered if the fires made a run. Williams knew that time spent early on with the locals was always good. They knew the roads, the canyons, the wind patterns. Besides, part of an incident commander's job is always politics. When you ride to the rescue of a besieged community, you take the time to talk to its leaders and its citizens.

Williams and Huffman went door-to-door, knocking and talking. The ranger warned homeowners to be prepared to flee if the fires kicked up. Williams helped a bit with that work, easing anxieties where he could, even as he analyzed the difficulties that fire would pose if it funneled up the river's canyon toward Lowman. In late morning, he and Huffman were carrying the word to Enchanted Valley, an isolated rural neighborhood above Lowman. Smoke began to curdle and thicken in the sky. Sensing that fire behavior was picking up, the pair hurried back to Lowman, planning a helicopter scouting flight.

*Above: Day and night,
the pace never slows in the fire camps,
the command centers of big Western forest fires.
The open-air cafeterias are hubs where the troops
of wildland fire swap war stories and the generals
take the pulse of their armies' morale.*

■ ■ ■

*Left: Bob Dunnagan,
a National Park Service fire specialist
and the leader of an interagency command team
for major forest fires, surveys the results
of infrared aerial photography as he contemplates
the next move against a growing fire
in Washington state.*

Then, two miles from the town, a fire along a small stream known as Smoky Creek blew up. In less than half an hour, it converted from a creeping ground blaze to a galloping crown fire. Embers from the fire carried into eight hundred acres of wind-downed, dead timber, a heap of dry giant jackstraws waiting for ignition. Wind speeds rose. Flames erupted in the deadfalls. Suddenly a monster firestorm galloped for Lowman, brandishing flames two hundred feet high. Williams' routine reconnaissance patrol evaporated. Cut off from his command post, he faced a real and present danger. The onrushing fire was only minutes away from the community. Strategizing could wait. With the fire roaring upriver, the urgent need was to get people out of homes and out of town.

Huffman dropped Williams on Highway 21, the road that snaked along the river. While the ranger went to rush people out of Lowman, Williams attempted to cope with the scene on the roadway. For the rest of his life, he would remember that bizarre and frantic tableau. Westbound cars were heading unknowingly into the teeth of the fire, and he had to force them to turn back. Other cars were pulling over to the side and stopping on the road. His experience told him that the gawkers and the tourists were minutes away from incineration. Oblivious to it all, they piled out of their cars, wearing shorts and tank tops, and aiming their cameras at the dreadnought of fire that was roaring toward them. Pushing and yelling, Williams tried to keep them moving, tried to get them back into their cars, tried to make them understand how fast big fire can move.

Soon enough, they understood. The winds screamed to eighty miles an hour. A hailstorm of fiery embers carried into Lowman, crossed the river and touched off hundreds of spot fires. Flames erupted on roofs. The tourists headed east at flank speed, some of them forced to flee so quickly that they had to abandon their own vehicles and catch rides with others. Huffman returned. He and Williams raced upriver ahead of the flames, banging on doors, getting people into their cars and onto the road. Downstream, homes were burning. Over the radio, Williams learned that one of his engine crews was trapped back there, surrounded by fire but safe, unable to move until the blaze passed them.

A row of houses on the south bank of the river was marooned and beyond help, cut off when the fire swept over the Kirkham Hot Springs Bridge and a connecting road. Williams and Huffman had checked the homes before the bridge was blocked. Speeding along the north bank and looking across the water, they could see fire bearing down on the houses, and they believed that all of them were empty. Then they were flagged down by an approaching car. The man and woman in the car,

Randy and Sandy Greer, pointed frantically toward the river. Williams and Huffman saw Murton Blackler on the opposite shore, in front of the houses.

He was eighty-two years old, confused and scared, standing on the riverbank while the fire roared down to take his home. He had driven a half-mile downstream, and found the Kirkham bridge swept by fire. Now he was stranded. He had retreated as far as he could go. The fire, preparing to take the row of homes, was showering embers around him. Huffman pulled his pickup to the bank. Williams jumped out of the truck and yelled to the others to find a rope. He did not fear the fire, but he feared the river. He ran to the stream's edge and looked across fifty yards of swiftly flowing water, snow-melt from the mountains above. He debated taking off his heavy, lace-up boots, but decided he would need them if he made it across.

A mountain stream, even in midsummer, is a numbing, breathtaking, strength-sapping adversary. Williams waded until the water reached his chest, then cast off and began swimming. The rushing water carried him downstream, away from the old man. But Williams made a sort of diagonal progress across the river, getting closer to the opposite shore even as he was pushed down the river. Finally his feet touched. He clambered out of the water and made his way to the bank. Chilled as he was, he could feel the heat rolling ahead of the fire.

Murton Blackler was in shock, barely coherent. The embers were falling thicker and heavier now, driven by a hot, roaring wind. Firebrands nested on the roofs of the homes and began their work. Williams knew he could never get the old man back across the section of river he had just crossed. He considered not attempting a crossing, but simply dragging the man into the shallows and riding out the fire with him. He looked across the water and saw Randy Greer yelling and pointing upstream. Williams hurried the old man in that direction. He reached the spot that Greer had found. Less deep but more swift, it offered a chance.

Across slippery boulders and rushing water, he started into the stream as homes roared into flame behind him. Greer came from the opposite side and they met in the center, where the numbing water was chest-deep. Arms linked, they made a fence of their bodies, holding Blackler on the upstream side, picking their way carefully toward safety and trying to avoid the fall that would send them all tumbling downstream. Huffman and others met them as they walked out of the shallows. In the battlefield confusion of the moment, Blackler was whisked away. Williams never saw him again.

■ ■ ■

Somewhere, thirty years off in the future, a raging forest fire awaits—a land-gobbling, tree-consuming monster that threatens homes, dominates headlines, and strains the resources of the West. And somewhere in the here and now, packing a pulaski on a Western fire crew of the 1990s, just as Bill Williams did in the 1960s, is the young groundpounder who will run that battle. He, or she—for it is all but a foregone conclusion that by then women will be fixtures in the top echelons of wildfire command—will preside over a camp of two thousand firefighters and be beset with a thousand problems.

Homes will have to be evacuated under protest. The national logistics coordinators in Boise will announce that the system can offer no additional hotshot crews until next Tuesday. A section of fire line that cost a million dollars to establish will be overrun in a half-hour fire blowup. The mayor from the town down the road will huff into camp to demand that more local hires be put on the fire line. A ranch kid from a Wyoming fire crew will punch out a college kid from a California fire crew. Cabinet secretaries and congresspeople will show up expecting kid glove treatment and instant air tours of the battle line. The impossible will be heaped upon the merely imponderable, and all of it will demand resolution by afternoon.

In a very real sense, the making of fire generals begins each spring when rookie groundpounders are shepherded through training. In wildland fire, there is no true officer corps, no entry to the game as a commissioned second lieutenant. Every firefighter begins, figuratively speaking, as a buck private, wielding a hand tool, throwing dirt, sleeping on the ground, and, almost always, viewing the whole business as a temporary detour en route to the real work of life.

Many, of course, will hang on for a decade or more of seasonal work. To their own surprise, a few will find a full-time career in fire and, of that number, fewer still will rise to fill command-level positions on the great fires of the West. For the tiny cadre of those who will become fire generals, hints of the future are there. "I realized even as a young groundpounder that I liked the big fires and the whole scene that goes with them," said Dave Liebersbach, a BLM manager who leads an Alaska-based national command team that is dispatched to fires around the country. "Even when I first began, I liked the big fire camps. I liked being out on a project fire for multiple days. I liked dealing with the fires that were a big problem."

Throughout the federal wildfire system, and in most of the Western states, every rookie firefighter who completes training is handed a "red card" of official certification. In a system that confers no collar insignia, no shoulder stripes, no hash marks,

the red card is the definer of rank and ability. For as long as the firefighter stays in the game, the card will reflect increases in experience and training. From firefighter to crew boss. Then onward and outward in dozens of possible directions, to strike team leader or division fire line supervisor or operations chief.

For the tiniest handful, the card will someday read: Incident Commander, Type I. In the modern world of big wildland fire, the IC title attaches to the traditional job of fire boss. Long-gone fire bosses like the colorful, pistol-wielding Edward Pulaski might find the new sobriquet a bit bureaucratic, but would be pleased to know that the old one still gets heavy use around fire camps. The new designation flows from the incident command system that was created after the disastrous Southern California wildfires of 1970. ICS, with its simple organizational charts and its progression of scaled-up responses to emergencies that grow in size, is the framework in which wildland fire is battled in the West.

"One of the interesting things about the command in the wildfire world is that people sometimes have two careers," said Liebersbach, the incident commander who works as a BLM resource manager. "Like me, you can be in a regular job with your agency, a job that has nothing to do with fire. And you work at two levels. One is your GS level, your civil service pay grade, your regular job. And the other is your red card for fire. And one doesn't have to match the other. You can be a low-grade seasonal with very high fire qualifications. You don't have to be a GS-twelve to be an IC-one. You can be a lowly GS-nine and still be up in the top red card levels, running important fire operations."

Incident commanders come in grades, certified on their red cards to direct operations of a given size and complexity. Each fire, no matter how small, gets one, even in the initial attack stage. If two smokejumpers parachute to a half-acre lightning-strike fire in the Bitterroot Mountains, one is technically the incident commander. If a Bureau of Land Management hotshot crew or a Nevada Division of Forestry engine crew takes on a fire, the crew leader or the engine foreman becomes fire boss, and handles all command functions. In some locales, even the initial attack can be huge. In California, with its monumental interface problems and its history of giant fires, the standard response to even the tiniest wildland fire start involves multiple engines, crews, and aircraft.

Should a fire grow in size and complexity, additional resources are marshaled to fight it. Among the resources will be additional management talent, or overhead, in fire camp parlance. The fire will be handed off, perhaps more than once, to a more qualified incident commander as it expands. Along the way, command will metamorphose to a team function. Branches such as planning, operations, logistics, safety, and finance will acquire their own managers, working under the incident commander. If the fire continues to grow, more specialists will arrive, so that a full-blown campaign fire will be buttressed with fire behavior specialists, meteorologists, air operations commanders, mappers, public information officers, medical unit managers, helibase managers, dispatchers, food unit leaders, and intelligence officers.

In most of the West, those overhead positions are drawn from the ranks of full-timers in the public lands agencies. Scattered throughout operations such as the Forest Service, the Bureau of Land Management, and the California Department of Forestry are professionals who hold administrative or technical jobs year-round, but who are trained in various fire management specialties and are on call during the annual fire season. In Alaska, where variations on the standard fire themes are common, both the BLM's Alaska Fire Service and the state Department of Natural Resources use part-time specialists in many of those overhead jobs. Their training matches that of their colleagues in the Lower 48, but they join the agency payroll only for the fire season.

Large fires are handled by incident command teams that are designated as either Type I or Type II, depending on their level of training. The teams are usually interagency outfits, with a mix of members from federal and state land agencies. The Type II teams usually work only within a geographic region of two or three states, and most often handle fires that require up to two hundred people. Trained to handle fires involving forces of a thousand or more, the Type I teams are national resources, and can be dispatched on short notice to fires anywhere in America. When the team is mobilized, its members drop their regular jobs and head off to tackle the assignment. They will be based in some large fire camp, often at a park, a public school, or a county fairgrounds. If they are the first team assigned, they may get the job of creating the fire camp, building an instant city to accommodate the hundreds of firefighters being dispatched from around the West.

A firefighter takes a wind velocity reading with an anemometer from a tiny field weather kit. The commanders of wildland fire operations depend upon weather and fire behavior intelligence flowing up from the field.

· · ·

The national wildfire system fields eighteen of the Type I incident teams. The typical team has eight or nine key members, but may add twenty-five or more specialists in a major fire where it covers all possible functions. On every front, an imported command team has the task of converting chaos to order. "It is a big, confusing, stressful job," said Tom Harbour, a Forest Service fire manager who leads a California-based Type I team. "Who else would sign up to be awakened out of a dead sleep and be jerked out of their home at two in the morning for the opportunity to do something like go to Lewiston, Montana, and sleep in stall number 17 of the country fairgrounds for three weeks? You get all the variations of temperature and noise, you get to work twenty-two hours a day, and you get to sleep in the dry sheep manure. It's a great life."

The ICS system pumps in additional variations for monumental fires. A fire that crosses the boundaries of several agencies may get a unified command structure reflecting the multiple jurisidictions. In fire busts so large that several command teams are at work, each with its own fire to fight, an area command level is superimposed to coordinate their efforts. At those upper levels, where the task is defined as orchestration rather than direct strategic and tactical management, two or more co-equal commanders may represent their agencies. The Yellowstone battle of 1988, for example, involved fires burning in the national park and in adjoining national forests. So the area command function was handled by co-commanders, one from the National Park Service and one from the Forest Service. Together, they managed the efforts of thirteen incident command teams battling individual fires in that conflagration, the greatest wildland fire in American history.

"There is nothing new about what we do," said Rick Gale of the National Park Service, who pulled a long stint as one of the two area commanders for the Yellowstone battle. Like many of the fire commanders, he is a student of military history. "Some of us like to think that fire people invented this incident command system," he said. "If you look at what's really in it, you see it was invented by General George Patton. If you look at some of his battle orders to the Third Army, the terminology is stuff you recognize. And I suspect that if you really look at it, the history of ICS goes back to leaders like Tamburlaine and Alexander the Great. The principles of fire are the same as the principles of warfare. You have the principle of the objective, the principle of the defensive, the principle of simplicity, and, probably most important, the principle of reserves, the idea that you don't commit everything. It's all the same. The only difference is that we're not shooting bullets."

In timber regions, the fire command structure extends into the private sector. Every large timber company has a detailed fire operations plan. Typically the companies own brush engines and deploy their logging crews as firefighters. A few even put on seasonal fire employees. Often fires that begin on timber company lands become joint operations with state or federal agencies. In the largest firms, such as the Weyerhaeuser Company, logging foremen and forestry superintendents are versed in the incident command system and can quickly marshal a hundred or more firefighters. On big multiagency fires, those woods bosses work in the fire command structure, beside their counterparts from the government agencies. In Washington, Weyerhaeuser fields a sort of company hotshot crew, a squad of loggers who volunteer for the assignment, devote extra time to fire skills and are on call during fire season. "They're into it for a variety of reasons, but it's partly a thing of emotion and the excitement of it," said Tom Miller, head of the company's land and timber operations in Washington state. "There's definitely some esprit de corps with it."

Opportunism is perhaps the cardinal virtue of fire generals. Most of them acknowledge that a roiling conflagration marching across the landscape with two-hundred-foot flames cannot be stopped. Much of fire tactics is a waiting game. Work the flanks. Assemble your resources. Do your best to protect homes. Bide your time. And be prepared for the break in the weather that will inevitably come your way. It may come as a cool night or a couple of cloudy days where the humidity rises and the fire behavior moderates. And then you hit it hard. It is a philosophy reflected in the fire camp dogma: "You don't fight a big fire, you herd it. And you make damn sure that you're ready when the weather gives you your break."

On many big Western blazes, fighting fire is the least of an incident commander's problems. The politics that swirl in the smoke of big fires can be intense. The prime difference between Type I and Type II command teams probably is not fire management ability, but political skill; the much-traveled Type I groups

have had regular exposure to the situations that demand Solomon's wisdom. Allan West was plummeted into one of those conflicts on a historic California fire. Until his retirement in 1993, West was the Forest Service deputy chief for state and private forestry, the branch that directs all fire operations within the agency. But, much earlier in his career, he was a part of the epic Marble Cone Fire.

At Marble Cone in 1977, West worked with the command team, handling political problems. The fire perimeter encompassed tens of thousands of acres. In the midst of the battle, a light plane with two passengers crashed somewhere in the fire zone. Because of thick smoke, the wreck could not be located from the air. But it was in a broad area where a huge backfire operation was about to be touched off. The backfire was a crucial tactic needed to prevent the fire from marching over a ridgeline and into the Carmel Valley, home to thousands of people.

"The pilot's family came to me, pleading for us not to do the backfire," West remembers. "It just tore me apart. They were sure that he was such an outdoorsman that he would have survived the crash, that he was alive out there somewhere. It got a little bit violent. The sheriff had to take them away. And there was more to think about than that. I was going to be jeopardizing some firefighters' lives if I asked them to stop the main fire without the backfire. I would have to put them right in front of it. In my own mind, I felt that the plane had crashed within the area that had already burned. I needed to make the decision to backfire, and I did it." Later, after the backfire had saved the Carmel Valley, and Marble Cone had ebbed into the mop-up phase, the aircraft was found at a spot that had burned before the backfire. Its two occupants had died on impact.

Even generals do not operate in a vacuum. Command teams mobilized from afar are handed broad marching orders and carefully defined limitations when they march into a fire camp to take over a big fire battle. The parameters are fashioned by those who represent "ownership" of the land. Typically a national forest supervisor, a national park superintendent, or perhaps a state forester will spell out guidelines or priorities for the imported command team as the fire is handed over to them. In the best of situations, the agency manager is an old fire hand, perhaps even a former incident commander, who understands fire; in the worst, the manager has only a vague idea of the difficulties.

Sometimes the agency priorities are obvious and understandable—a rural community or suburban neighborhood must be defended at all costs. Or the fire boss may be told that protecting a stand of virgin timber, a scenic watershed, a wilderness boundary or a historic trapper's cabin is a prime objective. Sometimes the requirements seem more political than practical, as when an incident commander is told that community good will depends upon local restaurants getting the lucrative job of preparing thousands of sack lunches for the fire lines, even though the fire camp kitchen is perfectly capable of putting them together.

The best known, and most controversial, set of ownership guidelines came from the administration of Yellowstone Park in the 1988 fires. Bulldozers were barred from most parts of the park, fire engines were largely required to remain on roads, and digging of fire lines or the use of chain saws was prohibited in some areas. The Yellowstone position, not wholly indefensible, was that the philosophy of the National Park Service found the natural scars of fire, which would heal, easier to accept than the unnatural scars of fire fighting, which could last for centuries. At Yellowstone, firefighters and incident commanders—particularly those who had never fought fire in a national park—chafed at the restrictions and at the mind-set that sometimes seemed to accompany them. On one occasion, an engine crew that drove across a Yellowstone meadow to head off a fire was issued a warning citation by park police. On another, some battle-

fatigued hotshots who had spent over forty continuous hours on the fire lines were reprimanded by a park ranger for soaking their feet in a mountain stream.

Political awkwardness is involved anytime a local agency manager hands over a piece of turf to an imported fire team. Real or imagined, the stigma that local forces were unequal to the task, perhaps even that local fire bosses made bad decisions, can hang in the air. Groundpounders and tanker pilots who come from afar to fight the battle are invariably lionized. Communities nail up testimonial signs to honor them. But the imported fire commanders can be subjected to the sort of second-guessing usually reserved for local high school football coaches, especially in rural areas where critics with outdoor knowledge are in great supply.

Sometimes local fire and public safety operations, and local politicians, mesh smoothly with the visiting giant in their midst, and the incident commanders and their troops all finish the battle as community heroes. At Mammoth Lakes, California, a 1992 fire was halted at the outskirts of town. Before the firefighters shipped out, the community threw a massive party, complete with food, live music, and testimonials.

But command teams know that if the politics of fire do not play out well, they will be convenient, in absentia scapegoats once they have gone. "When you take a team in on a fire, you really come to understand that you're a hired gunslinger," said Brian Barber, a career Forest Service fire management officer based in northeast Utah and the commander of a Type II team. "Sometimes it's just like the Old West. Everybody wants you around until the bad guy is dead. And then, the sooner you leave town, they better they like it."

■ ■ ■

A malevolent lightning storm triggered three thousand fires to launch the Northern California-Southern Oregon fire bust of 1987. Quick response nipped all but forty or so of the starts in the bud. But the survivors of the Labor Day weekend storm lived to become giants, and they made the Siskiyou Mountains their playground for two months, until winter rains blew in off the Pacific.

For firefighters, it was the best and the worst of times. The college students had signed off to go back to their classrooms. For those groundpounders who remained on crews shored up

■ ■ ■

A 250,000-acre Alaska fire devours spruce trees between the Toklat and the Teklanika rivers. Giant blazes bring into play all the elements of the forest fire world's command and logistics functions.

A mix of Forest Service and California Department of Forestry crew bosses are briefed before taking their outfits into battle at California's Fountain Fire. Like the military organizations that are its model, the forest fire command system is designed to percolate information downward from commanders to troops in the field.

■ ■ ■

with replacements, fire burned on every quarter. Big late-season paychecks were a certainty. But the mountain nights were cold and the days were hot. As the weeks rolled on, the fires never seemed to give ground. The National Guard was pulled onto the fire lines, and then the Army. The country was so rugged, so remote that some fire crews could not be brought back to camp each night. Instead, they were "spiked out," sleeping in the open on ridges high in the mountains, living on canned military rations or the occasional hot meal delivered by helicopter or by mule pack-strings, which remain an essential element in the era of high-technology fire fighting. Once a week they would be hauled into one of the fire camps that blossomed that fall and given a day off to take showers, do laundry, and make telephone calls. Draining fatigue was a fact of life, but the big overtime rolled on and on, and no one wanted to go home.

In every large fire camp, banks of pay phones sprout after a day or two. Western telephone companies are geared to in-

stall them on short notice when big fires hit. On a Friday in the midst of the long campaign, April May, a Forest Service firefighter from Washington, stood in the interminable line at the phones in the Longwood fire camp, a few miles above the Oregon-California border. She fell into conversation with the weary, yellow-shirted firefighter ahead of her. He had been hauled in from a spike camp for his day of rest and was preparing to head back to the lines.

"Got to call my girlfriend," he said. "Got to tell her that we're gonna have to postpone our wedding until this is over."

"That's too bad," May said. "When was it going to happen?"

"Tomorrow," he said. "I sure hope I can reach her."

Fire camps are the venues of the generals, the instant cities they create when campaign fires bring firefighters from around the West. Though each is different, all are tapestries of humanity in extremis, with heat, dust, exhaustion, and a war-zone sort of urgency as the common threads. Like the circus lifting its canvas in some pasture at the edge of town, a Western fire camp rises almost overnight, whole and complete, with its own government, transportation system, cafeteria, communications network, weather station, police force, clothing outlet, garbage service, public relations office, medical clinic, post office, and corner store. But more than all of that, it becomes the crossroads where the equipment and technology and expertise of the Western wildfire system meet. Tossed up outside a school, in a forest park, at a county fairgrounds, or somewhere in the vastness of the desert, fire camps are communities with frenetic life histories that may span less than three weeks.

"In two days we build a city to provide all the things any city would have," said Fred Dutli, logistics officer on a Pacific Northwest national command team. "But where you decide to put it is crucial. If you're not careful, you might choose a spot where the fire will be coming through in a day or two." The typical camp is temporary home to no more than two thousand firefighters. Additional camps are thrown up if a fire pulls in more troops. The seasonal and full-time wildfire force in the West, numbering fifty thousand in peak years, is a community small enough that a gathering of its troops always will have an element of reunion. A hotshot crew from Washington will renew acquaintances with a hotshot crew from Arizona. A New Mexico Apache will encounter a Montana Sioux she last saw on a fire in Colorado. A portable shower contractor will deal for the third time in four years with a command team's logistics officer.

"After a few years at this, you go to a fire camp and you know what's going to happen," said Steven Alarid, a firefighter from Oregon's Siuslaw National Forest. "You see people that you've known over the years. They're from all over, from all the fires you've ever been to. They're friends, but they're from everywhere, and you only see them at fire camps. The place turns into a neighborhood, a little community. It's really one of the best parts of doing this. It's part of what makes it meaningful work for me."

A camp established adjacent to public buildings may use classrooms or a park headquarters for its command functions. But the typical built-from-scratch fire camp will have at its heart a compound of garage-sized squad tents and jerry-built plywood offices with tarp roofs, a center for all the quasi-military functions of operations and planning and mapping, as well as the crucial business of running the camp itself. Within sight will be a portable kitchen capable of cranking out up to eight thousand meals a day, a truck that provides hot-water showers, a supply cache that can furnish everything from paper clips to chain saws. The medical unit, the timekeeper's tent and the camp bulletin board with its collection of newspaper clippings and official pronouncements will be clustered near the camp's heart.

Somewhere nearby, a commissary will peddle such essentials as toiletries, socks, and boots. It will be operated by a private contractor, but under an arrangement that may permit cash-short firefighters far from home to charge the purchase of necessities against their paychecks.

Beyond that impromptu civic center, as distant as possible from the noise of trucks and generators and refrigeration units, row upon row of tents will bake in the sun. Backpack-style dome tents have become popular with some fire crews. But plastic tarps, rope, and two-by-fours, artfully combined to make an open-sided shelter large enough for a twenty-person fire crew, remain the architectural material of choice at most fire camps. Often crews decorate their group sleeping areas with homemade signs. A few who have come from great distances, especially Eastern fire crews dispatched to Western fires, may fly a state flag. Big fires run on two twelve-hour shifts. In the daylight hours, when the temperature is often somewhere above ninety degrees, the night shift is always seeking shade and sleep in fire camp. Its weary refugees will cluster under sun-blocking tarps or beneath trees, trucks, buses, and cardboard lean-tos.

Somehow, despite the punishing work, a few firefighters maintain an excess of youthful energy. Hackysack, the simple game where a tiny leather bag is kept aloft with fancy footwork, is the unofficial game of fire camps. At every camp, the off-duty scene will offer groups of firefighters, some of them Nureyevs of the game, circled up, spinning and kicking, keeping the bag in flight. Hackysack is defined as noncompetitive recreation, but some hotshot crews add their own macho twist and demand twenty pushups from a player who flubs a pass. Sometimes park and schoolyard fire camps offer basketball goals and, no matter how punishing the fire line shifts, the courts are busy.

Like a town anywhere, a fire camp is not immune to humanity's failings. The typical large camp will have a police force of up to a half-dozen officers. Usually the group is headed by a uniformed law enforcement officer from one of the federal or state land agencies, and it may include off-duty local police hired for camp patrolling. Petty thefts, fights, and vehicle accidents are the most common problems. Drugs and alcohol show up occasionally, despite the fact that their presence is prohibited in fire camps. In the tight confines of the camps the agencies, especially the federal agencies, react swiftly to instances of racial or sexual harassment. An incident is enough to get an offending firefighter or crew shipped home immediately.

Fire camp law officers find that their problems multiply when a camp is plunked into a populated setting, such as a city park. Every fire crew, it sometimes seems, has at least one member willing to try sneaking into camp with a six-pack of beer from the convenience store down the street. Opportunities for friction with local residents abound in such situations. "The setting of a fire camp makes a major difference," said Jim Keefer, a Forest Service law enforcement officer from Oregon. "If you put it out in the sagebrush, miles from anywhere, all kinds of problems just seem to go away."

On the very largest fires in the very busiest seasons, real generals stride through fire camps. Soldiers, Marines, and National Guard units and their commanders come to the lines when the West has more fires than its seasonal army can handle. Through a U.S. Army office empowered to mobilize military resources for civilian emergencies, troops of any major service branch may be dispatched to forest fires, a triggering of the same federal linkup that activates the military for hurricanes and floods. National Guard units, activated by their state governments, are found even more often on the fire lines of the West. In all the military units, the troops find that fire provides them with an abundance of war stories to haul home. "The troops like fire because there's a variety to it," said retired Army Major General Todd Graham, who took three thousand soldiers onto fires in Idaho. "They see it as something more than a couple of weeks of training on a military range."

The military generals sometimes regret the interruption of their regular training and preparedness cycles. And they are occasionally vexed by the consensus-style management used in such high echelons as the National Interagency Fire Center. But they also admit that, from a military standpoint, the fires become valuable real-life exercises in transportation, planning, and operations. And they have found much to praise in wildfire organization and its paramilitary style. When military troops are activated for fire duty, each platoon, each company, each battalion gets a designated training and liaison officer from one of the fire agencies. That officer stays with the troops through their period of fire duty. On the big fires, a general is blended into the top command structure, and other officers work with their counterparts in the fire organization.

"That's the part of the system that works the best," said retired Army Major General Thomas Cole, who oversaw the movement of more than eight thousand soldiers and Marines to the Yellowstone fires in 1988. "When you get to the level of the fire crews and the incident commanders, it goes very well. Our troops found a lot to respect there. We were in it for weeks. Our people pulled some very tough assignments. But what came out of it was a great deal of mutual respect between the two organizations."

Most fire commanders, like their military counterparts, worry about the morale of their troops. In fire camp, they take the pulse of their army. "You can easily become isolated," said Tom Harbour, the Type I commander. "Any good incident commander knows how to break the bubble. You get out and walk around camp. You talk with the groundpounders. You ask them about the food. You look to see how tired they are. You find some of those hotshot bosses that have been around forever on fires in the West—the Paul Gleasons and the John Wills. They'll tell you. And they'll be short and succinct. Because they know. They understand what I want."

In very long-running fire campaigns, morale becomes a command concern of increasing priority. Crews may catch a day off after two weeks on the line. If civilization is so distant that rest and recuperation time must be spent in camp, the command team may move in some mild diversion, perhaps a big screen television and some movie videos. Sometimes a local country or bluegrass group will swing through a camp and donate a few hours of music, or a chiropractor or masseuse may volunteer a few hours of service. The longer a fire camp operates, the more trappings of home it takes on. Someone in the facilities unit, the group that oversees the camp operation, will erect a tall post in the center of the camp, and throw out some precut signboards. Within a day, the post will bristle with hometown signs.

Not everyone is enamored of the fire camp scene. Older hotshots and smokejumpers sometimes prefer being spiked out in the bush with a few crewmates, avoiding the long lines, noisy generators, and layers of authority, even if it means eating packaged military rations and doing without creature comforts such as showers. "The camp scene has gotten so big," said Jon Curd, the BLM smokejumper based at Boise. "Sometimes it seems like there's twenty people in support for every one person on the line. It's like going to a big city somewhere. People seem to be worrying more about portable toilets and caterers than about fighting the fire."

But occasionally the luck of the draw on fire assignments serves up camp accommodations beyond a firefighter's wildest dreams. In the catastrophic fire season of 1994, Oregon's Union Hotshots racked up nearly sixty days on the road before they were posted to fires raging around Wenatchee and Chelan, Washington. Their assignment, they learned, would be a long spikeout to the Lake Chelan National Recreation Area, a remote Cascade Mountains site accessible only by aircraft or boat. Usually such an assignment means a week or two of existing on prepackaged military rations. But not this time. On the lakeshore at Stehekin, at the edge of the recreation area, were a resort and a guest ranch, which quickly made the switch to feeding firefighters after fires drove off most of the tourist trade. Early each morning the road-weary 'shots would head for the dining rooms, enjoy breakfasts that included such niceties as bread pudding and scones, then helicopter off to the fire lines with lunches packed by the resort chefs. When the crew tumbled

Above: A fire camp, such as this installation at Burns, Oregon, is an instant city, erected overnight to serve as home for a thousand or more firefighters.

■ ■ ■

Left: On the first night of a fire camp operation, an outdoor food line provides dinner. Twenty-four hours later, a full kitchen operation will be in place.

Above: On long-running fires, crews find time to decorate their sleeping areas. Some take their artwork home and maintain a crew collection of the signs they have posted in fire camps around the West.

. . .

Right: When fires run for weeks, camp facilities officers look for ways to boost morale; erecting a couple of posts and providing the makings for hometown signs always works.

. . .

Below: Hotshot firefighters from Idaho and California work off surplus energy. Hackysack, the footbag game, is the unofficial sport of fire camps.

into camp after a long day, sumptuous dinners were waiting. The kitchen staffs even managed to come up with that Southern staple, grits, for a contingent of Mississippi firefighters who were dispatched to Stehekin to provide standby structure protection.

In the early decades of this century, fire camp food often was served up by church ladies and forest rangers' wives. The Civilian Conservation Corps crews of the 1930s had their own camp cooks. In the years just after World War II, the Forest Service and some of the state forestry departments operated field kitchens at big fires. It was a cumbersome business, usually built around a huge cast iron cookstove that was trucked into the woods to become the center of a tent mess hall. But the technological and tactical explosion that swept the wildland fire world in the 1960s blew through the kitchen, too.

In the middle of that decade, Hugh Ferguson, a retired Air Force mess sergeant from South Dakota, began contracting to serve fire camps with mobile kitchens and cook crews. He was followed into the business by John and Wayne Keener of Seattle. Now eighteen western companies compete for annual fire camp contracts, offering not only staffed kitchens, but such camp necessities as portable showers, potable water systems, mobile laundry units, satellite telephone hookups, generators, and floodlighting.

About twenty-five of the two-hundred-thousand-dollar commercial kitchen units operate around the West under federal contract, pre-positioned in strategic locations during the fire season. In addition, several of the state forestry departments and Indian tribes run mobile camp kitchens. Food operations are one of the many areas where the U.S. military establishment acknowledges taking a lesson from the wildfire world. The Army was so enamored of the mobile kitchen units used by the California Department of Forestry that, during the Persian Gulf War, it commandeered and shipped to the Middle East a half-dozen new kitchen units that were bound for California.

In the standard twelve-hour work shift of a fire operation, firefighters eat breakfast and dinner in camp, and draw a sack lunch for the middle of their shift. Fire camp food is usually basic fare, served in large quantities. But the fire catering operations, like most restaurants of the 1990s, offer expanded salad bars and an alternative menu of vegetarian meals. Kitchen crews are expected to play the attitude game, too, because some incident commanders say food is the single most important morale factor on a long-running fire. The camp kitchens will serve up birthday cakes on occasion or offer a Chinese meal complete with chopsticks. "In eighty-six, we were on a fire that was winding down at Prairie City, Oregon," said John Keener. "The incident commander threw a vaudeville show and asked our crew to help. So our bunch pulled together an act. We try to be part of the fire camp community. And we absolutely demand of our

people that they are smiling and cheerful and pleasant when those firefighters come in off the line, even if it's three o'clock in the morning.

"Except in Alaska" is an axiom of the wildfire world. The frontierish state, where the spruce bough is the tool of choice for beating out tundra fires, plays many parts of the game in ways distinctly its own. Alaska seldom throws up fire camps, at least not the big, sprawling, commodious camps replete with electrical generators, hot showers, and full-service kitchens. Such camps are built by trucks and the tonnage they can deliver. In the vast, roadless reaches of the northernmost state, firefighters see themselves as necessarily leaner and meaner. Delivered by helicopter or airplane or parachute into the bush, they travel light. They toss up tents or crude shelters and, on occasion, spend a month or more in their rude bivouacs. They bathe, when they bother, in the cold water of creeks or muskeg ponds. Provisioned by the ubiquitous paracargo operation of the BLM's Alaska Fire Service, they receive fresh food from the sky every three days, dig refrigerator pits in the permafrost, and cook for themselves.

■ ■ ■

"The first year I was an IC, I had a fire and was making a point of walking around camp one day," said Brian Barber, the Utah command team leader who blends the savvy of the modern fire general with the crustiness of yesteryear's fire boss. "I saw a firefighter come walking up to supply. This kid was black from head to toe. He'd probably been out on the line for thirty hours. He was whipped. His shirt was ripped. His pants had burn spots. He's standing at the supply counter asking if he can get a new Nomex shirt. The guy behind the supply table is wearing brand new Nomex, but he's telling the kid that they don't have any more to issue. I stepped around the corner. I looked at the guy behind the table. And I said, 'Take it off. Give it to him.' It may have been the most important thing I ever did on a fire."

The logistical and organizational stream that ends at the fire camp supply table is fed by many tributaries. Just as fires are managed first by local incident commanders, then handed off to imported management teams if they grow large, so the equipping and manning of a fire operation is launched as a local effort but ripples outward through the system as the demands of the fire grow. In the West, virtually every local BLM resource office, national park, Forest Service ranger district and state forestry field station has a fire cache, a place where the tools of initial fire attack are stored. At a local district or park ranger station, it may be a space smaller than a two-car garage—home to a collection of pulaskis, Nomex shirts, hard hats, gasoline-powered pumps and fire hose.

But progressively larger caches wait further up the organizational chain, at such places as the headquarters of a national forest or at the main fire building of a large national park such as Rocky Mountain. At the top of the system are eleven national interagency caches, all but two in West. In those vast warehouses, the multimillion-dollar stock ranges from canteens to computers to medical kits to first aid gear to sleeping bags to radios to pencils, supported by year-round staffs of repair and reconditioning experts. Much of the material is prepackaged into kits designed to serve a fire of a given size—two hundred people, five hundred, a thousand. For reasons of time, distance, and geography, some of the regional caches operate strategically placed satellites, so that their resources are not all in one place.

Fighting fire is an intricate ballet of command and supply, with a choreography that leaps across the miles of the West. Once it has received its broad objectives from the agency that controls the land, the command team imported to handle a growing fire calls the shots on strategy and tactics. The general and his planning and operations chiefs decide where to deploy their troops, where to make a stand, where to sacrifice acreage. But they do not control the resources. They must ask others for the crews, helicopters, and airplanes they need to fight the battle. The command team has only one fire to worry about, but those who dispense the materiel and the manpower may have many. Sometimes they must say, "No," or at least, "Not now." Invariably, supply intrudes upon strategy.

"There's a lot of wheeling and dealing when things are busy," said Dolly Davis, a logistics coordinator in a regional center in Portland, Oregon. "Everyone who calls you thinks that their need is the most urgent. Sometimes I have to explain to them that they're not the only show in town. Sometimes you have to say, I can't give you any Type I crews for thirty-six hours, so what do you want instead? We have what we call tanker wars. You've got several pretty hot fires in the region and maybe three or four tankers flying on each one. And then you get a new start. And you have to decide who's going to lose a tanker. We all have to play the game. Nobody gets all the toys."

Unlike the bad old days before interagency cooperation, most Western wildland fire is now attacked on a "closest resource" concept. So, a state forestry crew, if it is nearest to a fire outbreak on federal land, may be the first to roll into action. If a fire grows, the closest resource concept will cover its early hours or days. The agency that has primary protection responsibility for the land will take over after a day or so, but it may fight the battle with help from any agency that is an immediate, contiguous neighbor. By the time the fire outstrips the resources of those nearby units, a Type II or Type I command team has probably been imported and the extended logistical system is being tapped. The more the fire grows, the greater its needs will be and the farther into the system it will reach. But the concept of the closest resource will still be the guiding principle.

In the logistical extension of the closest-resources concept, the regional logistics coordinating centers and regional caches each provide for the needs of fires within their area, most often two or three Western states. The Albuquerque coordination center, for example, and the regional cache at Prescott, Arizona, tend to the needs of fires in Arizona and New Mexico. The coordination centers, because they tap all agencies, often have interagency staffing, with both state and federal representatives from their regions. The same is true of some of the caches. The caches ship the hand tools, power equipment, and camp supplies needed for the battle. Meanwhile, the coordination center drums up crews, engines, aircraft, food and shower caterers, and any additional overhead personnel needed to run the fire.

The coordination centers have the feel of military situation rooms, with computer consoles and wall-sized maps, studded with moveable colored lights that represent planes and crews. During a big fire bust, the dispatchers split up the task. One handles airplanes, another moves crews, another brokers overhead specialists. For days on end, they are busier than stock exchange floor traders. They spend shifts of up to twelve hours on the phone, fielding requests from fire sites and wheedling equipment or manpower from local jurisdictions that can spare them. Some resources, such as hotshot crews, air tankers, and larger helicopters, are designated as national resources. They can be assigned only through one of the regional coordination centers. No local district has claim on them. They belong to the system.

To bring some balance to that system, most coordination centers assign an intelligence officer, who develops information on all fires and assesses comparative needs. Bob Lee handles that job at the Albuquerque center. "When it's going heavy with lots of fires, there's definitely some gamesmanship in it," he said. "You get the people who don't have a fire on their district, but don't want to release their people or their equipment because they're afraid they might have a fire. And you get the people who will ask for more than they need because they know their request will get cut back. All those games get played."

Ultimately, when fires grow huge and the numbers increase, all roads lead to the National Interagency Fire Center in Boise. When regional coordinating centers and regional caches can no longer meet their own needs, they turn to the national center. The generals of transport and supply work there. The center, a fully interagency operation, brokers equipment, aircraft, firefighters, and fire management specialists on a national scale, drawing from regions that are not busy to help regions that are. The center's dispatchers and logistics coordinators work with the same intensity as those at smaller regional and local dispatching centers, but they play the game on a chessboard as big as all of America. As the wildfire world's version of the Pentagon, NIFC alone can send a Montana air tanker to California or move an East Coast fire crew to Oregon.

Two national coordinators, Skip Scott of the BLM and Woody Williams of the Forest Service, oversee the process, making their deals with the regional coordination centers, rushing people and equipment through the pipeline in a complex game that relies heavily on jet transport aircraft and over-the-road trucks. Typically a push on resources begins with an order for crews. They are located and dispatched. If the distance is too great to be driven, air transport is arranged on

commercial airlines, chartered planes, or, perhaps, aboard the two jetliners the center keeps on contract through the summer. The number of crews mobilized defines much of the rest of the work, so dispatchers then turn to the task of moving a camp setup, caterers, showers, sleeping bags, radios, and tons of equipment to the fire. Anywhere in the West, the system can put in place a thousand firefighters in a single day, most of them people who began that day not knowing that they would finish it hundreds or thousands of miles from home.

"A thousand people is fifty crews," Williams said. "If we can't move fifty crews in a normal day, we're not doing our job. If we can see it coming, if we have just a little bit of lead time, we can get close to a hundred crews in that time. Once we had a Friday evening with orders for two hundred twenty crews,

■ ■ ■

On big fires in Alaska's tundra country, where every piece of equipment must be helicoptered or air-dropped, comfort is defined by rude shelters fashioned from poles, plastic sheeting, and canvas.

over four thousand people. There was already fire in a lot of places—the northern Rockies, the Northwest, the Great Basin, California—so we were really scratching for crews from other places. We had eighteen dispatchers working every shift that weekend. I felt sorry for them. They hardly got out of their chairs to go to the restroom or get a drink of water. The logistics problems were incredible. But by Sunday evening we had virtually all of those crews moved."

The center's directors, representing all the federal agencies involved in wildfire, sit as a multi-agency command, or MAC, group. Despite their overarching responsibility, they still define their role as logistics, not strategy. But more than any other place in America, they deal with the big picture, because wildfire updates from all over the nation flow constantly into NIFC. In practice, the MAC group is a governing body making decisions

on application of policy or resolving tough questions as fires are under way. Williams and Scott, the national coordinators, run the day-to-day operation and bring their actions to the command group for review, advice, and consent.

Jack Wilson, a BLM veteran whose career and management style are the stuff of legend in the fire community, chaired those command meetings for years until his retirement. "The pattern's always the same," he said. "Wherever they are, the fires kick up in the afternoon. Along about dark, the incident commanders all over the West are wringing their hands and saying, 'Hey, we can't catch the son of a bitch,' and they start yelling for help. So we spend a big portion of the night looking for a solution.

"It takes special people to sit in there and make the tough calls. You're aware that when you make decisions, you may be

■ ■ ■

In search of dinner fixings, Sean Farley delves into a natural refrigerator dug in the permafrost of Alaskan tundra. The vast, roadless reaches of the forty-ninth state preclude the sort of well-equipped fire camps found elsewhere in the West.

deciding that forests in Oregon are going to burn so that houses in California will be protected. You have to have some principles to stand by, and yet you have to be flexible. You can't always go by the book. There were lots of times when we did things without waiting for the authority to do them. You run into some great attitudes. Everybody knows that the Forest Service is far and away the biggest player in the resource game. But I can remember a Forest Service director in one of those meetings, saying that those who have more simply have to give more."

The NIFC command group meets at least twice daily during fire season, and its second meeting can run until midnight. The regular routine includes briefings by Rick Ochoa, who is based at the center and heads the National Weather Service system of fire weather forecasting. His staff coordinates the assignment of fire weather specialists to big fires, reviews their data, and builds it into maps that become part of wildfire probability forecasting for the nation. That work can effect logistical decisions. A predicted lightning storm for the Southwest, for example, means that crews should be left in place there and not pulled off for fires elsewhere in the West. When multiple fires rage around the West, representatives of the state foresters, the U.S. military, and the General Services Administration, the purchasing arm of the federal government also sit in on the sessions.

The world of forest firefighting includes radio communications, infrared photography, and sophisticated meteorological systems, but it rgularly encounters conditions where horse and mule pack strings remain the best way to supply remote fire crews.

■ ■ ■

"The extra people in those meetings are going to be there to talk about what bothers them," said Dick Stauber, the Forest Service representative who serves as the command group's chairman. "The Army guy will want to know if we're facing such high demand that he should start anticipating a call-up of troops. With the GSA representative it's different. We know that in a big fire bust, we go through a quarter million double-A batteries a day for radios and headlamps. Can he keep them coming if we run out in the caches? How many can he get? Where will they come from? How will he get them to the fires? Out of our meetings will come decisions that will put some American factories on overtime immediately. The GSA guy can walk right out of our meeting and make that happen."

In late summer of a busy fire season, the national fire center vibrates with activity. Located beside the runways of Boise's airport, it is home to a smokejumper operation and such technical marvels as a lightning detection system that covers all of the contiguous western states, a twin to another that covers all of Alaska. Hundreds of crews from around the West jostle through the place every summer, often laying over and bivouacking on the grounds as they're being flown from one fire to another or held in reserve for the fire of greatest need.

In the Boise supply cache, seasonal teams of equipment specialists load pallets of fire gear for rush transport by truck or plane. A team of experts will be checking, repairing, and shipping gear from the largest collection of portable emergency communications equipment in America. Periodically, small, high-speed planes jammed with infrared photography equipment will leave for missions that may involve late-night flyovers of as many as a dozen fires in four states. The filmstrips are in incident commanders' hands by morning.

Boise stands as the pinnacle of a technology, supply, and manpower system that can seem bottomless. A few who work in the system confess that they once believed that was true. But in 1988, the year fire swept Yellowstone Park and much of the rest of the West, demand emptied warehouses from the tiniest ranger districts to the largest interagency caches. "You'd think it couldn't happen, but it did," said Chuck Sundstrom, manager of the huge national cache at Missoula. "We were scratching for everything. We were literally out of things like sleeping bags. I was sending people into downtown Missoula, to places like K-Mart, and buying every sleeping bag in the store. And that was happening all over America."

But even then, there were reserves, because the wildland fire community is capable of linking hands across international borders. American fire crews and equipment are occasionally dispatched into Mexico and Canada. In 1988, Canada jumped at the opportunity to return the favor. "One day in the middle of it, when we were getting close to rock bottom, we got a big aircraft from our military, and we made a huge run through Canada," said Jack Wilson, the former chairman of the inter-agency fire center. "All the way across the country, that plane landed and picked up pumps and pulaskis. The Canadian fire center, our counterpart, set it up. They just said, 'We'll round it up and it will be ready when you get here. Come and get it. Take what you need.' It was quick. They handed it over, and we sorted out the paperwork later."

■ ■ ■

Storm Creek. Apt name. In the generations ahead, old fire hands will say, as they have already begun to say, that either you were at Yellowstone for the big one, or you weren't. You either made it to the most memorable war of all, or you didn't. And if you were at Yellowstone, you either made it to Storm Creek, the biggest battle in the war—or you were glad you hadn't. Joe Stam, an operations chief on a Type I command team based in Alaska, flew out of the northland to do Storm Creek. Stam is fire operations manager for the Alaska Department of Natural Resources. The Type I team on which he served was an inter-agency outfit headed by Dave Liebersbach, the veteran BLM fire hand who, like Stam, is from Fairbanks.

"We were taking over from a Type II team that had just been getting their butts kicked," Stam said. "Usually when you take over a fire, the team you're relieving doesn't want to let go, doesn't want to give up what they've been running. When we got there, they had their bags packed. They wanted to leave right away. I could barely talk their ops chief into doing a flyover of the fire with me, so that he could brief me. They just wanted to get out of there. There was an argument, and finally his IC let him take the flight with me. I saw amazing things. And when we got back on the ground, the other guy just looked at me and said, 'Good luck.'"

Storm Creek, which would soak up more than eight million dollars before it died in the early snows of fall, burned at the northeast corner of Yellowstone Park. Like so many of the other fires that stalked through the park that summer, it would go where it wanted to go. In the tenure of Liebersbach's team, it would march out of Yellowstone and make a frontal attack on the communities of Silvergate and Cooke City. The towns would be evacuated, amid factional cries that park management had permitted the fires to grow too large, and that the wrong tactics were being used to stop them. Every day and every night in the forests around the two tiny communities, crews grubbed fire line, worked themselves to exhaustion, and returned on the next shift to see their efforts overrun by fire. Being trapped in a meadow by surrounding fire or being chased out of the woods at a dead run were common occurrences.

"It was a third generation forest, and it had never burned," Stam said. "Not for three hundred years. One generation of trees had grown and then blown down or fallen over. Then another generation on top of that. And the third generation was already good-sized. It was ripe. And when it burned it was like nothing you ever saw. We had flames up a thousand feet and mushroom clouds that would go up every afternoon to forty thousand feet. It was like Hiroshima. The fire behavior was unbelievable. You'd see these mature trees bending over horizontal and snapping off at root level just from the fire winds. When our team got there, I had started building a plan. You always build in lots of contingencies. I had seven contingencies that allowed for the worst possible cases of things going wrong. Three weeks later, I was down to the last one, the one I thought I'd never use. I was burning out big-time to save Silvergate and Cooke City."

Liebersbach's team had at its disposal twelve hundred firefighters, twenty-seven engines, six bulldozers, seven heli-copters, and five mammoth C-130 air tankers. It would not be enough, just as all the other measures tried in that summer were not enough. Thick smoke kept the tankers out of the air and curtailed helicopter use. Despite the precaution of a wide bulldozer trail that had been laid down outside the park to flank the two communities, a wind shift sent Liebersbach's burnout pushing and spotting back toward the towns, denying it the opportunity to merge effectively with the oncoming main fire. In the ensuing fight, the towns were saved, but a few homes were lost. And the fire took Liebersbach's camp.

"We got a thousand people out of that camp in an hour," Stam said. "We abandoned it to the fire. I was one of the last people there. It was a *Grapes of Wrath* scene. The outhouse doors were banging in the wind and sleeping bags and paper were blowing along the ground. The fire was coming. It was eerie. We were moving the fire camp and trying to have a meeting of our team in the bus. We stopped to talk. It was night and the fire was chasing us. It had run us out of our camp and now it was chasing us. While we were talking you could see the horizon get red behind us. Then it was red on the right flank and red on the left flank. And then we had to get moving again."

Experience would have suggested that Liebersbach and his team, taking over from a previous command group, should have had an easier time of it. The generals of fire agree that few situations deliver more stress than walking in as the first com-mand team on a big fire. Fire command groups most often do stints of three weeks on big fires. By then, fire management philosophy says, endless eighteen-hour days have taken their toll, and a handoff to a fresh team is in order. So, over the years, most teams occasionally enjoy the relative luxury of taking over a fire where an organizational structure already has been crafted.

The business of being the first team in means inheriting chaos. By the very definition of its role, the team is handed a deteriorating scenario. Few tasks are more difficult than trying to bring order to an escaped fire situation as crews and equipment are pouring into a newly forming camp.

"For some reason, my team has never had the luxury of taking over a fire from another team," said Steve Raddatz, the Boise National Forest fire officer who leads a Type I team. "We have always had to take over from the local initial attack crew. Those poor people have been out there since some time yesterday, the fire has escaped them and grown way past their capabilities. In that situation, there's no lag time to sit back, get organized, and formulate a plan. You have to hit the ground running. That's the million-dollar shift, that first shift when you're getting set up. You can either catch the fire and save a lot of money, or you can lose it and have it become a long, long event, with a lot more people and a lot more money."

An incident command team will labor around the clock in the early days of a major fire. The operations position is doubled—one operations director and support staff for each of the daily twelve-hour shifts. But all of the team members will often work shifts of twenty to twenty-two hours. Though the fire boss and key members of his team will "fly the fire" and visit some spots on the ground, much of the information they need to create a plan of battle flows up from the fire line through the chain of command. The perimeter of the fire is organized into divisions, each with a supervisor. In addition, groups of fire crews or engine outfits may be headed by strike team leaders. All of them feed observations and progress reports into the system.

The intelligence coming from the field on the fire's progress and behavior is laid onto maps and hammered into a plan for the next twelve-hour shift, and details for air and ground operations are refined. The operational plan is played out in a briefing for crew leaders, division supervisors, and other overhead at the start of each shift. There the complex interplay of the command team's responsibilities becomes obvious.

As wildfires swept into Altadena, California in 1993, military involvement came on short notice. Marine regulars Leslie Grey and Freddie Polk were dispatched from their staff positions at a reserve unit to help with the evacuation of St. Luke Medical Center.

■ ■ ■

"It's like you're putting together a dance," said Harbour, the veteran California fire boss. "The rep for the agency that owns the land has given you some broad direction. He says the dance is going to be at this hotel. You can choose the ballroom, and here's your choice of dances. The IC says we're going into the grand ballroom, and we're going to do a waltz. And the ops chief says, 'Well, I want people coming through this door, not that door.' And the planning chief says, 'We'll do it at seven-thirty, and I'll see that the band is there on time.' And when it works, it's like Arthur Murray has laid the steps out on the floor, and you have three thousand people out there doing what they should."

Sometimes it does not come together easily. In 1991, multiple fires erupted in a two-hundred-mile stretch of eastern Washington, from the Canadian border south through Spokane. Bill Wilburn, a veteran fire boss with the Washington Department of Natural Resources, found himself at the epicenter of an event that would be known later as Firestorm '91. Though he wore the uniform of his state's forestry operation, he drew the task of protecting the Spokane urban area. The fire was a two-day catastrophe, so explosive and so accelerated that the business of creating order from chaos was mercilessly compressed. Wilburn had state, federal, and municipal fire units flowing his way from around the Pacific Northwest. Also shuffled into his deck was a huge collection of local fire departments from the Spokane area. Many of them had little experience with large-scale interface fire. One refused to be represented in the multiagency attack Wilburn was racing to stitch together.

"I had seven fire command teams coming at me and ninety-six fires, almost a ring of fire around the city of Spokane, and it seemed like the whole world was falling apart," he said. "In the middle of it, I literally had to teach people how you dealt with

■ ■ ■

Right: U.S. Marines, retrained as firefighters, march to work during the 1988 Yellowstone National Park fires. The military is activated for forest fires under a Defense Department program that makes troops available for civil emergencies.

something this big. We had ten major fires that were really big. We had an arsonist running around in the middle of the thing. At one fire we discovered the body of a homicide victim. We had one fatality. It was just an amazing thing. We were doing triage all day, just writing off one place after another and letting the fire have it. I built about four different command structures the afternoon Firestorm blew up. That night, I finally came up with the one that worked. It was the wildest thing I ever did."

Despite its track record, the incident command system is not without critics. Old fire bosses complain that it often seems to produce a scale of operations far greater than the fire of the moment may require. In the trenches, experienced hotshot bosses, helitack foremen, and smokejumpers say that reliance on the command structure often forces them to stand and wait for the system to assemble itself while the fire grows. A common criticism is that a day of battlefield momentum is lost whenever a lower level Type II command team is handing off responsibility to a Type I team.

"It happens," said Paul Hefner, a veteran BLM fire hand who manages the interagency Western Slope Coordination Center in Grand Junction, Colorado. "And it's getting worse. I believe that the incident command system is a top-notch, well-designed, well-planned method of managing any emergency. But we've missed something. We get into these situations where the initial level of response is in place and the top level of command hasn't arrived yet, and we're sort of paralyzed until it gets into place. We've just missed something there. It happens at that intermediate level, where the system is trying to shift gears and elevate to the next level of command. And it's frustrating."

Here and there in the fire community, a few iconoclasts ask hard questions about the scope and the mindset of the system. Don Ferguson, a well-read, thoughtful fire management specialist with the BLM in Southern Oregon, occasionally is booked to explore those questions before professional forestry and fire audiences that agree with little of what he has to say. "We're real brave about this, talking about fire and our ability to suppress it," said Ferguson, whose fire career began as a groundpounder in the early 1970s. "We give the idea that it's all a manageable process. I think in the long run we're grossly mismanaging. We're spending a lot of money for very small results. We've built a myth of prediction and control. I think that the one percent or two percent of fires that go outside the model disprove the entire myth. Most of the time we gather a lot of people and resources around and wait for the fire to do what it was going to do. Then when it's done, we draw a line where it stopped, and we say we won."

If the making of fire generals begins in rookie camps around the West, it almost always concludes in one spot. In Arizona, out on the wide-open stretch of Interstate 10 between Phoenix and Tucson sits the hamlet of Marana, home to a one-time Army airbase. In the shadow of the Santa Rosa Mountains, the long runways and aged hangars wear the cloak of clandestine history.

Through the Cold War, Marana turned up often in accounts of covert activities of the Central Intelligence Agency. The planes of Air America and other dummy airlines that the federal government has since acknowledged as espionage carriers swooped regularly onto the tarmac at Marana. Some of the BLM and Forest Service smokejumpers who were recruited into Air America and into the CIA itself passed through the guarded gates in those days and, sworn to secrecy, left for faraway places. Outside the chain link fences of its two thousand acres, locals told stories of giant planes that flew in with one set of tail markings and flew out the next day with another. Even today, planes with strange insignia, and with no insignia at all, nest around the hangars. But this odd and mysterious place, set on an ironically treeless plain, is where the generals of forest fire hone their skills.

In Marana's undercover heyday, some of its buildings stood empty and available. In the mid-1960s the Forest Service began conducting fire command classes there. Over time, the service settled into many of the non-aviation buildings, the collection of barracks and office structures identified in military fashion—Alpha, Bravo, Charley. That real estate has become home to the National Advanced Resource Technology Center. Still administered by the Forest Service, it is shared for training purposes by such federal agencies as the Bureau of Diplomatic Security and the U.S. Customs Service.

In the business of wildland fire, only the few pass through Marana's gates. Candidates for the command courses taught there must have years of lower-level experience in fire. They have been hotshot superintendents, district fire management officers, mid-level fire behavior or operations specialists. Some have spent most of their professional lives aiming for the opportunity to sit in Marana's classrooms. They may come back several times in their careers to be tutored by veteran fire bosses and to collect the skills that will enable them to work as staff officers on big fire operations.

For the very few, the ultimate objective at Marana will be the course known in the trade as generalship. The crux of generalship is a two-day simulated fire, where a command team of trainees is isolated in a room with phones and radios, then bombarded with "inputs" that demand decisions. Though the students are all professionals who have survived a fine-toothed selection process just to step through the door, many find the course brutal. The washout rate in the generalship course has approached forty percent.

"With the simulations, they make life as hard for you as they can," Raddatz said. "You're hooked up with people you've never met, and you have to work as a team. Everything is in compressed time frames, just like a real fire incident. You're being bombarded with information. You can't spend time chasing rabbits or not focusing on what you have to do. You *must* organize and delegate. They'll pop rabbits out there for you to chase. And if you bite on them, they'll set the hook, and you're lost."

Phil Parks is Marana's assistant director, a two-agency firefighter who was a groundpounder with the Forest Service and a smokejumper with the BLM. His job casts him as a sort of associate dean in a small and exclusive college. A small staff of professionals like Parks manage the curriculum at Marana, but the faculty is drawn from the ranks of veteran fire bosses around the country. They design the courses, monitor the programs, select the candidates. Parks can talk expansively about how the curriculum emphasizes regional fuels, topography, fire behavior, weather, personnel management, and a hundred other considerations. But with him, as with everyone who passes through generalship training, the conversational path always ends up at the simulations.

"It is truly where the rubber meets the road," he said. "In one room are fifteen or twenty role players, hooked up with phones and working from a scenario. There's a fire, like a real fire with a real name, and it starts at six o'clock. And in another room is a mock command team. It's given a briefing and it starts running this thousand-acre fire. And then a little wrinkle gets thrown in, maybe just a little piece of incidental information about a lost hiker. It's just one of the many pieces of information. But somebody needs to call it to the attention of the incident commander. And if that doesn't happen, the role players take it from there, and it will get worse and worse. Maybe they'll burn that person up because the team didn't jump on the problem. To watch the simulations is amazing."

In the exercise, the mock command team may be handed four crucial messages simultaneously—the food trucks are late, a crew has failed to show up at a rendezvous point, the helicopters are out of fuel, another fire has started. The evaluators who stand quietly around the room's perimeter see stress that is almost palpable. "When I went through generalship, a guy on my team had a heart attack right in the middle of the simulation," said Lynn Andrews, a Type I IC from Washington. "It was real. They had to stop everything." Through it all, the evaluators

look for the ability to stay in control of events, to anticipate problems, to delegate wisely. Those who have been through it never forget.

"Marana is a unique experience in any life," said Harbour, the California fire boss. "When you get in that room with all the inputs and situations coming at you, you are truly on that fire they have created. I remember watching another team go through it. They had an ops boss who tried to do too many things himself. The instructor team saw the weakness and exploited it to the fullest. Here was this guy with two radios, one in each hand, getting all these inputs that were just pouring in on him. They weren't trying to bury him, but they were trying to get him to the point where he had to delegate. And he never saw it. He wouldn't do it. The room was air conditioned. But I'll remember this guy with sweat, just rivulets of sweat pouring down his face and his neck as he attempted to keep up. And they were working him unmercifully."

Though the lore of generalship training has cemented Marana's legend, those who have watched the place operate over the years say that its collegiality may be just as important. The windswept Sonoran Desert offers few diversions, and the base is small. For junior fire officers, the place serves up an unparalleled opportunity to rub elbows for a week or two with each other and with the Pattons and Eisenhowers and MacArthurs of their trade. The lessons passed down by the veterans in after-hours sessions at the Roadrunner Lounge, the on-base watering hole, are pearls without price. The friendships cemented around the tables bear fruit years later, when Marana alumni find themselves tossed together on fire command teams, like military academy graduates meeting in the trenches of some distant battlefield.

The pressures of becoming a fire general are exceeded only by the pressures of being one. Around the West, those who fill the job of fire general are not given to braggadocio. They seldom miss the splinter of humor that can arise from even the worst situations. But mostly, they tell their tales with a mix of marvel at what they've been through and of gratitude for the opportunity. "First of all, before everything else, it's thrilling in the sense that you're allowed to play the game," said Hank DeBruin, a fire commander who climbed to high Forest Service positions before retiring to Maryland. "I loved to play the game. The game is the thing. And as a commander, you got to play the key role in the game. There was nothing better."

CHAPTER 9

The Sisterhood

EVERY AFTERNOON, ALASKA CALLED. The BLM smokejumpers in Fairbanks were ringing up their soul brothers at the Forest Service jump base in McCall, Idaho. Down two thousand miles of line, the voices of the Alaska brethren rattled glum and sour. On the other end, the brethren from McCall stood angry, confused and a bit defensive. The boys club—their version of the last, best macho job in America—was under assault. They were neighborhood urchins in the treehouse, once masters of all they surveyed. And in those strident calls that came daily from their buddies on the next block, the jump base at Fairbanks, they stood accused of having failed to pull up the ladder soon enough.

"Is she still there?

"Whadda you mean she hasn't washed out yet?"

"What's *wrong* with you guys?"

While the phone line buzzed in that spring of '81, Deanne Shulman marched ever nearer to becoming a smokejumper. Around the West, the jumper grapevine crackled and rankled with the news. She was twenty-seven then, with six years of fire behind her. She had been a hotshot. She had rappelled from helicopters. If ever a woman was to take on fire by stepping out the airplane door, this might be the one. With each day she notched in the training cycle, the jumpers saw the unthinkable loom larger. They had squeezed her out two years ago—got her not because she couldn't blast through the mile-and-a-half run, not because she couldn't crank out the requisite pullups, but because she couldn't make the needle on the scales swing past 130. But dusting off the old minimum weight rule had been a wink-and-a-grin deal, a bit of selective regulatory application in the good old boy tradition, so obvious and so abrasive that a few veterans predicted it would come back to haunt the jumper corps.

Shulman wanted the chance to be a smokejumper. Only the chance. The other baggage, the first-female-ever baggage, she would gladly have done without. It would have suited her to be the hundredth or the thousandth. But for her, jumping was the next logical step. It was time. Out on the fire lines of the West, she had paid her dues and left in her wake a trail of male crew bosses who counted themselves as former skeptics. She was, in her own thoughtful way, a bit of an adrenaline junkie, and this was the challenge she had chosen.

Where she was headed, no women had walked as pathfinders, none waited as role models. But she had two mentors. One was Mark Linane, who ran one of Southern California's most aggressive and respected hotshot crews. He was an unlikely confidant, because by look and style he was a John Wayne sort, a traditionalist who could have been sergeant-at-arms in anybody's boys club. On the

Above: Four California firefighters take a break at a training camp. As more and more women find places in wildland fire, the experience of being the only female on a crew becomes increasingly rare.

■ ■ ■

Left: Oregon smokejumper Gretchen Hoenig doffs her helmet after a successful descent. Since women broke into parachute fire fighting in 1981, about fifty have qualified as smokejumpers.

first day they met, when she was a candidate for a lowly rookie's spot on an engine, he had explained the pecking order of fire. He had told her, as if it were an unalterable geologic truth, that there would never be women on hotshot crews. Three years later he offered her a spot on his. And later, when she decided she wanted to move on to jumping, he encouraged her.

Her second advisor was a jumper named Mouse Owen. He invited himself into her situation after the horrible three-day trip to McCall, where she passed the physical qualification test, tipped the scales at 125, and was sent packing. "I was very distraught," she said. "They had made it very clear that they didn't want me there. They all had a reaction, and all but a few were very negative."

Owen caught up with her in the aftermath. "He was four-eleven and weighed maybe one hundred twenty," she said. "He had fought in Vietnam, and then had come back and decided he wanted to be a smokejumper. When they said no, that he had to weigh one hundred thirty, he took them on. He fought it and got a congressional waiver. He was great. He was already kind of a legend as a jumper, this little tough guy, and he just called me out of the blue. He really put it to me. He told me I had a right to prove whether I could do the job, and that I couldn't give up. He said I had to fight it. He told me about other men who'd gotten in under the official weight. And then he sent me his packout bag to practice with, because that's the hardest part."

Though it was not the course she preferred, she filed a legal complaint, charging that the height and weight standards were discriminatory to women, and that she was being treated differently than lightweight men. By then, the U.S. Forest Service was in inglorious retreat. A settlement offer came quickly. "What happened to her wasn't fair," said John Marker, a veteran Forest Service fire hand and public affairs specialist. Marker, now retired and a respected consultant on wildland fire, was in the group of top officials who quietly but firmly informed the smokejumper world that the twentieth century had dawned. "Even some of the jumpers felt that she had been wronged. There was never any doubt that she was qualified. So some people around the system sat the jump community down and made it very clear to them that she was going to get another shot, a fair shot."

The interruption had chewed up two years. But in 1981, Deanne Shulman had walked back into the McCall base. A day at a time, she began marching through rookie training. And the news that went up the telephone line to Alaska was all bad. She passed the physical fitness test again. She mastered the parachute landing fall and did well on the training tower. They were sure that tree climbing would do her in, but it didn't. She stepped

out the airplane door on her first jump without hesitation. The packout test—hauling 110 pounds three miles in ninety minutes—awaited her. "It was the last thing," she said. "I heard later about what happened the day that I passed it. The word was in Alaska almost immediately. They say that some jumper walked out of the lunchroom and threw up."

The training was over, but the personal testing went on. With the men in her rookie class she forged strong friendships. With the veterans, it took longer. "I heard more negative things after I made it through than I did before," she said. "It was like it was okay to say anything then. So I always had people coming up and telling me straight out that jumping was a fraternity, and that I didn't belong, that I would never belong. But for me the big pressure had been learning to jump and looking out that airplane door for the first time.

"With guys who come into jumping, real acceptance comes after the second year. It took me three, but then I realized that I had become very well-liked, except for a few diehards I didn't care about. My fourth and fifth years, my last years, were just wonderful. There was no question that I belonged. There were a few more women jumping then, and I was a mentor for them whenever I could be. I felt almost like a cult figure. When our McCall group would go to different jump bases, other jumpers—men and women—would want to have their picture taken with me. It came full circle. When I left, I could hear the McCall guys bragging about how their base had the first woman jumper."

■ ■ ■

In the sisterhood of wildland fire, only a little is known about the woman who showed up first of all. The sisterhood has a history that is fresh and young, but vague. Its pathfinders in those first seasonal jobs were so scattered, so young, so temporary that they left a scant trail. They fought fire for a few summers, and mostly moved on to other lives. Hence, their history is largely unwritten and so sprinkled over the geography of the West that it plays like a misty legend of tribal beginnings, as if it had been blurred through traversing centuries by word of mouth. But, like a tribal ancestor tale that might be called First Woman, there is a passed-down Alaska story, from that long-ago year of 1971.

Her name was Kara, as the story goes. Only Kara—her last name has been lost somewhere in the tellings and retellings. Some BLM personnel clerk, perhaps one with a sense of the preposterous or one who had been brushed by the stirrings of the newly born women's movement, accepted Kara's application and told her where to report for work. The awful truth of inferior gender was quickly obvious, so it is told, and the crew boss fired her at the end of the first day. But media intruded, and the bureaucracy responded to adverse publicity by promising that it would create an all-women's crew, in the unlikely event that enough interested women appeared. Twenty-four signed up, and the crew fought fire that year.

The myth, if that is what it is, dovetails conveniently with some known historical fact. Among a few of the male old-timers in Alaska fire, there's a different recollection of a first female firefighter—her name may have been Virginia Vain, some say—and no certain memory of a hired-fired-and-rehired sequence of events. In any case, the BLM did start all-female fire-fighting crews in Alaska in 1971. And the Forest Service put some females on the fire lines a year or two later in the Lower 48, sometimes by upgrading crews of women who had been hired for brush disposal and prescribed burning.

The records of the women who first hired on seasonally for fire in that era have long since disappeared. Male fire managers, perhaps hoping that they were dealing with a passing fad, didn't track the opening rounds of the new social phenomenon erupting in their midst. No one thought to document what has since become regarded as a milestone. And the federal wild-fire agencies, though now aggressively affirmative in their hiring policies, have been too busy looking ahead to look back and recapture beginnings.

Those who care enough to pursue the stories always give a nod to the earlier, temporary corps of women who took on wildland fire during the manpower shortage of World War II. Rosie the Firefighter, not as famed as her airplane-building sister, Rosie the Riveter, dug fire line and packed hose in the temporary spirit of the war effort. Though her motivations may have been different, she is the spiritual ancestor of the women who began showing up on the fire lines twenty-five years later. Unlike Rosie, there was nothing temporary about that new group that began turning out in the early seventies. Only a few had career aspirations in fire, and most were focused on earning college tuition or indulging a yen for adventure. But none expected the number of women coming into wildland fire to diminish or to disappear. All anticipated the sisterhood would grow. And it has. Though there are no firm figures, somewhere over five thousand women now stand in the ranks of those who fight the summer battles of the West. Many are with the state agencies that, mirroring the history of much of wildland fire, followed the federal lead.

In the prelude years of the late 1960s, there was resistance. It was fierce, and it was seldom subtle. Women who applied for fire work were shunted to recreation and forestry jobs. They were organized into units that were always held in fire camp and never sent to the line. They were told that, no matter what they might think, they did not really want to take on the dirty, exhausting, demanding, and exclusively masculine work of fighting fire. Much of the running debate over their presence and their aspirations foreshadowed the national debate that came just a few years later over the question of women in military combat. Women heard that they did not have the strength or the temperament. Though some of them had been camping and backpacking and mountain climbing with other young adults for years, they were told that the land agencies could not consider placing them in threatening outdoor settings with mixed company and no provision for toilet facilities.

But after the door began swinging open in 1971, progress came swiftly, if not always easily. In 1974, by the best estimates, the women in wildland fire units numbered a few hundred. In short order, they began to escape the pigeonholing of all-female crews, and were working side by side with men. But mostly they were clustered on engine crews and low-experience Type II outfits. Many worked as the only woman on a crew and suspected that the arrangement was a pressure tactic. In fire camps, there were whistles and obscenities and jokes about cooking and face-to-face confrontations with fire bosses who told them they were in the wrong place. There was, at least once, a rape of a female firefighter by some of the men on her own Forest Service crew.

The sea change which would double and then treble the number of women working outside the home had begun. Newspapers of the time were filled with a new genre of feature stories, the tales of women stepping into traditionally male jobs, hiring on as carpenters, as truck drivers, as railroad engineers. But it was the sort of change that did not always sit well in the hidebound, traditional, paramilitary world of wildland fire, led in those years by men from the World War II generation. Change was in the wind, and the dinosaurs were in full roar. For twenty years, the fire shops of the West would keep their barricades well-manned, and they would always lag behind the changing hiring practices of other departments in their agencies.

Among those who felt the fire world could, and must, resist that change, none stood more boldly at the ramparts than Carl Hickerson, who was head of Forest Service fire operations for the Pacific Northwest in the early 1970s. For a year or so he delivered to enthusiastic male audiences of senior fire managers a popular speech, titled "Should Firefighters Wear Petticoats?" He characterized the arrival of women in fire as a disruptive influence, an aberration spawned by a permissive society, a step that was certain to diminish the stature of the corps of wildland firefighters. In his arguments, it was a given that women lacked emotional stability and the ability to make logical decisions during moments of mental and physical stress. He invoked their natural responsibility to bear and raise children.

"I simply cannot imagine a truly feminine woman even considering fire suppression work, and all the adversity, filth, and hazard it entails," Hickerson said. He promised that if fire managers would have the courage to resist this bizarre social experiment they could keep the forest fire ranks free of women and, he hinted, preserve men's jobs in the process. "The tide is beginning to turn on the radical lib movement whose espoused goals include the invasion of every profession, and the storming of every craft and skill, the undermining and ultimately the destruction of the American family and home."

To others, including the Forest Service brass who eventually squelched Hickerson's bookings for the infamous petticoat speech, social Armageddon did not seem to be at the doorstep. Whether, as Hickerson suggested, they were caving in to political pressure, or whether they were simply recognizing the in-

evitability of one of the most sweeping social changes in American history, they opened more and more places for women on fire crews. A rift of sorts began to widen in the fire shops, with a few younger male managers braving the dinosaurs and hiring women regularly.

By 1978, women had cracked the ranks of helitack units and hotshot crews. And in 1981, precisely a decade after that first woman, whoever she was, hired onto an Alaska fire crew, Deanne Shulman stepped into the sky over Idaho. Since then change has come so quickly that less than twenty-five years of fire-fighting history seems to encompass three or four uniquely different generations of fire-fighting experience. In many ways, wildland fire is a microcosm of the women's movement itself: Those who walk through open doors often do not stop to think about how they were opened or the price that was paid. "When you try to tell younger women what it was like just a few years ago, they can't comprehend," said Kelly Esterbrook. An Oregon smokejumper of Shulman's generation, she has also been a hotshot crew boss. "You can't always make the newer women understand. You feel like a grandmother. After a while, you quit talking about it."

The women who marched off to fight forest fire in those early years shared experiences much like Deanne Shulman's. As they stepped into a macho, male-dominated world, they found both opposition and support, met both mentors and monsters. In the sisterhood of wildland fire, the axiom about the brotherhood goes: "Some will help you. Some will change. Some never will." Most often, the opposition seemed commensurate with age and seniority. At the crew level, most women learned that matters would generally go well if they could perform and if they could convince their crewmates and their bosses that performance standards would not have to be lowered to accommodate them. Most felt supported within their crews; a few even had the experience of seeing a brother crewmate flatten some obnoxious fire-camp chauvinist. But they would still reap scowls and patronization from older fire bosses and local fire management officers.

■ ■ ■

Right: Far from home,
Kori Kirkpatrick, a former U.S. Navy firefighter
serving with the Flagstaff Hotshots of Arizona,
takes on the Cub Creek Fire
in Idaho's Boise National Forest.

Left: California Department of Forestry engine crews
are home to many women,
who learn the rigors of dragging
heavy hose up steep slopes.

Among those early fire-fighting women, the array of personality types was wide. Some were quiet, shy, almost apologetic for their presence. Some wielded wit that was more than a match for any harassment that came their way. Some reveled in the dirt and the sweat, but nonetheless made a point of maintaining a touch of femininity, perhaps by always sporting earrings or by wearing their smoke-eater's bandanna like a fashion accessory. And some swore like stevedores, lined up at the guard position in touch football games, and always finished in the top five on crew training runs.

"Before I went on a hotshot crew, I never dreamed of myself as being macho," said Sherry Reid, a wildland fire dispatch chief in Tucson, Arizona. She worked in California and the Southwest in her groundpounding days. "When I was a teenager, I saw myself becoming a stenographer in a courtroom. But when I got into fire I realized that I loved to see the human body, my body, pushed to extremes. How much can you push your body? How much can you continue to push after you think you've reached the peak? I liked challenging myself against men and what they could do. You could call that macho if you want. I chewed tobacco. I arm-wrestled. I did the whole nine yards. I loved it. I loved the chainsaw, the dirt, the exhaustion, the traveling, the risk, the adrenaline. I thrived on it. It was the best time of my life."

Sometimes in those days, disapproval was manifested indirectly. Even after women had been showing up in fire camps for several years, some fire bosses would deliberately make no provision for shower facilities for them. They would not schedule a women's hour at the shower truck nor would they bring in a separate unit. Some women worked through ten-day fires, growing filthier with each passing day, watching their male crewmates head off to the showers at the end of each shift. Within the spectrum of female personalities in fire lurked enough moxie to call management's bluff on the business of showers. Without any coordinated plan, the matter was addressed spontaneously about 1977. A few women in a few fire camps demonstrated that they were going to take showers with or without men. By the time that they marched out of the shower trucks, toweling their hair, the bureaucracy was in full fidget, worrying about scandal and repercussions. Thereafter, separate shower facilities became a priority and a standard of fire camp organization.

Though it was sometimes years in coming, many of those earliest women in the game, just like Deanne Shulman, reaped the satisfaction of having a male coworker or boss admit to a turnaround in thinking. Sometimes the admission came as a compliment, sometimes as a sincere apology. For some of the men, the process rearranged fundamental assumptions. "When I was an eighteen-year-old stud, I used to sit around and laugh about the idea of women being on fire crews," said Paul Gleason, who ran a premier Oregon hotshot crew for years. "The idea was hilarious. But then I started getting women on my crew. It really came home to me how much wildland fire is an endurance game.

"All the people who know about human performance talk about women as endurance performers. I've seen it. It's true. I get these big guys, the studs. They go out fast. They roll trees and dig line for a few hours and they're done. If they miss a meal, they're really done. The women keep going, all day, all night, it doesn't matter, on just a little bit of food and no rest. Not the fastest, not the strongest, but persistent. The work output is really there. One year I had seven women on my hotshot crew. All of them could carry and run a chainsaw. I felt there was absolutely no loss in crew performance by having that many women."

Mike Fitzpatrick's memory is even more distinct. Now the operations director of the Forest Service smokejumping center at Redmond, Oregon, he was a BLM jumper in Alaska when Deanne Shulman was pounding her way through training in Idaho. He was among those who screamed down the phone lines at the jumpers in McCall. He lived to become unabashedly critical of those old attitudes.

"I'm not proud of the attitude I had back when Deanne was training," he said. "We had this club. It was like big guys pretending they were twelve years old. We were crude. We were slobs. It was fun. It was arrested development. It's odd when you look back. Anyone who has a wife or a mother or a daughter has a stake in that kind of equality. But we were at that point in time where we could believe in equality for the women in our lives, but we didn't want other women joining us in jumping. And then we saw these women succeeding. And most of us recognized how hard it is to succeed as a jumper even when everyone around you is pulling for you to make it. And they had done it without that support. At some point you just could not avoid recognizing that."

For many of the women who were in fire early, no such testimonials were needed. It was enough to be a player, to be in the game. "I broke in on the Lassen Hotshots under a guy who was a typical, traditional 'shot boss," said Sue Husari, who went from California groundpounding to fire management posts with the National Park Service and the Forest Service. "He yelled and screamed and made us work hard. But he was an equal-opportunity abuser. He treated us all like dirt. Even when I was furious with him, I appreciated him."

■ ■ ■

Maybe it was the wrong thing to do. Maybe it was exactly the right thing to do. Katy Nesbitt, fresh from her first year of Western fire fighting, was sitting through an anthropology lecture in a big amphitheater class at St. Mary's College on Maryland's Chesapeake Bay. The professor's presentation in that winter term of 1988 evolved into a discussion of women in combat, a topic once again being hotly debated a few miles away in the nation's capital. The professor noted that soldiers are expected to hike ten miles and carry forty-pound packs. Clearly work beyond the capacity of women, he allowed. Suddenly, before the huge audience, Nesbitt found herself standing on her amphitheater seat. "I carry a forty-pound pack," she yelled. "I'm only five feet tall. And I hike ten miles a day. I do work that's so dirty and so hard you can't imagine. And it's not so different from combat." The professor shifted the direction of his lecture for the remainder of the period.

Katy Nesbitt was a gymnast, a skier, a runner during her high school years. In the 1990s, that makes her like virtually all of the other young women who are stepping onto engine crews, rappelling from helicopters, finding places on hotshot outfits, tackling the rigors of smokejumping. The first generation of female firefighters went through high schools that offered few, if any, athletic programs for girls and no emphasis on the competitive experience. Deanne Shulman, Kelly Esterbrook, and Sue Husari came from the schools of that era.

But in 1972, at almost the same moment that women stepped onto fire crews, a new federal law, Title IX of the Education Act, changed the U.S. athletic world forever. Title IX remains much in the news as the springboard for rancorous debate among college presidents, athletic directors, and coaches. But those are programs for the few. The law's most sweeping effect has been in middle schools and high schools, where local school boards were forced to create meaningful athletic opportunities for female students. As a result, the number of girls on athletic teams—and the number of sports offered to them—skyrocketed. Before Title IX, fewer than one percent of high school girls participated in sports. Afterward, the national figure rose to thirty percent. In some high schools, more than half of the female students were in organized sport by the late 1970s. For the world of wild land fire, the effect was profound.

"Most of the women who make it in fire, and almost all of the ones who really do well, have been athletes," said Mark Linane. "Not necessarily stars. But they know about discipline. They know about teamwork. They know about pain. The know about competition—some days you beat the fire, some days the fire beats you. It goes beyond the physical part. The ex-athletes seem to be better able to handle the joshing that goes on with any crew."

Leslie Anderson, who became a smokejumper in 1984, was six years younger than her mentor, Shulman. Just enough difference that she had the opportunity to play basketball in high school. In first a helitack operation, then the jumper organization, she found a teamwork spirit that was familiar and valued. "I liked the adventure of fire," she said. "At that point in my life it was important that I was doing something that women didn't normally do. And the camaraderie was real important. In the jumpers, that took a little longer to come, but it was good. People really took care of each other. It was something they beat into you in training. Whether you like the person you're with or not, you take care of them on a fire."

Under circumstances she did not seek, Anderson was to find the truth of that maxim. She was with twenty jumpers who took on a risky, rugged section of a Southern Oregon conflagration. On landing, Anderson sprained her ankle so severely she was unable to walk. Her fellow jumpers packed her to a helispot, but the fire exploded and overran the landing zone. The fire chased them down a long, precipitous ridge in a race they thought they would lose. "I couldn't walk," she said. "They were carrying me. It was an impossible situation, an awful situation. The fire was getting closer all the time, and we were running out of ridge." Just before nightfall, a helicopter tiptoed in through the smoke, and lifted her and four others out. The others tried to make their way off the ridge. In the blackness, one of them kicked a rock. "They heard it go clink, clink in the dark, and then just nothing—off into space so far that they never heard it hit the bottom," she said. "And they sat down right there in the rocks and spent the night."

If there is a sector of wildland fire that women have claimed as their own, it is helicopters. No one knows exactly why. It may be because the Pacific Northwest, after Carl Hickerson's retirement, developed a reputation for willingness to hire women; it also had one of the largest helicopter fleets in fire fighting. For whatever reason, women remain well-represented in federal helitack operations and fill over half the positions on some crews. "We did an evaluation tour of all the helicopter rappel bases in California in 1993," said Lanny Allmaras, the national director of Forest Service helicopter operations. "What we saw was so obvious and so unexpected that we constantly found ourselves talking about it. The women on those crews knew more about the program, were more interested in what was going on and had better suggestions for improvement than most of the men we talked to."

Above: New Mexico firefighter Cheryl Boyd of the Smokey Bear Hotshots spent enough time in wildland fire to learn that her feet deserve the best treatment she can give them.

■ ■ ■

Left: At a rookie fire school in Oregon, veteran Laura Robson explains the complexities of a hose valve to newcomer Donna Ellis. Women who have followed the pioneering 1970s generation of female firefighters speak often of the value of having other women as trainers and mentors.

■ ■ ■

Below: Slinging forty-pound packs down the line, Christen Dedrick, Julia Ondricek, and Cindy Bartlett help unload the plane that brought their Winema Hotshots crew from Oregon to a big Arizona fire.

Above: In the middle of a grueling week in Oregon's Siskiyou Mountains, Kim Steele of the Union Hotshots spreads fire down a ridgeline on a lengthy burnout.

■ ■ ■

Right: In the tight physical and psychological confines of a fire crew, many women meet and grow to like the most grueling manual labor they have ever experienced.

Women remain a strong presence on Alaska village crews and on Native American crews in the Lower 48. In the Northern Rockies and in the Northwest, they work most often on mixed crews. The Southwest tribes have mixed crews, also, but the tradition of all-female crews continues there. Among the Apache and some other tribes, a few women spend decades in fire. The historical timetable for Indian women in fire fighting played out the same as for non-Indians. They began seeking places on crews in the early 1970s. All-female crews were created to accommodate them. In some tribes, for reasons related both to culture and reservation politics, the separate crews have endured.

"Some of us would be on welfare if it wasn't for fighting fire," said Rose Phillips, a San Carlos Apache. A veteran of women's crews, she has been leaving her Arizona reservation for fire duty for twenty years. "Some of the men and the elders didn't like it when the women first started. My dad didn't like it when I was young and just starting. He said it was a man's job. But the money I brought home looked just like the money the men brought home. That made a difference. Now you get a lot of respect from the elders if you are a woman fighting fire. If you ask them, you'll find out they know who all the women firefighters are."

Although women on fire units regularly speak with pride of the acceptance and support they have won from male crewmates, they also complain, or joke, about a sort of benevolent patronization. It manifests itself most often in either a big-brother protectiveness, or in the assumption that some task is too heavy, too dangerous, or too complex for a woman. "Nothing will make a bunch of male firefighters move faster than a woman reaching to pick up a chainsaw," Leslie Anderson said.

Scott Blecha, a college engineering student, was an ex-Marine from an elite combat reconnaissance unit. He had never worked with women until he stepped into Oregon's Prineville Hotshots in 1991. "When I started, I believed that there were a whole bunch of things that women couldn't do," he said. "But I have learned that these women on hotshot crews can do the same things any guy can do. It has been a real discovery and a surprise. I've also noticed that at the start of the season, the guys will pay special attention to the new girls on the crew. You notice that one's really pretty and one's really sweet. That changes in about a month, after you've all been out and gotten dirty and tired on a fire. After that, she's your sister, and anybody who messes with her is in trouble. And that's not always something the women appreciate. They don't always want someone looking out for them."

Women who have spent a few seasons in wildland fire often speak of redefining their limits, of discovering levels of physi-cal and mental strength that surprise them. For some it is finding the ability to work a thirty-hour shift and to come back six hours later to work another. "I learned that most of the limits are mental," said Judy Reese, whose fire-chasing career has taken her from Montana to California to Alaska, where she works for the state's Division of Forestry. "I found that when I thought I couldn't go over one more ridge, I had it in me to go over ten more. The experience constantly expanded what I thought I was capable of doing. The interplay of the physical and the mental made me feel very powerful, almost invincible."

The most recent generation of women on the firelines is seldom apologetic or shy about its role. The young women on today's fire crews grew up in an era when friendship patterns outside of dating relationships were expanding among teenagers. That social change, so often noted by high school educators, manifests itself on fire crews, where women claim their niche without much deference to any sort of traditionally submissive gender role. Blecha, the ex-Marine, sees it often.

"Everybody has peaks and valleys," he said. "On a fire, the men go out strong at the start. But what I notice is that, about the middle of the shift, it's the women who are pushing, yelling the things that get us going. That's where tempers might flare. At the start, the guys are wanting to get everything done, right now. You're digging line and they're swearing and yelling, 'Move, move, move.' The women are wanting to just work through it and might get mad at the guys. Later on in the day, when the guys are very tired, it's the women who are yelling at us to get going. There are some hard looks that go back and forth. But mostly it's a team thing—you lean on me now, because I'm gonna lean on you later."

Blecha's observations on his female fire-fighting compatriots were made in 1993, during a slow day at his crew's headquarters in a tiny town in the Central Oregon desert. Less than a year later, Blecha and eight of his colleagues from the Prineville 'shot crew would die on Colorado's Storm King Mountain. Among them were Tami Bickett, Kathi Beck, Terri Hagen, and Bonnie Jean Holtby. The four fit the hotshot profile and the profile that has come to mark women in wildland fire—young, athletic, adventuresome, and interested in the outdoors. Bickett and Holtby had been successful high school athletes. Beck, a year away from a psychology degree, was a mountain climbing instructor. Hagen had been a U.S. Army medic and paratrooper.

The four women were not the first female wildland firefighters to die. The records show three others, one each in Montana, Idaho, and Arizona. But never before, in either the structural fire community or the wildland fire community, had more than one American woman died in a single incident. Thirty years earlier one of the ways in which the debate over women going to battle in wildland fire had foreshadowed the national dialogue over women in military combat was the use of the social impact argument: American society is not prepared for women to die in action. In the wake of the Colorado fire, some female firefighters expressed fears that the argument would surface again, that perhaps the agencies or Congress or the public would begin to think about pulling women off the fire lines.

But it did not play out that way. In Prineville, in the rest of Oregon, and across the West, Bickett, Beck, Hagen, and Holtby were memorialized as firefighters, four among the fourteen who had die heroically in the Colorado fire. Though some eulogies marked their accomplishment as extraordinary women, few distinction were made, and there were no public calls for policy changes. The handful of media stories that took special note of the women's deaths were mostly dispassionate accounts of the history and the numbers of women in wildland fire. And the friends and parents of the four women said things that were not so different from the sentiments expressed by survivors of the ten men who died with them. Across the West, those families were a Greek chorus of tragedy and pride, and Beck's father, Ernest Walsleben, echoed them all when he said of his daughter, "She was ecstatically in love with fire fighting. She had called us and told us over and over how much she loved doing it."

■ ■ ■

The snag burning on the edge of the Thompson Creek Fire was ugly and dangerous. Towering above the line in that Montana summer of 1991, it threatened anyone who walked near. It was a monster, leering with tongues of flame, and promising to breed embers and spot fires. But Holly Maloney and her partner from the chainsaw squad of Missoula's Lolo Hotshots knew that it had burned too much, was too fire-weakened in its core to be felled. For anyone who might put a saw to it, the tree held the potential to explode and crumble, sending down tons of broken, splintered, charred wood. They would have to watch it and chase its spot fires. But the division supervisor for their section of the fire would have other ideas.

Confident and articulate, Maloney was a veteran of fires all over the West. Though petite, she was a University of Montana heptathlete, a competitor in that difficult combination of the shot put, high jump, long jump, javelin, hurdles, and two running events. Small wonder that she had a reputation for toughness on her fire crew. She was regularly handed leadership positions and given such difficult technical and physical jobs as being a sawyer.

Like other female firefighters, however, she was saddled with a sort of dual citizenship. On her crew she was a first-class citizen. But on fires far from home, when she had to deal with male authority figures outside the crew, she knew she was likely to be challenged, questioned, doubted, and patronized. When she was a designated leader, she could expect some division supervisors and fire bosses to look through her and address the nearest male, even if he was a rookie. Or worse, she could be given an order that would never be given to a male. The sisterhood had taught her to recognize female-baiting, the macho quicksand game that never seemed to offer an easy out and that so often seemed to ignore the fundamental fire line principle that any firefighter may raise a safety issue.

The division supervisor for the line approached Maloney and her male crewmate. They discussed the precarious snag. Maloney had the chainsaw. She told him her crew had agreed that the snag was too dangerous to be approached or cut. Even as she spoke, she sensed the inevitable gender standoff coming. The line boss smiled the baiting smile. "I think you're going to have to cut it down," he said. Maloney was polite, though she suspected that she had cut hazardous, burning snags far more often than this authoritarian clipboard warrior in the clean yellow shirt. She repeated chapter-and-verse of the manual on danger trees, and made it clear that the snag was patently unsafe for felling.

"Cut it down," he said, enjoying the moment. Maloney paused. She took the big saw and set it in the dirt at his feet, then looked him in the eye. "I don't think I will," she said. "Maybe you can." Bluff called, the supervisor looked at the saw. He looked again at the towering, flaming tree. Then he turned and stalked off. It was the sort of encounter that can send consequences rattling back along the chain of command. But they never reached Maloney. That night, in camp, her male crew bosses backed her judgment.

"The thing women have learned in doing this work is that you have to take pride in what you do, you have to believe in yourself, and you have to know the job," she said. "If you do that, you can find out that you really belong to a crew and that you pack some weight in that setting. I'm only twenty-seven, but I'm kind of a grandma now. I try to make the younger women coming onto the crew understand this. I try to raise their expectations, but I also try to make them know that they have to learn and they have to carve out a role for themselves. Just being here because it's good money on a good summer job is not enough to get you through a season. It's too tough."

So often in the early years the women who stepped onto fire crews were alone. Frequently, they were the first female on their crew, or in their district. They endured all the official and unofficial rites of training and initiation without mentors. It

seldom plays out that way now. And the difference is often crucial. It was for Jenny Houchin of Santa Maria, California, who began her stint in wildland fire with a Forest Service hotshot crew in 1990.

"Everyone was fair to me, but it was very harsh physically," she said. "I had a tough time. I threw up a lot. I cried every day—but not in front of people. There were four women on the crew. One of them was experienced, Kathleen Lowe, a sawyer. Really strong. The woman could do seventeen pull-ups, more than most of the guys. Amazing. And she'd sit me down every evening and say, 'You can do this.' She pushed me through. And there was another woman on the crew. Really small. About five feet tall and thin. A beautiful, cute little gal. She would do the kind of work that just seemed impossible. She would go up hills carrying a five-gallon gas can in each hand. That's forty pounds apiece. She'd take them because the guys would sidestep them and just carry tools. It was hard for her. And I kept telling myself that if someone her size could do it, I had to do it. It was a neat year."

The pathfinding women who found their way into wildland fire in the 1970s sometimes talk almost apologetically about the slights they let pass. In an era when their right to even apply for such jobs as fire fighting or smokejumping was in question, other issues had to wait. Verbal assaults, frontal and often obscene, were commonplace; physical harassment was not rare. "In some respects, ignorance was bliss," said Lael Gorman, a hotshot and helitack veteran who works now as a BLM fire dispatcher in Grand Junction, Colorado. "Back then, I knew I was in a job that was basically a man's world. I told myself that I had chosen to be there, so I accepted a lot. I consider myself adaptable. I accepted things in that time that no woman would accept now and that most men would find objectionable. The problems aren't all solved, but the world has changed."

Left: Most women who show up with state and federal agencies on the fire lines of the West are under age thirty. But some, such as Patricia Wescombe, who turned out for battle into her sixties at Glencoe, California, have built up decades of experience on rural volunteer departments that take on wildland fire.

■ ■ ■

Right: Suited up and awaiting a jump plane's departure, Montana smokejumper Kim Maynard savors a relaxed moment.

One of the ways in which it has surely changed is that what was once widely experimental now sometimes becomes narrowly legalistic. On the state and federal wildland fire crews, affirmative action programs, equal employment opportunity regulations, and diversity goals overlay the simple process of a woman stepping onto a fire crew and carving a role for herself. In the 1990s, both women and men make the observation that when a Deanne Shulman or a Lael Gorman fought her way into the game, the gauntlet to entry and acceptance was so harrowing that there remained no doubt about the ability and qualifications of any woman who survived it.

But now there is almost universal agreement that hiring and performance standards were lowered or sidestepped for several years in the late seventies and early eighties to push women and minorities into the fire game. Some of those who say it most loudly are women who feel that they did not need lowered standards or hiring quotas and that their own status is diminished by the fact that other women may have gained entry only because of reduced requirements. The federal land agencies, especially the Forest Service, now operate with hiring goals that seek approximately forty percent representation of women and minorities. In their fire shops, where huge numbers of seasonal hires are made, the emphasis is especially strong. Some of the state forestry and fire branches have similar policies.

Forest Service crew bosses and fire management officers in the Pacific Northwest, the Northern Rockies, the Great Basin, and the Southwest have found it relatively easy to live with the policies. Geography and demographics have assisted them. Small towns and ranches of the nonurban West have provided a steady supply of interested, outdoorish young women. Invariably, crew bosses who seem to be the least troubled by the brave new world are the ones who have created innovative recruiting programs. They have, for example, learned that contacts with college athletic departments can bring in women who have little trouble meeting physical performance requirements. Rural Native Americans and Hispanics, often engaged in lifestyles that make them accustomed to the outdoors and to manual labor, have provided another recruitment pool.

But problems come with goal-oriented hiring, too. Nowhere have those problems been more vexing than with the Forest Service in California, which has been in court since 1972 on issues related to the hiring of women. For much of that period, the agency's California record for hiring women was described as lackluster, even obstinate. Often, the fire shops lagged farthest behind in compliance with the directives. For fifteen years the California branch of the agency operated under a court-ordered consent decree. The decree and a subsequent settlement agreement called for forty-three percent representation of women in all Forest Service job categories in the state. Litigation on hiring policies there is expected to continue through the 1990s.

While Forest Service affirmative action policies generate occasional friction elsewhere in the West, in California they are a constant tension. Men and women on fire crews talk about them often, and so do their managers in the fire shops of ranger districts and national forests. White males argue that they've been denied jobs and advancement opportunities because of the court decree. Many men step into the work seasonally and grow to love it, but come to the conclusion that hiring policies will block them from long-term opportunities.

"No matter how much you like it, it's really hard to find a permanent position in wildland fire in the Forest Service," said Chris Amestoy, who works on a Forest Service engine crew near San Bernadino. "I'm a male. I really shouldn't mention that, but that's the way it is. I don't see a future here. It's too bad. I'm going to miss it when I leave." Fire crew bosses defend the abilities of most of the women who wind up on their crews, but complain about passing up eager, qualified men while working twice as hard to find and hire qualified women.

Even the most talented women who have landed Forest Service jobs on California fire crews or who have moved up to fire management posts know that their abilities often are in question. The shadow of the court order hangs over whatever merit or ability they brought to their position. "It is not easy," Husari said. "The California consent decree has produced difficulties for women everywhere in the Forest Service. There are a lot of women who feel tremendous guilt for what the consent decree has brought them. I don't feel guilty. I feel personally that I never got a damn thing because I was a woman. I proved myself in every fire job I had. I think what's happening is good for the agency, but I know there's a lot of short-term pain. I know that there are a lot of really talented, really frustrated men in fire. Some of them have an easier time dealing with their careers being stymied than others."

In the corps of four hundred smokejumpers, the number of women remains small. In any season, no more than fifteen women are scattered among the rosters of the nine Forest Service and BLM jump bases. A dozen years after Deanne Shulman stepped out the airplane door, the total of women who had followed her had not reached forty. The smokejumper world has mostly adapted to their presence, although a few older jumpers still grouse that performance standards were lowered or bent in the 1980s and never rebounded.

Rod Dow, a veteran Alaska jumper who is often described as the archetypal blend of smokejumper wit, intelligence and machismo, is one who has adapted. "I've pretty much reached the conclusion that the only guys who are threatened by the idea of women jumpers are the guys who have their entire manhood wrapped up in the fact that they're smokejumpers," he said. "I liked this work better when it was all guys. But I'm accustomed to what's happened. The women who are here are my friends. They are doing the job. They were not given any favors. They made it on attitude and on desire, at the same time that big, strong stud guys were washing out because they just didn't want it bad enough."

Around the world of Western wildland fire, even outside of California, the issue of women moving from seasonal fire-fighting jobs to command and management positions simmers vigorously. In some locales women say that the glass ceiling is thicker than ever, that the system is unwilling to let them move beyond the seasonal work of digging line and throwing dirt. But from the other quarter, from both men and women, comes criticism that fast-track advancement has moved inexperienced women into critical fire management positions, sometimes with almost no ground-level fire-fighting experience. "I'm a firefighter and I expect to be in this work for a long time," said Kelly Martin, an assistant foreman on a helitack crew in Idaho. "I've worked on building my experience gradually. Sometimes the fast track sets people up for failure. I've seen these women marooned in higher positions in fire, and wishing they were back down in the field, gaining the experience."

More and more, among women in wildland fire, that view is beginning to prevail. Many women talk of resisting the fast track, or have decided to step off it before it carries them too far too soon. Michelle Ellis is an assistant fire management officer, a career position, for a Forest Service ranger district at Entiat, Washington. Though she spent some time working in real es-

tate management for her agency, fire was her love. She was a Forest Service groundpounder in Colorado and later a dispatcher. She moved up quickly through the system. But ultimately, she felt the need to slow the pace.

"The agency tried to accelerate things for me and invested a lot of training in me," Ellis said. "They were moving me along pretty quickly, and there was talk about giving me a district fire job on my own. I started to think about it. If I messed up a land appraisal when I worked in real estate, the government might lose two or three million dollars. So what? If I make a mistake in fire fighting because I've been pushed along too fast and too far before I really have the skills to be there, the consequence could be that someone doesn't come home. That's unacceptable. So I've told the people who've been so good to me not to try marketing me as a fire management officer. I'm not ready yet."

Still, women have been on the fire lines of the West for nearly twenty-five years now. Some of them have paid their dues and have clearly earned the full-time fire management jobs they hold in the federal and state agencies. The best of them are being recruited onto the command teams that tackle the West's largest wildfires. Those who watch the fire game at its upper end see the last hurdle approaching. It waits at Marana, Arizona, where the generals of forest fire are trained and certified. "They're coming through now," said Phil Parks of the Marana staff. "The first ones were training for the finance positions on Type I command teams. In ninety-one, we had a woman qualify as a plans chief. I'm waiting for the time when we have a woman go through as an operations chief or as an incident commander. Those will be watershed events. And they'll happen. We'll see it. We're not that far away."

CHAPTER 10

The Fires of the Future

LIKE THE CREASES THAT DEFINE THE FUTURE for a palmreader, the surgeons' tracks on Mark Linane's knees tell the stories of his past. Here on the left is the tiny mark for the patch job of 1988. And here on the right, fresher than all the others around it, is the one that runs from ankle to thigh, summing up twenty-five years of accumulated insults from pounding the mountains of the West. Behind that one are steel pins and rerouted ligaments and snipped cartilage and bones deliberately fractured on the operating table to rejigger the geometry of a joint gone bad. As the boss of the Los Padres Hotshots, a crack crew on the most fire-active national forest in America, Linane is something of a legend. His fiftieth birthday is behind him. He has been in wildland fire at ground level since the age of eighteen. He has been the ramrod of his crew for more than twenty years. He is the oldest hotshot boss in America. In the entire history of wildland fire no one has ever run a 'shot crew longer. And still the business of pounding up and down mountains goes on for him, along with relentless physical conditioning and the occasional surgical invasion to splice another ligament or trim some more cartilage or add some more hardware inside the creaking knees.

"It gets rougher each year," he said. "It's five major knee operations now. I've got pins, I've got scars that run all over. It's tough. You get past forty and it's double-tough. There's no time that I can get by without physical training now. I can never stop. I have to stay at it all the time. Every year I have to take those young bodies up the hill. Some of them are always going to be new and fresh, twenty or maybe twenty-one. It's like the crew doesn't get any older, but I always do. I'm still always with them or ahead of them going uphill. Downhill is harder. Downhill is what gets firefighters and their knees."

Someday the knees will quit. Someday the surgeon will sigh and say, "Not this time." Someday the fire world will be done with Mark Linane, and when the day comes that he can no longer climb the hill, it may have nothing else for him. Along the trail, he passed up the opportunities to slide behind a desk in the fire shop. The enticement of going out to meet the dragon claimed him season after season after season. In a Forest Service that is downsizing under federal budgetary strictures, the options are no longer there waiting. As a full-timer, not a seasonal, he has a retirement package waiting, if the knees will take him there. It is not a handsome package, and quitting early is hardly an option, because all the years that Linane spent as a seasonal will count for only a little. He is still, in many ways, emblematic of how the game uses up young bodies.

The vast majority of those bodies, in the Forest Service and in virtually all of the other wildland fire agencies, will never be more than pure seasonal employees.

Above: Forest fire commanders, with decades of experience in plans and operations, have begun to find their skills in demand for a widening variety of civil emergencies.

■ ■ ■

Left: Simmering beneath the world of seasonal wildland firefighters in the 1990s is a vigorous debate in Congress and in federal agencies over such issues as risk, injury, long-term health effects, and fairness.

Like cowboys who drift back to the ranch every fall for roundup, they will go on season after season, putting in perhaps six months a year in the summer battles of the West. They will do what they must to stay in the game. This year an engine crew in California, next year a hotshot crew in Montana. If they hang around long enough, a few of them may get medical benefits for the months they work, and the right to accumulate a modest pension benefit based on their part-time labors. But only a tiny fraction will ever find the payoff of a full-time job in fire. Many will stay with it as seasonals on the fire lines for five years, ten, fifteen. They will be warned.

"I'd get these people who came back year after year as seasonals," said Paul Gleason, the veteran crew boss who left Oregon's Zig Zag Hotshots at age forty-five to take a job as a fire management officer in Colorado. "After four or five years, I'd sit them down and I'd say, 'Look, there's no career opportunities here. You've got to understand. This isn't going to produce anything permanent for you. I'll give you a job as long as you keep coming back. But all you're going to get from the government is that we're going to blow out your knees, we're going to give you arthritis in your hands and maybe some complications in your lungs. And then, on the day when you can't stand up straight and do this work, we're going to say goodbye.' But they'd come back the next year. And I'd give them the talk over again. And it went on and on and on. They knew I was right. But they kept coming back."

The federal government, however, has shown some pangs of conscience. James King, President Bill Clinton's director for the Office of Personnel Management, publicly declared in 1993 that the government's policies toward firefighters and other temporary government workers were creating a "public service sweatshop." In Congress, the Civil Service Subcommittee began weighing in regularly with complaints about treatment of temporary workers by various federal agencies. Proposals to increase benefits, job security and advancement opportunities are afoot.

In the federal fire shops, a corollary debate has begun on the rightness of relying on—some say exploiting—the esprit that brings the low-paid, ever-available militia back season after season. Some have come to question a system built on the passion of part-timers. However, there is no denying that the alternative, a full-time wildland fire force, would be monumentally expensive. The zealous temporaries who pick up pulaskis and come back season after season to work in low pay grades save the government billions. And yet, their enthusiasm and their commitment have exacerbated the problem. Indeed, it was no problem at all during the decades in which fire fighting was only a youthful rite of passage, an interlude of two or three seasons during the college years.

But scores of forty-year-old smokejumpers and thirty-year-old hotshots change the equation and crystallize the question of fairness. And, to many fire managers, moving out the seasonal graybeards and returning to the high-turnover hiring of the past is no answer. In an era when fire and technology have grown more complex, and the training investment in every groundpounder is high, the old idea of rotating virtually an entire work force every few years seems fraught with problems. The portents of slipping back to a system where hotshot crews might average only two years of experience unnerves some fire and safety experts.

Seasonal firefighters have testified in Washington, D.C., and at a special Congressional hearing held in Missoula, Montana, perhaps the West's preeminent fire town. They called for change—especially in such matters as the granting of medical benefits, the creation of opportunities to advance to full-time positions, and the possibility of alternate work if age or injury take them away from the fire lines. In 1994, the government floated the first cautious proposals to actually limit the number of seasons that a firefighter could work.

The proposed regulations were intended to force the agencies' hands by making it necessary for them to offer more full-time positions. The idea reaped a harvest of protest. Some of it came from the fire managers. But a surprising amount of it was offered by the seasonals. "It was kind of amazing," said Kathy Burger of the federal Office of Personnel Management. "It's a situation where the government was showing concern about doing what's right and fair. But there were all these letters that showed so much commitment, all these seasonals writing to say that we couldn't change the system because they wouldn't be able to get the job done." The battle to inject a quotient of fairness into the seasonal equation is a political fire for the future. The debate will likely run through the 1990s, and its outcome may reshape the ranks of the armies of summer. However it plays out, the results will probably percolate from the federal wildland fire agencies to their counterparts in the states, just as so many other developments in the fire game have done throughout the twentieth century.

But some think that the reshaping of the armies of wildland fire will come from another direction, that budgetary pressures on federal and state governments will carve an ever-increasing role for firefighters fielded by private contractors. A few, noting the growing number of top government wildfire careerists who take early retirement and find roles in the private sector, even speculate that the future may bring contract fire generals. They raise the possibility that entire fire command teams might be assembled, trained, marketed, and hired. If that happens, the lead in the hiring most likely would come from the Forest Service, which almost always is the pacesetter in the world of wildland fire.

"There is a tremendous change in the culture of our organization," said David Aldrich, the Forest Service national branch chief for fire training. "Thirty or forty years ago, everybody in this agency had a fire responsibility. No matter what your job title was, you did fire when the need came. But that was when everyone in the Forest Service had either a woods or a ranch background. It was a logical expectation. Today we have people with more diverse backgrounds. We talk about our 'ologists'— the biologists and anthropologists and other specialists. Fire may be in their vocabulary, but they're not really interested in learning how to fight it. It's a huge change. Because of that, I think we may see contractors doing things in fire that seem unimaginable to us now. It seems possible to me that, beyond hand crews and engine crews, we may actually have a contract overhead team, running big fires. It's partly a result of downsizing and budgets, but it's also part of that big cultural change in the agency."

But the contractors themselves think it unlikely that mercenaries from their payrolls will someday dominate the armies of summer. Lou Jekel, director of Scottsdale, Arizona's Rural/ Metro Corporation, probably the nation's largest wildland fire contractor, sees his company as a one-of-a-kind exception to the normal order of business. He argues that the forces of federal and state government will never relinquish the white hat job they have come to enjoy so much. And Mike Wheelock, who offers firefighters from his Grayback Forestry operation in Oregon, makes the point that, as the Western timber industry shrinks under political and environmental pressure, the contract forestry firms are downsizing in parallel fashion. "I think we saw the peak of contract fire fighting about nineteen ninety-two," he said. "If the other work isn't there, you can't keep a lot of people on payroll just for fire calls."

Lawrence Amicarella, who retired in 1993 as national director of forest fire operations for the Forest Service, sees the pressures and knows the difficulty of marshaling the army that will fight the battles of summer. Across a long career, he was an agent for change in the fire world, and he can see that more change is in the wind. But he does not expect the fundamental equation to shift. He argues that fire has its own way of creating esprit and that it will attract the people who see in it something they can find nowhere else. "Fire will always get the people it needs," he said. "The best of them, the smokejumpers and the hotshot crews, they will get caught up in it. They'll be the soul of what we do. It will become their life. That won't change. They are still going to be finding that there's enough excitement out there to keep them going. The dragon, the wild dog, the devil—all the things that we've called fire—will always be there for them."

■ ■ ■

When the Exxon Valdez hit Bligh Reef and spewed oil into Prince William Sound in 1989, when Hurricane Andrew slammed into South Florida in 1992, when the Mississippi River spilled over its banks for long months in 1993, wildland firefighters and their generals rolled into action. More and more often, the incident command system, the wildfire arena's gift to the larger world of emergency services, tugs its commanders and its groundpounders into situations that lie far beyond the forests and mountains of the West. The trend is established, and it is growing. Many of the fires of the future may not be fires at all.

That expansion is welcomed, even fostered, by the federal agencies, especially the National Park Service and the Forest Service. With approval from Washington, D.C., they have taken the position that a system that represents an immense reservoir of skills and equipment should not sit on the fence during major national disasters. The Forest Service, in fact, has an international arm that has even fostered development of the ICS system overseas. After the earthquake that devastated Mexico City in 1985, hotshot crews were dispatched from Southern California to help dig victims from the rubble, just as some Western fire crews were assigned to sandbagging operations on the flooded Mississippi in 1993.

In Alaska, state government has also taken an activist role in pushing its fire expertise across new frontiers. When the Exxon Valdez spilled its cargo of crude oil, the state's Department of Natural Resources teamed up with the Bureau of Land Management and the Forest Service to swing three interagency fire command teams into action. "Some people pushed the edge a little bit there," said Frenchie Malotte, who heads Alaska's state fire operation. "We had a federal Type I command team come in from Colorado. They were an hour out of Anchorage when people started saying that there might not be any federal authority for using them up here on a non-fire emergency. But somebody somewhere must have figured out a way, because the Colorado folks were here for weeks, helping us with our problems." The three overhead teams coordinated big pieces of the cleanup work. Just as they would have done on a fire, they provided the planning and worked out the operations schedules for researchers, animal rescue volunteers and oil removal experts. They issued media releases, coordinated transportation, dovetailed local officials into the command structure, and provided huge measures of savvy for an unprecedented emergency.

Rick Gale of the National Park Service was one of the area commanders—the top leadership position—for the Yellowstone Park fires of 1988. More than any other general in wildland fire, he has been on the cutting edge of the business of taking fire expertise into places where there are no flames and no smoke. The expansive thinking he represents is called "all-risk" response. It is built on the concept of finding new ways to use fire command teams and sometimes ground troops. Gale works regularly with the Federal Emergency Management Agency, the U.S. Coast Guard, and local emergency officials. Out of his work flows training and methods that will prepare fire commanders to handle other emergencies. He explores ways to meld the diverse units of federal, state, and local officialdom that may confront an offshore oil spill or an earthquake. The task is a familiar one for the commanders of big wildland fire operations.

"This isn't a change of mission for the wildfire community," he said. "We will still be geared to fire, and that will mean that there will be some times of the year when we won't be much available for these other things. But more and more, FEMA has been coming to us. They've been activating pieces of the wildfire system for other emergencies. That tie seems to be getting stronger. It clear to a lot of people that some sort of management structure is needed for these big emergencies. And a lot of people have begun to see that the wildfire community has developed that expertise. Why reinvent the wheel? We have a form and a structure that works. Our basic approach—planning, operations, logistics, finance—applies to just about any emergency that comes along. We're learning that we don't always need as many people for an emergency as you need for a fire. Sometimes we can take just a few of our experts and then blend in local people."

The mounting problem of interface fires will consume ever more attention as residential buildup continues in the rural and suburban West. A few experts say that, more than ever, such blazes will be the fires of the future. Some Western states already have enacted aggressive vegetation setback rules that require homeowners on the margins of forests, deserts, and mountain brushfields to remove trees and undergrowth. Failure to comply can result in criminal penalties.

In some locales, the fire agencies have detected a growing public awareness of the tradeoffs in battling interface fires. "People are starting to understand," said Karen Terrill of the California Department of Forestry. "We're beginning to run into situations where people are angry that a forest was allowed to burn because all the available firefighters had to be deployed to protect a house that someone chose to build in a bad spot." Increasingly, the issue of firefighter safety is injected into the interface issue. At Arizona's Dude Fire in 1990, six firefighters died on a line they defended between an onrushing fire and a rural subdivision. At Colorado's Storm King Mountain in 1994, fourteen firefighters died within sight of a set of rural homes, so close that residents there saw the fire sweep over them. Such fatal incidents have brought home the idea that those who choose to live in the forest can endanger lives.

• • •

Left: The wildfire that raged through Altadena, California in the fall of 1993 reduced expensive homes to rubble in minutes. The threats of interface fire are expected to grow with each passing decade in the Western zones where homes and wildland vegetation mix.

Right: In the 1970s, fierce debate raged over the adoption of the Nomex fire-resistant clothing that is now standard in wildland fire. The current debate is over protective respiratory equipment, which would be almost certain to reduce work output.

Other threats to firefighters—threats more insidious and less dramatic than a galloping firestorm—have begun to trouble the leaders of the wildfire world. In the 1960s, researchers began probing the respiratory effects of working for days and weeks in the forest fire environment. But the research was episodic and underfunded until the late 1980s. Then, in the Northern California fires of 1987 and the Yellowstone fires of 1988, thousands of firefighters turned up at fire camp medical tents with respiratory complaints. Those multi-fire events were both marked by weather inversions, which clamped an atmospheric lid over several thousand square miles and held smoke and particulates close to ground level. Many firefighters worked in those settings for weeks and even months. At Yellowstone, medical personnel handled twelve thousand respiratory cases.

Firefighters who have had heavy exposure to smoke regularly cough up sooty, black particles for days afterward. Tests have shown minor decreases in lung function that may last for several weeks. The list of harmful toxins and carcinogens in forest fire smoke is long. Invisible carbon monoxide, the basic by-product of all combustion, is as feared as any of the observable contaminants. Some veteran fire bosses believe that the mind-numbing effects of carbon monoxide may be at the root of dangerous and seemingly inexplicable decisions that veteran firefighters and crew bosses have made in the heat of battle. The effect of carbon monoxide is temporary. But seasoned hotshot supervisors tell tales of firefighters whose thinking processes become so clouded that they have difficulty deciding which boot to tie first.

In the medical community, it is a given that effects of insults to the respiratory system often take decades to manifest themselves. Long-range studies on lifetime effects are especially difficult to design because seasonal firefighters move on to other occupations and experience other airborne pollutants. Across a lifetime, the effects of a few seasons of intense exposure to smoke and particulates cannot be isolated. Because of the temporary and footloose character of the seasonal ground troops in wildland fire, no long-term study on cumulative effects of smoke inhalation has ever been attempted.

James Johnson, director of hazards control projects at the Lawrence Livermore National Laboratory in Northern California, is a scientist who has become passionate about the issue. For years he has argued that putting forest firefighters into protective respiratory equipment is overdue. "It's a crime that we continue to let those young adults function like that," he said. "They're a forgotten subset of people who have been ignored en masse. In all my years in industrial hygiene, I've never seen anything like it. These people, especially the hotshot crews, are young and adventurous. They sell their bodies. And we use

Experts are beginning to say that rudimentary masks, goggles, and ear plugs are flimsy shields against some health threats that lurk in wildland fire.

■ ■ ■

them. Even though we don't have any studies on cumulative effects of wildland fire smoke, look at what we know about passive cigarette smoke. We say it causes six thousand deaths a year. Well, passive cigarette smoke is nothing compared to what people endure out there on forest fires."

Official Forest Service research on firefighter respiration is headed by Brian Sharkey, an exercise physiologist at the University of Montana. He coordinates a team of researchers scattered in various facilities around the West. The work, under way since the early 1990s, is mostly unfunded. Several of the researchers do it on a rob-Peter-to-pay-Paul basis, stealing time from other projects so that they can conduct field and laboratory tests of smoke effects and prevention measures. Some of the tests involve respirators, filter devices worn over the nose and mouth or over the full face. On the lines, firefighters are openly skeptical of such equipment. They leave no doubt that the thought of wearing high-technology face gear runs against the macho grain of their trade. Those who have worn test models complain of struggling for breath during heavy exertion.

"I think that someday in the future, wildland firefighters will go into fires wearing respirators," Sharkey said. "But respirators decrease working performance significantly. It's work to breathe through one. You're inhaling against resistance. The respirator alters breathing patterns. A lot of firefighters don't like it. But I know a lot of professionals who think that if these firefighters were doing comparable work in private industry, they'd already be required to wear respirators."

In the here and now, though, the leaders of the world of wildland fire are more preoccupied with sudden death than with cumulative injury to knees and lungs. The fourteen deaths in the 1994 South Canyon Fire on Colorado's Storm King Mountain, the unwelcome centerpiece to a year in which twenty-seven firefighters died, refocused the question of safety. Storm King will reverberate in the fire community for years. Even before the season was over, the lessons of the Colorado holocaust were floating out to the fire camps. New protocols were promulgated for fire shelter training and deployment. When the investigation showed that ground-level temperatures at South Canyon had hit two thousand degrees—a figure far beyond the design capacity of shelters—the trickle-down effect made the question of running versus sheltering more of a judgment call than ever. Because the investigation showed that many of South Canyon's victims died carrying their chain saws, tools and packs, fire commanders and firefighter trainers began working to remove any onus that might attach to those who abandon equipment and gear when circumstances dictate a rapid retreat.

The fire shelter itself is expected to change dramatically in the wake of the Colorado fire. The Forest Service Technology and Development Center at Missoula is under way with development of a floored model of the tent, an ingenious, accordion fold design that should reduce flame and smoke intrusions into shelter interiors. The aerospace industry and the U.S. Department of Defense have weighed in, too, offering consultation on materials and design. In yet another manifestation of the long relationship between the world of wildland fire and the military, some exotic materials previously classified as military secrets may find their way into fire shelters.

■ ■ ■

The most important and perhaps the most controversial fires of the future may be those that are allowed to burn or are deliberately set by the fire community. The case for such fire is certain to build. So is the opposition. Prescribed natural fire of the sort started by lightning in wilderness and national parks took a severe beating after the Yellowstone fires of 1988. Some of the Yellowstone fires were touched off by lightning strikes in early summer and then allowed to burn for weeks. They eventually grew to raging, unstoppable conflagrations, burning beside other fires that were fought without success from the moment of their inception. Considerable evidence suggested that fuel and weather conditions were so extraordinary in the summer of 1988 that even early suppression action would not have headed off the fires and would have made no significant difference in the ultimate outcome.

In the Western fire community, allegiance to the concept of prescribed fire remains. However, some of its most ardent supporters suggest privately that the park service overplayed its hand in Yellowstone, strategically and politically, by allowing so many fires to gain so much headway in the face of severe drought conditions. In congressional hearings that followed the Yellowstone blazes, prescribed natural fire was preserved as a forest management tool for wilderness and national parks. But some new fences were erected around it, primarily limitations that call for suppression action to be initiated early and aggressively during drought conditions, or when other large fires are straining the national fire-fighting resource pool.

In Alaska, different as always, another version of prescribed fire will play out. Within the state, the Bureau of Land Management and the Alaska Department of Natural Resources began moving in the late eighties to an intricate system of graduated responses that was both an attempt to curb costs and to recognize fire's natural role in the state's ecosystems. Across the vast reaches of the state, 371 million acres are mapped and designated for a specific sort of fire response. In many isolated and uninhabited tundra regions, a lightning-ignited fire gets no response at all, other than periodic monitoring by aircraft. From that low level of interest, the system offers graduated responses, with fire starts near communities or critical natural habitat areas designated for a maximum suppression effort. The system is the largest wildfire planning effort ever attempted. Fire managers elsewhere in the West will be watching its long-term performance.

The Yellowstone fires, catastrophic as they were, did not stem the rising tide of interest in fire and forest health. Around the West, in fact, foresters, scientists, timber managers, and

Top: Still regal amid the ashes of his kingdom, a bull elk strolls through the Yellowstone National Park forest during the fires of 1988, the worst U.S. forest blazes of the twentieth century. Wildlife biologists are learning that animal populations sustain few losses in even the most catastrophic fires.

■ ■ ■

Right: Ecologists see fire, even catastrophic fire, as a step in the life cycle of forests. In a forest's rebirth, grasses and distinctive purple fireweed appear first, usually within weeks.

■ ■ ■

Bottom left: Using fire as a tool of forestry, two members of the Boise Hotshots work the perimeter of a prescribed burn designed to prepare a forest area for reseeding. Such "project work" keeps fire crews busy in the months before the summer fire season heats up.

■ ■ ■

Bottom: Catastrophic stand-replacement forest fires, which kill every tree in their path, are increasingly viewed as the fires of the future in the pine forests of the West. Insect infestation, invasion of non-native tree species, and fuel buildup caused by fire suppression itself all contribute to the hazard.

environmentalists are becoming converts to the new gospel. They've been forced to it in many locales by a preponderance of evidence. Before them spreads the sight of dying forests where fire control has changed the face of nature, encouraging unhealthy density, allowing minor tree species to dominate, ushering in lethal insect damage, and creating the buildup of dead and dying fuels that leads to catastrophic events known as stand replacement fires.

From Oregon to Montana to Nevada, the problem is epidemic in the pine forests of the West. In some regions the stands of dead trees run for miles. The fear of Yellowstone-style conflagration grows with each passing year. The irony is that fire once was the predator that thinned the herd. It came every decade or so, burned lightly in most cases and kept forests healthy. Now, with fire held at bay for so long, ton upon ton of dead fuel carpets the forest floor. Huge sections of western forest land are incendiary accidents waiting to happen.

Paradoxically, holding off fire's unwanted incursions into the tinderbox has become more crucial than ever, even as the experts seek noncatastrophic ways to return to the old balance and invite fire back into the forest. Now, foresters and fire bosses alike talk about gearing up for huge increases in prescribed nonnatural fire—fire deliberately ignited by man—to return the forests to a natural balance and to reduce fire hazards. They debate how much introduced fire might be too much. And they confront problems they had not anticipated. Seventy years of fire control has changed the vegetation of some regions so much that they now are the habitat for animals and birds that they previously did not support.

Around the West, managers speak with pride of their burning programs and talk of the brave new world of prescribed fire, of burning for hazard reduction and for forest health. But they admit privately that the amount of it they are able to push through the budgeting and political processes is minuscule compared to the need. The battle produces foes that range from air pollution authorities to homeowners. It creates allies and then divides them. In the timber regions of the Northwest, traditional foes such as the timber industry and the environmental community find agreement on the need for returning fire to the forest; but they part company over industry suggestions that large amounts of pre-fire thinning and post-fire salvage logging should be part of the therapy for ailing forests. In the Southern California brush fields that have been invaded by suburbia, official attempts to reduce hazards and create firebreaks through small amounts of controlled burning have been met with public outcry and legal action.

As a result of such opposition around the West, the land agencies admit that they often are burning less than a tenth of the amount judged necessary to restore ecosystem health or to head off future fire. "To be able to derive benefit from prescribed fire and vegetation management, you have to do it on a huge scale," said Richard Chase, a Southern California fire researcher. "These little pieces they're doing—thirty-five acres here and fifty acres here and one hundred twenty acres there—are only eyewash. They make great stories but they do almost nothing to reduce the possibility of catastrophic fire."

Recognition of fire's ancient role in forest health has delivered high status to fire ecology. One of the leaders in the field is Professor James Agee of the University of Washington. He regularly makes the point that much of the new vision of fire ecology is not new at all. It had been postulated for decades by a few of the West's renegade foresters and academicians. "In the last twenty or thirty years, we've had some major changes in the structure of the forests, changes that affect the fire behavior in those forests," Agee said. "The more effective you are at putting out fires in certain ecosystems, the worse the problem gets. Professionally I've been lucky to be in the generation where those ideas have become acceptable. My mentor at the University of California was ridiculed and laughed at to his face for what at the time seemed to the fire community to be a bunch of crazy ideas."

David Peterson, an associate professor at Washington and a colleague of Agee's, also subscribes to the importance of fire's role in forest health. But he sees some of the born-again fervor over allowing fire back into the forest as a misguided quest for what is perceived to be natural. Indian fire is a fact of history. It was a form of forest management that shaped the image of what modern Americans believe to be the natural forest. "But if Native Americans hadn't been here, what would the truly natural forest have looked like?" Peterson asked. "Nobody knows the answer to that question. In fact, forests change constantly, climate changes constantly. There may not be an easy answer. If we choose in the future to make the forests look like they did in the eighteenth century when the Native Americans controlled them, that may be a legitimate management choice. But it is not necessarily natural."

Thomas Quigley is an Oregon natural resources expert and the head of a consortium of government agencies and corporations. His group has set itself to the herculean task of saving the forests of the Northwest's Blue Mountains. The Blues, where vast stretches of the pine and fir forest are eighty percent dead, are the cause celebre of the current rethinking of fire and fire suppression. Historically, stand-replacement fires, the holocausts that take out everything in their path, have averaged less than four thousand acres in the Blues. But in the late 1980s the fuel buildup delivered several stand-replacement fires that exceeded fifty thousand acres. Quigley's role in attempting to stem that tide, in some cases by deliberately introducing fire, is ironic. His background is Forest Service, third generation. He comes from a long line of firefighters. In his youth, he was a dirt-throwing groundpounder himself. He cherishes the memory.

"We've gotten to be quite efficient in suppressing fires for fifty or sixty years," Quigley said. "The effect of that has been to increase the number of trees per acre in our forests. The open, parklike stands are gone. Instead, we have created a dense, tightly packed forest with fuels that go all the way from the forest floor up into the canopy. That's very different from what we had when fire was a frequent visitor to the forest. Ever since we started aggressively putting out forest fires in this country, small voices have been saying that it might not be the best course. But only in the past ten or fifteen years has that become the principal statement of the scientific community."

Though the idea of letting fire have its way more often is fast becoming the new conventional wisdom, support for the concept is not universal. One of the respected skeptics is Jack Wilson, the former head of the interagency fire center at Boise. Now retired from the BLM, he brings to the argument the perspectives of a career that began in natural resources management and evolved into a preeminent role in the world of wildland fire. Across a working lifetime, Wilson has seen his share of narrowly conceived, management-by-objective schemes purporting to hold the answer for the future of public lands. In the willingness to embrace prescribed fire as the savior of the forests, he thinks he sees another.

"I empathize with the scientists who want to let the decadent lodgepole pine stands burn," he said. "It is the only way to get a new beginning. But I don't support the decisions to let massive, stand-replacement fires do the job. Loosing mass fire that burns the lands of all agencies—and maybe ranches, home and even towns—is not the kind of management objective that is acceptable in the twentieth century. So few do not have the right to make that kind of management decision for so many."

The nation's state and federal land agencies once enjoyed a white-hat image that had no parallel in the West. But most of them, and especially the Forest Service and the BLM, have been buffeted by political and environmental controversy for more than twenty years. The heat has been turned up on such public lands issues as timber, mining, grazing, water rights, and wildlife habitat. Juggling the needs of diverse, demanding, and competitive constituencies has frayed the traditional image of benign, wise rangers guarding the natural treasures of the West. More and more often the agencies have found themselves ac-cused—too often deservedly—of auctioning the treasures to the highest bidder.

In the main, the raging debate over natural resources has not touched the fire branches of the land agencies. But in the difficult questions that swirl around prescribed fire, forest health, the mushrooming interface problem, and firefighter safety, the fire shop sees the possibility that its white hat could be knocked askew, its heroic image tarnished, and its momentum slowed.

"It is not so easy as it once was," said Bill Sommers, the forward-looking national director of forest fire research for the Forest Service. "The complexity of wildfire management has gone up many orders of magnitude in the past twenty years. Now it's routine for fire people to be in a catch-twenty-two situation. If you introduce fire in a controlled manner, you have public objections because of the smoke. If fire burns in an un-controlled manner, people lose their homes. You see something happening, rightly or wrongly, to all of these people who fight forest fire. The fire side of the operation is absolutely one of the last vestiges of the white hat that used to cover us all. But the the fire shop is very close to losing it, because of people's houses burning up. With the interface issue, there's just a bigger tendency to point fingers at the people in command positions. Maybe that will never happen to the ground-level firefighters, the dirt-throwers. Maybe they'll always be viewed in the same heroic way. But I'm not sure. Compared to other forest issues, fire has led this charmed life. And I don't know how long it's going to last."

Though society's outlook on forest fire is clearly in shift, the growing community of fire researchers and fire ecologists makes no argument that the yellow-shirted warriors have outlived their usefulness. Shifting public attitude notwithstanding, no one foresees a time when wildland firefighters will shuffle off to the dustbin of Western archetypes, like the trappers, gunslingers, homesteaders, wagon bosses, and dam builders of yore. Reviving dying forests is a task that will take much of the next century, with the threat of conflagration ever present in the dead-falls and debris. The delicate business of reintroducing fire to forests—forests that in the late twentieth century are almost always cheek by jowl with civilization—will regularly require firefighters as escorts. And for all the new thinking about fire, there will remain millions of Western acres where natural resource preservation, scenic values, the threat to life and property, and political considerations will dictate a rapid and aggressive response to fire. The armies of summer will still have battles to fight.

The Photographers

The work of more than fifty photographers made this book possible. Their ranks include young freelancers who chase forest fire with the same energy as firefighters, photojournalists at Western newspapers, frontline photographers with the fire agencies, and long gone professionals who hired on with the U.S. Forest Service to chase fire during the Great Depression.

Some of the best work in these pages came from firefighters themselves, because so many of the elite hotshots, smokejumpers and helitack crew members are serious and talented photographers who enthusiastically add the weight of camera gear to their heavy backpacks. In some few cases, the names of those who stood behind the cameras have been lost as their work passed into federal archives. The photographers and their pictures:

■ ■ ■

Roger Archibald, a free-lance writer and photographer based in Philadelphia, has been a Montana smokejumper since 1984. In winter, he is a merchant marine officer on sail training ships. Pages 72, 76 (upper right), 77, 80, 84, 85 (upper and lower right), 87, 149.

Joe Belcovson, an industrial photographer in Santa Barbara, California, also freelances in aviation photography. His workplace, near an air tanker base at the Santa Barbara, California airport, gives him a vantage on air attack operations. Page 101

Lynette Davis Berriochoa of Idaho's Boise National Forest has been a U.S. Forest Service fire information officer since 1988. She uses still photography and video to record fire action and its aftermath in the Boise area. Page 160 (lower left).

Leif Borgeson, who now lives in Colorado, crafted a much-traveled fire career by working on hotshot crews in Arizona, California, and Idaho. With the Boise Hotshots, he was the designated crew photographer. Pages 53, 152.

Alan and Sandy Carey, nature photographers based in Bozeman, Montana, have worked in South America, Africa and Europe. They stepped away from customary pursuits to document action at Yellowstone National Park in the historic fire year of 1988. Pages 88, 96 (top), 130.

Paul Carter is a staff photographer at *The Register-Guard* of Eugene, Oregon. Across a journalistic career in the West, he has photographed forest fires in Montana, Utah, and Oregon. Page 62.

F.E. Colburn packed his cameras to remote Forest Service installations in Colorado during the 1920s. Page 25.

Keith Cullom is a firefighter and department photographer for the Santa Barbara, California, County Fire Department, which oversees one of the most volatile wildland fuelbeds in the world. Pages 8, 38, 108 (top), 156, 157.

Carl Davaz, graphics director for *The Register-Guard* of Eugene, Oregon, has worked extensively in Montana's wilderness regions. He has covered forest fire in that state, as well as in Oregon and Yellowstone National Park. Pages 125 (upper left), 133.

Craig Elkins, who lives in Anchorage, Alaska, fought fire during his college years, first as a Forest Service crew boss in Oregon and then as a logistics dispatcher with the Alaska Fire Service. Page 163.

Kyle Engstrom, the nation's senior helicopter rappel firefighter and trainer, works for the Forest Service in Chelan, Washington, and frequently takes cameras aloft. Page 111 (lower right).

Robert A. Eplett is the senior photographer for the California Governor's Department of Emergency Services. His years of photographing wildland fire began with the state's Department of Water Resources. Pages 67, 148.

Thomas Evans, now a dispatcher for the Upper Yukon-Tanana Zone of the Alaska Fire Service, has campaigned with engine and helitack crews in Alaska, Montana, California, Colorado, Nevada, and Utah. Pages 120, 129.

Ken Franz has been a smokejumper with the Bureau of Land Management in Boise, Idaho, since 1975. His non-fire duties center on photography that documents smokejumper activity for historic and training purposes. Page 111 (top).

Ravi Fry, a former wildland firefighter in Nevada, is an outdoor photographer who has worked in the American West and in Asia. During fire seasons he signs on as a contract photographer for the Boise National Forest. Pages 49, 55 (lower left), 59, 141, 145 (bottom)

David Gilkey, a staff photographer for the *Daily Camera* of Boulder, Colorado, has worked on assignment for Knight-Ritter Newspapers in South Africa and Rwanda. He has shot forest fires in Wyoming and Colorado since 1988. Page 164.

Michael Ging, a staff photographer with the *Arizona Republic* in Phoenix, fought forest fire as a teenager in Arizona's Tonto National Forest. He has covered wildland fire throughout that state since 1977. Page 53 (upper right).

Tiana Glenn is chief still photographer for the National Interagency Fire Center in Boise, Idaho. Besides overseeing one of the largest forest fire photo collections in America, she annually tracks fire and firefighters around the West. Pages 76 (lower right), 160 (lower right).

Jeff Henry is a Montana outdoor photographer based near Yellowstone National Park. In 1988, he was a member of the park photography crew that documented the historic fires of that season. Page 118.

James Hughes photographed wildland fire action for the Forest Service in Washington State during the 1970s. Page 33.

Tom Iraci is a Forest Service photography specialist based at Oregon's Mt. Hood National Forest. A firefighter during his early years with the Forest Service, he now takes to the field each season to document fires in Oregon and Washington. Page 124 (top).

Steve Karkanen, the superintendent of Montana's Lolo Hotshots, began working in wildland fire in 1979 and became a full-time crew boss in 1990. He regularly carries a camera into battle. Page 2.

Dale Kolke abandoned advertising photography for outdoor work. Now senior photographer for the California Department of Water Resources, he works on assignment for the California Department of Forestry during major wildland fires. Cover photograph.

Robert Manis, a freelance photographer who specializes in air operations on wildland fire, is a retired firefighter who worked with the California Department of Forestry and the La Mesa, California Fire Department. Pages 44, 100 (top).

Dan McComb, a staff photographer with the Spokane, Washington, *Spokesman-Review*, was drawn into photojournalism through the images he saw in two years of work as a hotshot firefighter and five years as a smokejumper. Pages vi, 81, 85 (lower left), 93, 102.

Blaine Moore, who retired after a thirty-four-year career with the California Department of Forestry, flew as an air attack operations supervisor at Santa Rosa. He took cameras aloft to record aviation action in scores of California fires. Page 89.

Paul Morse worked as a staff photographer for the *Pasadena Star-News* before moving to the *Los Angeles Times*. He has covered Southern California wildland fire for seven years, including the horrific autumn fire season of 1993. Page 132.

Andy Nelson has covered wildland fire since 1988 as a staff photographer for The *Register-Guard* of Eugene, Oregon. Free-lance work has taken him to Romania, Kenya, Burundi, and Hong Kong. Page 144 (upper left).

Trent Nelson, a staff photographer at the *Contra Costa Sun* in Lafayette, California, covered wildland fire in Utah before moving to California's volatile chapparal country. Page 109.

James Peaco is the chief photographer for Yellowstone National Park. He has photographed fire in the park since the early 1980s and steered a crew which documented the 1988 conflagration in the park. Pages 55 (lower right), 125 (upper right), 161.

Chris Pietsch, a staff photographer for *The Register-Guard* of Eugene, Oregon, formerly worked on Idaho newspapers. Since the mid-1980s, he has covered wildland fire in Washington, Oregon, and Idaho. Pages 12, 45, 105, 136.

A.F. Potter photographed some of the earliest history of the U.S. Forest Service in the Northern Rocky Mountains. Page 22.

Bill Riggles, a Floridian who came West to fight fire, packed a camera through a dozen seasons with the Smokey Bear Hotshots of Ruidoso, New Mexico. Now he operates a studio and field photography business from the same town. Pages 35, 115, 144 (upper right).

Roy Rodriquez of West Covina, California battles wildland blazes as a helitack firefighter with the Los Angeles County Fire Department. He has been photographing fire action since 1988. Page 104.

Dan Root, a world-traveling multi-media photographer and producer based in Portland, Oregon, covered forest fires in Montana, Oregon, and California during six years as a photojournalist. Pages v, 6, 145 (top).

Tim Sexton is a fire management officer in Oregon's Winema National Forest. His twenty-five-year fire career includes a stint as a hotshot crew superintendent and duty as an incident commander for one of the historic Yellowstone National Park fires of 1988. Page 97.

John Simpson is a staff photographer with the *News-Journal* of Mansfield, Ohio. While a student at Western Kentucky University, he covered forest fires as part of a summer internship with *The Register-Guard* of Eugene, Oregon. Page 58.

Bear Stauss of Missoula, Montana, is retired from wildland fire fighting for the U.S. Forest Service. In his two years, as a hotshot and and nine years as a smokejumper, he packed cameras into remote fire scenes around the West. Page 76 (upper left).

W.E. Steuerwald photographed smokejumper training and missions in Montana during the 1950s. Page 28.

Tom Story, a staff photographer at the Arizona Republic in Phoenix, gravitates to fire assignments, with a special interest in hotshot crews. He has followed them through Arizona, Idaho, Nevada, and California. Pages 15, 41, 48, 52, 53 (lower right), 63, 96 (bottom), 125 (bottom), 144 (bottom).

K.D. Swan trailed Civilian Conservation Corps firefighters during the Great Depression and became a fixture in the forest fire camps of Idaho. Pages 18, 27.

Mark Terrill of Tarzana, California, chases wildland blazes for Associated Press in the nation's most fire-active state. His first fire photographs were published in the mid-1980s, when he was a sixteen-year-old high school student. Page 13.

Bruce Turbeville is a public information officer and chief photographer for the California Department of Forestry. With extensive background as a fire information officer, he has been involved in wildland fire photography since the mid-1970s. Pages 100 (bottom), 137, 140.

Ted Veal, who died in 1994, was public relations director for Columbia Helicopters of Portland, Oregon. He was often on location with Columbia's crews in missions that ranged from famine relief in the Sudan to forest fires in the American West. Pages 108 (bottom), 111 (lower left).

Roger Wallace is fire management officer of the Leavenworth Ranger District in Washington's Wenatchee National Forest. In a fire career that began with work on ground and helitack crews, he has always packed cameras into the field. Pages 66, 128.

Karen Wattenmaker, an outdoor photographer based in Garden Valley, Idaho, has worked in South America, Asia, and Antarctica. She follows wildland firefighters each summer as a contract photographer for the Boise National Forest. Pages ii-iii, ix, 40, 70, 158.

Hans Wilbrecht was a photographer for four years at the Missoula Technology and Development Center, a Forest Service facility that constantly refines such equipment as fire shelters, smokejumper parachutes, and field gear. Pages 121, 124 (bottom).

Joe Wilkins, a staff photographer for *The Register-Guard* of Eugene, Oregon, worked as a White House photo intern before coming West to take on forest fire assignments each summer. Page 55 (top).

Yuen-Gi Yee, the director of audio-visual services at Forest Service headquarters in Washington, D.C., periodically shows up with his cameras on the fire lines of the West. Page 114.

Bill Yensen of St. George, Utah, was a U.S. Forest Service smokejumper for thirty seasons in McCall, Idaho. His photographs became part of the McCall base archives after he retired from jumping at age fifty-three. Page 53.

Tim Zelazo, who works for the state forests and parks system in Massachusetts, fought Western forest fire for eight seasons with Forest Service hotshot crews and engine outfits in Colorado, Wyoming, and California. Pages 3, 34, 47, 153.

Institutional credits: Associated Press Wide World Photos, page 13; Boise National Forest, pages ii-iii, ix, 40, 49, 53, 55, 59, 70, (upper right), 141, 145 (bottom), 152, 158, 160 (lower left); California Department of Forestry, cover and pages 67, 100 (bottom), 137, 140, 148; National Interagency Fire Center, pages 46, 76 (lower right), 160 (lower right); U.S. Department of Agriculture Archives, Beltsville, Maryland, pages 18, 19, 20, 22, 27, 28, 33; U.S. Forest Service Air Center, Redmond, Oregon, page 73; U.S. Forest Service, Denver, Colorado, page 25; U.S. Forest Service, Portland, Oregon, page 23; U.S. Forest Service, Washington, D.C., Page 114; Yellowstone National Park, Pages 55 (lower right), 118, 125 (upper right), 160 (top), 161.

Index